Black White Blue

Black White Blue

The Assassination
of Patrolman Sackett

WILLIAM SWANSON

BOREALIS
BOOKS

Borealis Books is an imprint of the Minnesota Historical Society Press.
www.mhspress.org

The Minnesota Historical Society Press is a member of the
Association of American University Presses.

Manufactured in the United States of America

10 9 8 7 6 5 4 3 2 1

♾ The paper used in this publication meets the minimum requirements
of the American National Standard for Information Sciences—Permanence for
Printed Library Materials, ANSI Z39.48-1984.

International Standard Book Number
ISBN: 978-0-87351-870-3 (cloth)
ISBN: 978-0-87351-871-0 (e-book)

Library of Congress Cataloging-in-Publication Data

Swanson, William, 1945–
Black, white, blue : the assassination of patrolman Sackett / William Swanson.
p. cm.
ISBN 978-0-87351-870-3 (cloth : alk. paper) — ISBN 978-0-87351-871-0 (e-book)
1. Sackett, James. 2. Murder victims—Minnesota—Saint Paul—Case studies.
3. Murder—Minnesota—Saint Paul—Case studies. I. Title.
HV6533.M6S93 2012
364.152'3092—dc23
2012018637

For my family

. . . and the boys move against the traffic as though they are moving against the enemy. The enemy is not there, of course, but his soldiers are, in patrol cars, armed.

JAMES BALDWIN

There had always been rules in the game. One had to have a good reason to kill a cop. . . .

JOSEPH WAMBAUGH

Contents

Black White Blue

Young Men and Murder

—*Police. Kinderman.*

—*Yes. I was wondering if you could send a squad car down to 859 Hague.*

—*What's the trouble?*

—*Uh, my sister's getting ready to have a baby, and we have no transportation.*

—*Okay, just a moment. Eight-six-nine?*

—*Eight-fifty-nine.*

—*Eight-five-nine.*

—*Hague.*

—*Eight-five-nine—is that correct?*

—*Yes.*

—*Hague. What apartment number?*

—*It's on the first floor.*

—*Okay. How close is the baby due?*

—*Well, she's having pains . . . two minutes apart.*

—*Okay. What is the last name, please?*

—*Brown. B-R-O-W-N.*

—*Phone number, please.*

—*I'm at the phone booth now.*

—*Okay, 859 Hague. First floor.*

—*Yes.*

—*Thank you. 'Bye.*

1

The young woman's voice was soft and unhurried, with a trace of a languid drawl. She did not ask for, much less demand, a squad car—she *wondered* if a car could be dispatched. She might have been ordering a pizza or, if it wasn't already a few minutes after midnight, a blouse or a pair of shoes she had seen in a Dayton's department store ad in the paper. On the other end of the line, the flat, midwestern male voice bore the patient air of a desk-bound cop who answers hundreds of such calls in a career and knows from experience that the situation at 859 Hague, first floor, will more likely than not be all in a night's work for the officers directed its way.

In 1970, more than a decade before the adoption of the 911 emergency call system, a citizen needing help or having some other urgent reason to call the police in St. Paul, Minnesota, dialed 224-7391. (Callers using a pay phone got their dime back.) In addition to their law-enforcement responsibilities, the police provided crisis medical service in the capital city, responding in Chevrolet station wagons called "stretcher cars" or more fully equipped International Harvester "emergency trucks" to everything from auto accidents and domestic violence to heart attacks and premature babies.

On most nights there was either a stretcher car or an emergency truck available in the area, but because of the midnight shift change none was in the vicinity when John Kinderman took the call regarding Mrs. Brown at 12:04 on May 22. The nearest patrol car was Squad 337, but patrolmen Edward Steenberg and John LaBossiere were investigating a theft from a car at Grand Avenue and Oxford Street, eight blocks away, so the dispatcher queried Squad 327 for its location. Despite the response—"Right in front of the Capitol"—327 was told, at approximately seven minutes after midnight, to proceed to 859 Hague to take care of an "O.B." When patrolman Glen Kothe pointed out that 327 was a traffic car, not an emergency vehicle, the dispatcher replied, "Three-twenty-seven, you're the only one I have available right now." With no further discussion, Kothe confirmed, and 327 proceeded toward the Hague Avenue address, about two miles away.

St. Paul was a middling city, with a population, according to the 1970 census, of 309,980, and comprised fifty-six square miles in a rough horizontal rectangle abutting the Mississippi River and the city of Minneapolis, its larger, flashier "twin." In the wee hours of a Friday morning, with scant traffic and benign weather conditions (for the moment), it would take a squad car little more than five minutes to travel from the Capitol, just north of downtown, to Hague Avenue at Victoria Street.

Squad 327 was not representative of St. Paul's familiar dark-blue-and-white police department fleet. It was a factory-new Plymouth 440—a rakish two-door, burnt-orange muscle car—on the street that night for the first time. Its unusual color and the fact that its only exterior marking was a police shield the size of a dinner plate on the passenger-side door would presumably make it a stealthily effective traffic car. But manned by Kothe and another young patrolman, James Sackett, Squad 327 had made only a couple of routine traffic stops since coming on duty as part of the 8 PM "power shift." Free to roam, the partners—a couple of frisky gearheads enjoying the improbable car they were driving that night—cruised the downtown Loop, took a swing through the East Side, and, in Kothe's words, "ran in on a call or two and stuff like that." Sitting in the shadow of Cass Gilbert's monumental Capitol for maybe three-quarters of an hour, they had little to do. Later, Kothe reckoned they made only a single stop at the site that night.

St. Paul was hardly a wild town, though by 1970 it had begun to feel the tensions that had been tearing at the fabric of larger, more fractious communities for the past several years. It was a time of conflict and change. The escalating war in Vietnam was unpopular across the United States, and antiwar demonstrations had turned increasingly violent. Activists among African Americans, Native Americans, and Latinos had become strident in their demands for equality and respect and were joining radicalized women's and youth groups in the streets of the nation's cities and campuses. Street crime, from purse-snatchings to murder, had risen almost everywhere during the 1960s, including in St. Paul. When, during the "long, hot summer" of 1967, African Americans torched storefronts and skirmished with police on the North Side of Minneapolis, St. Paul remained calm. There was little concentrated violence in either city, for that matter, when other cities burned following Martin Luther King Jr.'s assassination in April 1968. During the Labor Day weekend that year, however, St. Paul was shaken out of whatever complacency it might have enjoyed when a dance at Stem Hall, a dingy downtown arena, got out of hand—predictably, there were conflicting accounts of what sparked the disturbance—and young blacks fought a running battle with the police between downtown and the Selby-Dale section of the nearby Summit-University neighborhood.

Nothing like that had recurred, but St. Paul had been put on notice. Meanwhile, its police department was busy dealing with the uptick in crime. Incidents of aggravated assault, robbery, burglary, and auto theft had risen dramatically during the 1960s. The city that reported only three murders in 1961 recorded nineteen in 1968; in 1970, the total would drop slightly, to fourteen. By the end of the year, St. Paul patrol officers would respond to more than 108,000 calls for service. Sometimes fresh-faced cops such as Kothe and Sackett put on tie-dyed T-shirts and bell-bottom slacks and cruised for illicit drug buys. Sometimes, in a used car borrowed from a University Avenue auto dealer, they staked out a rumored stickup site. On other occasions, they joined raids on Selby Avenue after-hours joints. Compared with making adhesive tape at 3M and delivering cases of Pepsi-Cola—the officers' previous lines of work—policing their urban bailiwick was high adventure and offered, on most nights, at least the possibility of some action.

The action could be dangerous. The fatal shooting of Keith Barnes, a young African American, by a white plainclothes officer at a University Avenue bar in February drew a large crowd of aroused citizens. As it happened, Kothe and Sackett were the first uniformed officers to arrive on the scene and were greeted by jeers and threats from the bystanders. There was also the night, in March 1970, when Sackett shot and wounded a burglary suspect in the Frogtown neighborhood north of the Capitol. The suspect's wound was not life-threatening, and Sackett was not sanctioned by the department, though afterward he spoke solemnly with his wife about the stress of firing his gun at another human being. In 1970 officers were generally operating within both the law and departmental guidelines when they shot at someone they believed to be committing or fleeing a felony. St. Paul cops, by their own admission, did a lot of shooting in those days.

Kothe (pronounced *ko*-thee) was twenty-four years old, married, and the father of three small children. Sackett, though three years older than Kothe, had joined the department in the fall of 1968, about a year later than his partner. Like Kothe, Sackett was married and had a growing brood at home. In fact, that night was Sackett's first back on the job after taking three weeks off to help care for his newborn fourth child. The Kothes and the Sacketts were not especially close, but they were friends. Glen and Jim frequently shared the same squad car, and their wives, Patricia and Jeanette, were casual acquaintances.

Kothe and Sackett made each other laugh, which was a good thing since they often spent eight hours in a car together, sometimes doing little more than waiting for the occasional knucklehead to run a red light. They talked about their families, discussed the cars they were working on at home, and bitched as all men and women in uniform bitch about superior officers and organizational regs. Sometimes they talked about the future. Both men wanted eventually to take the sergeant's exam, with the ultimate objective of becoming a detective. Detectives, in Kothe's words, "could wear plain clothes, do pretty much what they wanted, and didn't have to put up with a lot of crap." Mostly, though, the patrolmen joked, pulled dumb-ass stunts—squirt-gun attacks, bumper tag, hiding another guy's car— and laughed a lot. Not three weeks earlier, when the two of them were visiting Jeanette and the Sacketts' new baby in the maternity unit of Mounds Park Hospital, they were enjoying each other so much that a nurse gave them an ultimatum: pipe down or leave the ward. Tonight, en route to the O.B. call, Sackett kidded his partner, a strapping six-footer, about the prospect of delivering a baby in the cramped back seat of their two-door muscle car.

Sackett was behind the wheel. He turned the key and revved the 440's powerful engine. With Kothe beside him, he pulled out into the almost nonexistent traffic and headed west, in the direction of the Hill.

Officially, it was known as the Summit-University neighborhood, but the cops referred to the area as the Hill—a conglomeration of about 180 city blocks bounded by University Avenue on the north, Lexington Parkway on the west, and Summit Avenue on the south and east. The governor's baronial residence and the Victorian row house briefly occupied by F. Scott Fitzgerald were situated along verdant Summit, as were dozens of the city's grandest old-money manses. Where Summit approached the bluff overlooking downtown, the massive Cathedral loomed, since the turn of the twentieth century the seat of the Roman Catholic archdiocese of St. Paul and Minneapolis. On gray, gritty, relentlessly industrial/commercial University, the enormous Montgomery Ward department store dominated the neighborhood's retail trade, while a dozen or more new and used car dealers for decades made the thoroughfare the Broadway of auto sales on the east side of the Mississippi.

But none of that was what most cops first thought of when directed to the Hill. The Hill was where most of the street crime was in 1970. In the minds of many white cops, it was no coincidence that the majority—an estimated 85 percent—of St. Paul's African American population lived on the Hill, making up about a third of the neighborhood's residents. Though the 1970 census counted fewer than eleven thousand blacks, or 3.3 percent of St. Paul's total population, they would account for 17 percent of that year's arrests of persons eighteen years and over and 12 percent of the juveniles; five of the ten citizens arrested for murder in the city that year would be listed in police tallies as "Negro." Most of the arrests were made on the Hill. Long restricted by the unofficial "rules" and redlining practices of Twin Cities real estate companies and lenders, the once closely knit and peaceable community centered on Rondo Avenue had been splintered in the early 1960s by the local leg of the new interstate freeway. The area's growing African American population was becoming younger and poorer. According to historian David Vassar Taylor, who grew up in the Rondo neighborhood during the relatively halcyon 1950s, unemployment in the Summit-University neighborhood by 1965 was above 9 percent for blacks—more than 50 percent higher than it was for their white neighbors.

Kothe had grown up on the Hill. He had run around with black and other white kids and got in his share of small-fry trouble. Sackett was an East Sider born and bred, coming of age in the days when that part of town was lily-white and somnolent from a crime-fighter's point of view. As patrolmen, both had already been on dozens of calls on the Hill and were familiar with the trouble spots. The cops, all but a handful of whom were white, knew they were not always welcome. Neighborhood groups, comprising mostly African Americans, loudly complained about police inattentiveness on the one hand and brutality on the other. The cops, for their part, were increasingly aware of the knots of surly youths on the street corners—and of those knots almost supernaturally mushrooming into menacing crowds at the site of an incident, such as Keith Barnes's shooting in February.

But a few minutes after midnight on May 22, Kothe and Sackett were rushing to the Hill to help deliver a baby.

Sackett could have taken the new Interstate 94 from the Capitol to within a few blocks of 859 Hague, opening up the 440 on the freeway. But it was a short trip and, given the dearth of traffic, one of the east-west through streets would be just as quick. Sackett switched on the car's red light and siren, crossed over the freeway on John Ireland Boulevard, then sped west on Marshall Avenue. At Victoria he turned left and raced south three short blocks to Hague. Because it was a maternity run into what was a mainly residential area in the early hours of the morning, he switched off the siren. At Hague, he mistakenly turned right instead of left, then slammed the car into reverse and backed across the intersection, stopping in front of the house on the northeast corner.

The neighborhood was silent and still. Running west to east a block south of Selby Avenue's small businesses and municipal bus line, Hague Avenue was a solid several blocks of two-story single-family homes, duplexes, and modest apartment buildings, most of them forty or fifty years old but generally well maintained. Neither Kothe nor Sackett, during their experience policing the Hill, had taken any calls at 859 Hague or anywhere else on the block. Eight-fifty-nine itself was a white, two-story frame house with an enclosed front porch and aluminum front door and windows that filled most of a narrow corner lot. Out back there was a garage (with access to Victoria) but no alley running between Hague and Selby. A large brick church, also dark and apparently deserted at that hour, sat directly opposite, on the south side of Hague.

There were no lights on in the house, nor was anybody waiting at the front door. Still wisecracking about tending to the expectant mother in the 440's tight back seat, the young cops emerged from the car. Like most uniformed officers, they considered their peaked caps as much a nuisance as a symbol of authority, and, once out from under the eyes of their superiors, they usually left the caps in the car. So bareheaded, yet unmistakably police in their pale blue shirtsleeves and dark blue pants, their heavy service revolvers holstered on their hips, the fan-shaped SPPD patch on the left shoulder and the silver shield on the left breast, Sackett and Kothe approached the quiet house.

Sackett climbed the short concrete stoop and rapped on the door. Pulling on the handle, he discovered the door secured, apparently fastened on the inside with a length of rope or wire.

Kothe backed away from the stoop and followed a narrow concrete walkway around the west side of the house. When he pounded on the back door and shouted "Police!" a dog barked loudly somewhere inside. Kothe leaned over the iron-pipe railing on the back stoop and hollered to his partner out front.

"Watch it, Jim—they've got a dog!"

At which instant their world exploded.

Jim Sackett had stepped down off the front stoop and turned toward the west side of the house—in the direction of his partner's voice—when the sniper's bullet tore into the upper left side of his chest an inch above the badge. If he saw anything more than the flash or heard more than the overlapping explosion, he did not have a chance to react. Though he would not be officially pronounced dead until almost forty-five minutes later, and though a few of the cops who converged on the scene immediately following the shooting reported detecting faint signs of life, others said later they were convinced he was gone before he hit the ground.

Glen Kothe crouched over his partner's body, shocked by the

amount of blood that was spreading across the sidewalk. He had heard Sackett scream, but until he came around the corner of the house, it hadn't registered that a shot had been fired, much less— for the moment—that the two of them were in the crosshairs of a sniper. Kothe's first thought, in response to the flash and percussion, was that somebody had set off an M-80 firecracker. Though illegal in Minnesota, firecrackers such as the large and hazardous M-80 were perennially popular and, though the Fourth of July was still six weeks away, the police were already getting complaints about the noise. But Sackett's prone body told Kothe that what he had seen and heard wasn't a firecracker. His next thought was that Jim had been shot by someone inside the house. The amount of blood indicated a shotgun fired at point-blank range.

Then he saw movement on other side of the front door and thought, *Oh shit, it's my time!*

Kothe yanked his revolver out of its holster and fired two shots toward the shadow on the other side of the door, then dashed down the short private walk, crossed the public sidewalk and another strip of grass, and dove over the trunk of the 440. With the car between him and the house, he hollered at whoever was inside to come out. Getting no response, he pulled open the car's driver-side door and fumbled for the radio phone. The car was so new the motor-pool crew hadn't disconnected the dome light, so when the door opened the inside lit up. But there were no more gunshots. Kothe grabbed the radio mic and broke into the police frequency's chatter, which instantly became a bedlam of shouted squad IDs, questions, and demands.

—*Three-two-seven, this is an ambush! Get us some help up here— my partner's shot!*

—*Three-one-seven?*

—*Three-one-seven. We're on our way. Give us some good location.*

—*Attention all cars! Eight-fifty-nine Hague, first floor. It's an ambush. We're supposed to have an O.B. One party was shot. Attention all cars! Eight-fifty-nine Hague, first floor. An officer was shot.*

—*Tell 'em to step on it! My partner's hit bad!*

Within seconds, all available squads on the streets of St. Paul were racing toward Hague and Victoria, as were cars from headquarters downtown, red roof lights ablaze and sirens caterwauling. Squatting behind Squad 327, Kothe heard the sirens almost immediately, but, as he would say again and again, "time was gone." Help would arrive within minutes, but to Kothe it seemed to take forever.

Ed Steenberg and John LaBossiere were on their way from the theft call to assist with the O.B. when they heard the chaos on the radio. When they arrived on the scene a few moments later, Kothe was back at the foot of the stoop, kneeling over Sackett. It wouldn't occur to him until later that instead of protecting himself when he had crouched behind the car, he was fully exposed, his back to the sniper, if the sniper had still been within striking distance.

The cops, however, saw nobody except other cops, who were rushing to the scene from all directions. LaBossiere joined Kothe with a first-aid kit, and the two men did what they could to stanch Sackett's bleeding. Someone retrieved Sackett's eyeglasses, which had fallen out of his shirt pocket and lay on the patchy grass near his body. Moments earlier, a man had called the police and on the verge of panic told Kinderman that a man had been shot outside his front door and that a second man was pointing a gun at him. "What should I do?" he asked the operator. Kinderman told him to turn on the lights, hold his hands out from his sides, and step out the door. "Move slow," Kinderman cautioned him, "and keep your hands in plain sight." The caller was standing on the front porch, hands extended as directed, when Steenberg put his shoe through the secured porch door.

Gerald Dexter and Daniel Bostrom were the power shift's sergeants that night. Dexter had put Sackett and Kothe in the new Plymouth traffic car a few hours earlier, a reward for their hard work and production. Somehow, in a perverse turn of events, the young officers had ended up in a front yard on the Hill, one of them either dead or dying. Now Dexter, brandishing a shotgun, joined patrolmen James Jerylo and Laverne Lee pushing through the back door of the house. Inside the door, he looked down a stairway that descended to the basement. A woman appeared at the bottom of the steps. He raised the shotgun. The woman screamed, and Dexter held his fire. The house, it turned out, was full of frightened people dressed for bed and a couple of wildly excited dogs. The occupants included a seventy-year-old man, his twenty-two-year-old daughter, and three related teenagers, one of whom was in fact pregnant. But the pregnant woman, who was seventeen and married to the man who had just called the police, was several weeks short of her due date and was not suffering labor pains. Neither she nor anyone else in the house was named Brown.

Outside, several cops were shouting into their radios for medical help. The absence of a stretcher car or emergency truck in the area was, of course, the reason Sackett's traffic car caught the O.B. call in the first place. Now its absence at the shooting site was delaying his evacuation. When, about ten minutes after the shooting, a stretcher car finally arrived from headquarters and Sackett was lifted aboard, LaBossiere crawled in beside him and began administering oxygen. He believed he could feel a pulse.

Dexter and Bostrom quickly decided that the shot had not come from inside the house. Which meant there was a gunman somewhere on the street. Potentially complicating the situation, a small crowd had begun to form, mainly on the west side of Victoria. But fears the incoming squads might have had for their own safety were almost immediately diminished by their own superior numbers and guns.

One of the officers on the scene was a thirty-year-old, Chicago-born Navy veteran named Joseph Corcoran, who arrived in the company of the police department's criminalist, Harold Alfultis. Corcoran had been a St. Paul patrolman since 1964. He had been so desperate to be a cop that he had repeatedly dangled from his mother's backyard clothes pole in an ultimately successful effort to stretch himself the quarter of an inch he needed to reach what was then the department's five-foot, ten-inch minimum. Recently, he had volunteered to work one of the emergency trucks that carried both basic medical supplies and rudimentary forensic tools. He had been trained in first aid, fingerprints, blood work, and photography. As it happened, May 22 was his first experience with the mobile lab.

Corcoran had caught the call at half-past midnight. "We've got a homicide scene, and it's one of our own," Alfultis told him.

The young officer, who was at home asleep when the phone rang, had difficulty comprehending what he'd heard. "They've killed one of *us?*" he asked.

Like most of the department's 460 sworn officers in 1970, Corcoran had not worked with Jim Sackett and knew him only as a name and a face in passing. Corcoran had joined the department three years prior to Sackett, and cops tended to establish their on-the-job relationships with those closest to their own age and level of experience. Often, the closest friends had signed on at the same time and come up through the academy together. But Corcoran, who was a devout Catholic at the time and a man of strong convictions, believed with all his heart in the brotherhood of police that existed from the moment officers take their sacred oath until they draw their final breath, regardless of age, rank, creed, or color. He was shaken to the core by news of the Sackett shooting.

The Hague Avenue crime scene was even worse than he expected. Sackett's body had been removed by the time he reached the site, but a three-foot splash of blood covered the private sidewalk. The shooter could have fired, Corcoran reckoned, from any number of spots. Later he, Alfultis, and homicide detectives would find and remove from a decorative oak plank on the front of the house the rifle slug they believed had passed through Sackett. They would use a simple dowel-like probe to figure probable trajectories and get some idea of the direction from which the shot had come.

Corcoran looked around the intersection. There were so many places a man with a rifle could hide. There was the church directly across the street, with bushes and a low retaining wall running in front and along the Victoria Street side. On the west side of Victoria opposite the church was a corner house with a garage and a waist-high chain-link fence along the front and side. Westward along both sides of Hague there were mature trees, overgrown hedges, and shadowed porches that could offer a concealed shooter a clean shot at the front yard where Sackett was standing. True, the nearest street lamps, on the northwest and southeast corners of the intersection, didn't offer a great deal of illumination, but there would be enough light for someone either good or lucky with a scoped rifle. Patrolman Kothe was fortunate he hadn't been hit, too.

That stretch of Hague was familiar to Corcoran. Only a week or so earlier, working a patrol squad, he and his partner had answered a noisy-party call at a duplex midway down the block. The two cops knew a young African American woman named Cheryl who lived there. When they were sitting at Selby and Dale, one of the edgier spots on the Hill at the time, they would see Cheryl walk by and chat with her. Sometimes, if she said she was hungry, they would give her a buck for a hamburger. Answering the noisy-party complaint on Hague, the cops were challenged by an angry black man. But before the situation could deteriorate, Cheryl came to the door and told the man, "Leave them alone—those are *good* cops." She promised to hush the revelers inside.

As for *who* might have fired the shot—well, it *could* have been anyone. A homicidal crackpot. A guy with a grudge against cops. Someone with a "cause." There was a lot going on around the country. Antiwar demonstrators, campus radicals, the Weathermen, the Black Panthers—all those groups out there raising hell and talking about overthrowing the government. And the cops, of course, *were* the government, or its agents at any rate, the part of it that many citizens encountered most often where they lived. The Panthers, with their "Kill the pigs!" rhetoric, public flaunting of rifles and carbines, and record of shootouts with police in other cities, were particularly worrisome to Corcoran. He had no specific information that the California-based group was active in the Twin Cities, but there had been rumors and rumblings, and who could say that that night's ambush wasn't the start of something in St. Paul?

Later that day, Corcoran, as the criminalist's assistant, would carry Sackett's uniform from the hospital emergency room to the crime lab at police headquarters. Staring at the blood-stained shirt, he noticed that the bullet had missed Sackett's shield—Badge 450— by scarcely an inch. "My God," he said to himself, "they were aiming at the badge!" Of course, he didn't know if the badge had been the sniper's target. It seemed apparent even early in the investigation that Sackett had been turning when he was hit and that he had probably turned into the incoming slug. Then again, the shield would quite possibly have caught the light from one of the street lamps and the reflection might have drawn the shooter's eye.

The thought sickened Corcoran, who believed that police officers were forces for good in the community. He looked down at his brother officer's bloodied shirt and thought: *They're killing us.*

In the several minutes following the shooting, a growing number of civilians had gathered on their stoops and front yards and in small groups mainly along the west side of Victoria. Some were residents of Hague Avenue, reflecting the ethnic mix of the day: blacks and whites mostly, with a sprinkling of Hispanics often identified by their neighbors as "Mexicans." Some had walked over from Selby, Laurel, and other nearby streets, roused out of bed or drawn away from the late movie on television by the revolving red lights and wailing sirens. Some were part of the amorphous crowd of mostly young people who always seemed to be on the street, no matter the time of day or night or what was going on.

There might have been some joking and jeering among the younger onlookers who resented the presence of cops in their neighborhood, but mostly the crowd was subdued and hushed, watching the scene the way most persons observed the immediate aftermath of fires, car wrecks, and other tragedies—with a bemused fascination that betrayed a range of human emotion.

It took a while for the police response to get organized. For the time being, Dexter and Bostrom were in charge at the site, attempting to save the victim, securing the crime scene, and directing the expanding force of officers into the immediate neighborhood to see what and who they could find.

Patrolman Steenberg, once he had helped determine that the residents of 859 Hague were not harboring Sackett's assailant, spotted a man and a boy standing on the front steps of the house next door. The man's name was Clair Kirkwood, and he told Steenberg he had heard a single shot, then, "a minute or two later," two more shots. Kirkwood's thirteen-year-old son, Jack, said he had heard the same three shots and when he'd run to his bedroom window he saw an officer with a gun and the orange car at the curb. Jack also saw, per Steenberg's report, "two male youths, approx. 18–19 yrs. old, wearing dark clothing, running from the S.E. quadrant of the Hague-Victoria corner. The two persons ran south on Victoria, crossing Victoria and heading west thru the alley (rear of 862 Hague)." A short while later, Cecil Westphall, one of the first homicide detectives to reach the scene, interviewed Kirkwood, his son, and his wife, who also heard the shots. Now, however, young Jack told Westphall that he wasn't sure if he actually saw the two men running away from the scene or if he had "imagined" it. Neither of Jack's parents said they saw any- · one running, and the boy conceded that the movement he observed might have been the officer (Kothe) sprinting toward his car.

Patrolmen Leonard Renfro and Donald Huisenga talked to

Hague Avenue residents on the west side of Victoria who heard a shot "that sounded like a big gun," then two more shots "in close succession," then, according to their report, "a man say ow-ow-ow 3 times." The residents said they saw one man on the lawn and another man "leaning into a rust colored car" in front of 859 Hague but saw nobody else until the other squad cars arrived. But they placed the time of the shots at about half-past midnight, at least fifteen minutes after the fact. Another neighbor told Renfro and Huisenga that she had heard "what sounded like thunder" but then heard or saw nothing else until the other squads rolled up.

Officers had begun a yard-by-yard search of the block bounded by Hague, Victoria, Laurel, and Milton—the block kitty-corner from 859 Hague. Judging by the position of Sackett's body and the initial trajectory estimates, the police believed the shot likely came from south or southwest of the Hague-Victoria intersection. Because a rooftop could hide a sniper or his abandoned weapon, the police requested a snorkel truck from the fire department. Climbing into the truck's elevated bucket, Dexter and Bostrom personally checked out the roof of the church—Shiloh Baptist—directly across the street as well as the roofs of nearby garages. Portable generator-powered floodlights provided dazzling illumination as cops prowled the yards and alleys within shooting distance. Later, investigators assisted by a crew from the city's public works department checked the sewers and catch basins around Victoria and Hague for evidence. But all the several dragnets of the neighborhood turned up were a dusty black cap with no identifying tags found along the side of a house on Laurel and two nondescript heel prints found on the Victoria side of the church.

Because there had been rumors involving out-of-town "militants" supposedly imported by local groups, the police department's brass, gathered downtown, directed a search of the Hill for cars with out-of-state license plates—cars that did not "belong," according to Dexter's report, in the neighborhood. But nothing substantive was discovered then or later. No weapon, no shell casing, no sight or sign of the shooter.

At 12:40 AM, Jim Sackett—possibly alive, but probably dead— was rushed into the emergency suite at St. Paul–Ramsey County Hospital, the city's central trauma center, located a couple of blocks east of the Capitol, not far from where Sackett and Kothe had begun their O.B. run. He was wheeled, unresponsive, into surgery room 10. His pupils were fixed and dilated, and he had no pulse. When the doctors opened his chest, the devastation was apparent. The bullet had shattered his sternum, severed two major arteries, and fractured two ribs and his right humerus before exiting his right shoulder. Despite their best efforts to find and preserve some spark of life, the E.R. doctors pronounced him dead at 12:54.

In the autopsy report signed by pathologist B. F. Woolfrey, cause of death was deemed "exsanguination secondary to [a] gunshot wound of the chest." In plain language, Sackett had been struck by a bullet and bled to death.

Jeanette Sackett was a self-described country girl who grew up in a large family in the tiny farming community of Effie, near Alexandria, Louisiana. She was Jeanette McNeal, a seventeen-year-old business college student, in August 1960 when she and a girlfriend were approached in an Alexandria bar by a good-looking airman from close-by England Air Force Base. He asked Jeanette to dance and they danced one dance and that was that, she thought—no big deal. The next day her girlfriend called and said, "That guy you danced with last night? He wants your phone number." He kept calling the girlfriend until the girlfriend said to Jeanette, "Can I give him your number so he'll quit bugging me?" So she did, and a short time later Airman First Class James Thomas Sackett, a jet engine mechanic from St. Paul, Minnesota, picked Jeanette up in his gleaming black Oldsmobile. He asked her to take off her shoes before she stepped into the car's immaculate white interior.

On their second or third date, Jim told Jeanette, "I think we'll end up getting married." He was still early on in his four-year Air Force commitment, but he had plans for afterward. He told her his dream was to be a policeman back home.

Jim and Jeanette were married in the air base chapel on April 29, 1962, and honeymooned in New Orleans. On their first anniversary they went back to the same motel and stayed in the same room, and that's when Jeanette figured she got pregnant. In February 1964, they moved to St. Paul with their six-week-old firstborn, James Thomas Sackett Jr., and two days after their arrival Jeanette experienced, awestruck, her first Minnesota snowstorm. They stayed with Jim's parents (his father, Melvin, tended bar at the venerable St. Paul Hotel downtown) for a few months, then rented an apartment, then bought a tidy three-bedroom bungalow on a leafy block of tidy bungalows not far from where Jim had grown up, a stone's throw from Lake Phalen on the city's East Side.

A civilian again, Jim worked odd jobs before landing a position with the local Pepsi-Cola bottler. He was driving a truck for Pepsi when he learned that the police department was hiring. He applied, passed the entrance exam, and happily entered its academy on September 3, 1968. There were eighteen members of his class, and in the official class portrait Jim sat first row center, straight as a sentry and sober as a judge. His first night on the street was Christmas Eve 1968. The holiday dinner was at his sister's house that year—the whole family was there—but when it grew near the time his shift would begin, Jim changed into his new blue uniform and said, "Gotta go. Gotta do my job."

That first night's work was limited to a few traffic stops. Jeanette began the habit of setting an early alarm and getting up for him when he finished his shift.

In the weeks and months that followed, Jim would put on his uniform, go off to work in the early evening, and then, relaxing with a beer or glass of whiskey when he returned home eight or nine hours later, tell Jeanette what had gone down on his shift. They whispered so they wouldn't wake the kids, who by the beginning of 1969 included, besides Jim Jr., two daughters, Jennifer and Julie.

It was obvious to Jeanette that Jim loved being a cop. There was more and more going on in the streets, even in St. Paul—more crime, more guns, and occasional threats to the police—but she didn't worry too much about his safety. Jim was fit and strong and knew how to take care of himself. He was well trained and he partnered with other good cops, including his pals Bob Winger, Joe Pelton, and Glen Kothe. But one night after a shift in early 1970, Jim somberly told her he had shot a man, a burglary suspect who had tried to flee the scene. The suspect had not been badly hurt, nor was Jim likely to get into trouble downtown, yet the incident had shaken him. And, despite the absence of outward concern for his own well-being, Jim would sometimes say unsettling things. More than once he told Jeanette that he would not live to see his thirtieth birthday, which seemed odd considering that he would also tell her, with equal seriousness, that his ambition was to be chief of police.

On the evening of May 21, after taking three weeks off to help Jeanette following the difficult cesarean birth of their fourth child, a boy they named Jerel, Jim had difficulty leaving the house for his shift. He always spread the love around before leaving for downtown, making sure he hugged and kissed each child before he drove off, but that night was different. Maybe it was simply having to go back to work after so many days off, but in any case Jeanette sensed an unusual reluctance. He kept hugging her and the children and telling her how much he loved them. Alarmed, she said, "What's wrong, Jim?" And he said, "I just love you all so much. I'm just so happy." But, when he finally left the house, she was seized by a small, insistent fear that something bad was going to happen that night.

When the doorbell rang sometime after midnight—Jeanette wouldn't remember the time—she saw two uniformed officers standing at the front door. She was quite sure she had never seen them before and didn't know their names, but she understood immediately why they were there. "I know," she told them at the door. "I know it's not good."

Jeanette called her in-laws. "Dad—" she began when Melvin Sackett picked up the phone.

"Oh, my God!" he exclaimed. Why else would his daughter-in-law be calling in the middle of the night? "Don't tell me! Don't tell me!"

"Dad, you need to come over," she managed to say before breaking down herself. "Something's happened to Jim."

In the early morning hours of May 22, Helen Miels, a registered nurse, was working in the emergency room at St. Paul–Ramsey County Hospital. Just about the time Helen's husband, Earl Miels, a veteran homicide investigator, was getting a call at home about the ambush of an officer on Hague Avenue, Jim Sackett was wheeled into the E.R. When, sometime later, Jeanette Sackett was brought into the hospital, Helen Miels was asked to give her Valium, something to calm her down. She could understand Mrs. Sackett's distress. The wife of a policeman and the mother of small children, she could put herself in Jeanette's shoes.

Jeanette Sackett insisted on seeing her husband. A doctor told her that her husband was dead, but she refused to believe him. Shown her husband's body, she exclaimed, "No, he's only sleeping!

He'll wake up! He'll wake up!" Lying there in the emergency room, Jim looked the way he did when he slept.

Someone finally managed to pull her away. "No, dear," the other person said gently. "He's gone."

In the hour or so immediately following the shooting, Glen Kothe recounted the details of the ambush for his supervisors and then to a handful of detectives, including Sergeant Miels (pronounced Mills), who had crawled out of bed, hurriedly dressed, and sped to Hague and Victoria. By two o'clock that morning, their number included Captain Ernest Williams, the commander of St. Paul's homicide squad. Williams told Kothe to take it easy, stay focused, and try to remember everything. The fact that Kothe, too, could have taken a sniper's bullet did not seem particularly relevant—except, of course, to the unnerved young officer himself.

Kothe was eventually driven to headquarters, where he learned that his partner had been declared dead. He then took other ranking officers, including acting police chief Robert LaBathe, through the pertinent information before finally being excused. There was nothing else to say or do, at least for the time being. The adrenaline rush was spent. The second-guessing and what some people call survivor's guilt had not yet set in, or maybe Kothe was too tired to acknowledge it. It was 4 AM. Numb and exhausted, he drove himself home.

The Kothes had purchased a small house on Plum Street, near the freeway east of downtown. Patricia Kothe was used to Glen coming home at four-thirty or five in the morning and usually didn't wake up. But that night, as Glen got ready for bed, he fumbled his shield while removing it from his shirt and it clattered on the dresser top, startling his sleeping wife.

"What's wrong?" she said, bolting upright.

"Jim's dead," he replied.

The couple talked quietly for a while before Glen fell into a brief, fitful sleep. Then the family's phone began to ring as word of his partner's murder started making the rounds.

2

I t had been a generation—twenty-one years—since a St. Paul police officer had been murdered in the line of duty, and the city,
waking to the news, was stunned.

Because of its modest size, its ethnic and religious composition,
and the sentimental self-regard of its neighborhoods and parishes,
St. Paul felt a close kinship with its cops. Until the late sixties, police
officers and firefighters had been required to live within city limits,
and, especially in its heavily Irish, Italian, and German Catholic pre-
cincts, many extended families boasted a cop, a priest, or several of
both. Sons followed fathers into the department, and brothers, cous-
ins, nephews, and in-laws were common at roll call. Many had been
encouraged by older officers they had grown up admiring in their
neighborhoods and congregations. The St. Paul Police Department
(officially, until New Year's Day 1971, the St. Paul Bureau of Police),
in the eyes of most citizens, provided an admirable way to make a
decent living. So for many reasons, even at a time of nationwide disorder, news of Patrolman James Sackett's murder coursed through
the city's arteries and organs like an electric shock.

The fact that Sackett's shooting had not been collateral damage—the by-product of an armed robbery, for example, or an instance of an officer getting caught in the middle of a domestic scrap
(the call that officers feared more than any other)—made it all the

more outrageous and difficult to comprehend. This was against the "rules," such as they were, that had long obtained between the police and criminals, who, out of fear of furious reprisal if not a weird sense of gamesmanship, were loath to attack cops with lethal intent if their freedom wasn't at stake. That day's papers, on the streets beginning at sunup, quoted police sources pronouncing the shooting "deliberate and cold-blooded" and described the phony O.B. call that drew the squad into the sniper's sights. The shot, according to the paper, was believed to have been fired from somewhere across the street, but so far, several hours after the shooting, no suspect, weapon, or eyewitness to the act had been found.

Few St. Paulites were more shaken by the murder than Sackett's contemporaries in the department, whether they were closely acquainted with him or not. The young cops of Sackett's cohort had not been in the department—most were not even out of knee pants—the last time a St. Paul officer had been shot to death. That had been Sergeant Allan Lee in 1949. Unlike more senior officers such as homicide commander Ernest Williams and veteran sergeant Paul Paulos, the young men who joined the force in the 1960s had not been hardened by combat in Europe, the Pacific, or Korea. Some of the younger cops had been in the "peacetime" military (the U.S. presence in Vietnam had begun to expand only in the mid-sixties), and a few had served as military policemen, but most had come to the academy from civilian jobs where the greatest occupational hazard was dropping a case of soda bottles on your foot. As recruits, they laughed nervously, probably not quite believing it, when told by an academy instructor that the odds were good that one of them would be killed in action. A St. Paul officer had been shot and killed on the job, on average, once every seven years since the first victim fell in the late nineteenth century, and it had been more than two decades since Sergeant Lee's death.

The young cops had been attracted by the promise of adventure—more adventure at any rate than they were likely to encounter driving a truck or peddling life insurance—and the idealistic if somewhat nebulous notion of making the community a better place to live. But the greatest appeal to the greatest number of them was the certain prospect of steady work starting at about six hundred dollars a month and the opportunity to retire in twenty-five years with a generous pension. Their parents had struggled through the

Great Depression, and they were brought up with a near-religious appreciation of a dependable job with solid benefits. The possibility of serious injury or death was not yet a preoccupation. "I don't think any of us were especially worried about our personal safety," Stuart Montbriand, who entered the academy with Jim Sackett in the fall of 1968, said much later.

There were, of course, the mundane yet often painful hazards of the job: the broken noses, slipped disks, dislocated shoulders, and lacerations a cop brought home after breaking up a bar fight or wrestling a 250-pound drunk into the back of a squad car. There were car wrecks during high-speed pursuits and tumbles from icy ledges during rescue attempts and nonlethal wounds from deadly weapons. Paul Paulos, who spent most of his forty years in the department on the street, was shot at on several occasions, grazed by a bullet while struggling over a .30-.30 with a berserk husband during a domestic call, and cut "quite a few times," most notably when he was slashed by a rapist wielding a butcher's knife in an alley off Victoria. A supremely fit and confident man who said he witnessed far more sanguinary situations fighting the Germans during World War II, he insisted the injuries were part of the job.

Even the supervisors such as Jerry Dexter and Dan Bostrom weren't that much older—most of them scarcely thirty—when Sackett was shot. Also still young were experienced patrolmen like Ed Steenberg, John LaBossiere, and Joe Corcoran, whose lives and careers would be indelibly marked by the murder. For many of those cops, including the men who *had* been around when Allan Lee was killed, the Sackett case was something special, a cop-killing that was unique in the city's history. Since May 18, 1882, when Patrolman Daniel O'Connell was fatally shot while investigating a burglary, twenty-five St. Paul officers had been killed on the job. Twelve had died of gunshot wounds. Ten had succumbed to injuries sustained in traffic-related incidents. One had been thrown from a horse, one had been fatally hurt in a fall, one had been accidentally electrocuted. Most died during or following contact with an apparent lawbreaker, say during the course of a robbery or while the suspect attempted to escape. Only one, James Sackett, had been assassinated.

Assassinated is a chilling term. It denotes the premeditated murder of someone because of *what,* at least as much as *who,* the victim is. John F. Kennedy and Martin Luther King Jr. were targeted because of their positions (president, civil rights leader) rather than for strictly personal reasons. St. Paul's cops quickly realized the shooter waiting in the shadows of Hague Avenue could not possibly have known who would answer that call for assistance. The shooter (and his or her accomplice or accomplices) could not have known that Kothe and Sackett would be directed there by the dispatcher. Indeed, patrolmen Kothe and Sackett, in their gaudy Plymouth traffic car, were accidental responders, filling in, as it happened, for the stretcher car that would ordinarily be sent to a medical emergency. If the outcome had not been deadly, it might have been amusing to imagine the sniper's confusion when the burnt-orange 440 rumbled up at the curb. But there was nothing funny about the inevitable conclusion drawn from the few facts at hand: the sniper wanted to kill a cop, and seemingly any cop would do.

That apparent reality, compounded by the fact that Sackett and Kothe were on what department spokesmen described as a "mission of mercy," cut St. Paul's cops to the quick and would haunt the case for the next forty years and maybe for as long as anyone remembered it.

Montbriand, who had gone off duty only moments before his friend was killed, was one of several officers who could have been excused for thinking *There but for the grace of God go I* that night. Decades later, Montbriand said the last time he saw Sackett was at the Dairy Queen at Sycamore and Rice, a few blocks north of the Capitol, where he and his partner swapped the Plymouth for the decidedly less flashy unmarked Chevrolet that Sackett and Kothe had been assigned, not long before Montbriand went home. The discrepancy between Montbriand's recollection and Jerry Dexter's version of how Kothe and Sackett happened to be driving the 440 was only one of many of the conflicted memories that would accrue around this case and perhaps says something about the lasting trauma of the event.

For officers such as Montbriand, Sackett's assassination was a deeply personal loss as well as a professional affront. "The last thing I heard Jim say that night was something like, 'Hey, you and me and the wives gotta get together for dinner.' The next thing I knew I started getting calls at home—first that Jim had been shot, then that he had died.

"The Sackett case had a dramatic effect on St. Paul's cops," Montbriand, who retired in 1992, continued. "There was anger, of course, but also a changed mentality, a sense of danger and vulnerability that hadn't been there before, or at least not for a long time. The idea that there had been a sniper, that it could be that sudden and unprovoked, how quick it could happen to you. . . ." His voice trailed off, his statement unfinished.

"Without a doubt, the Sackett murder was the defining moment of my career," Dan Bostrom told a journalist years later. Bostrom, who became a school-board member and city councilman after more than twenty-five years in the department, still lived on the East Side a few blocks from the Sackett bungalow. Sackett had worked under Bostrom for about six months and had impressed the older man both personally and professionally. "The way he handled himself— I considered him an extremely trustworthy, honorable, and hard-working fellow. Then he was gone. I don't know if the manner of his death would have made a difference to me or not—he would have been gone no matter what. *Still*"—and here Bostrom, like many of Sackett's contemporaries when recalling the case four decades later, looked back with a thousand-yard stare—"if you're in a shootout during a bank robbery, at least you have an opportunity to defend yourself. In Sackett's case, he was on a mission of mercy and didn't have a chance." Bostrom occasionally drove past 859 Hague and could see the young officer lying in that scrubby front yard as though the murder were yesterday.

Bostrom and Dexter, as power shift sergeants, were probably in harm's way more than the average St. Paul cop in 1970. The shift comprised mostly volunteers, and most of the volunteers were younger officers and supervisors. "We wanted to get into the thick of things," Dexter explained, "but I don't think we thought much about getting killed. We were cautious, but I don't recall being really frightened. We'd be prepared, but not afraid." Sackett's murder changed that. "This sort of thing had been going on around the country—officers being sniped at—and all of a sudden it happened in St. Paul. Before Sackett, we'd get word now and then to be particularly careful— people would be talking about the possibility of snipers. Our supervisors would say, 'We got word there are some people in town. . . .' But until Sackett, we weren't really on high alert." High alert equaled, among many of the young patrolmen, high anxiety, ratcheted up by the unmistakable sound of a bullet being chambered in a rifle as a squad car crept along a dark street late on a hot night on the Hill.

For Steenberg and Corcoran, stubborn idealists who were constitutionally inclined to believe the best about their city, Sackett's assassination was the end of a kind of innocence. "Not St. Paul," Steenberg—a large, courtly, well-spoken native who, well into his seventies, was pleased to don the department's 1880s-era tunic, silver star, and bobby's headgear at ceremonial functions—said to himself in the immediate aftermath of the murder. For Corcoran, the murder would forever be recalled as a "slap in the face."

Like most of that night's survivors, Corcoran was now also in his seventies, long retired and enjoying the robust pension that was part of the job's attraction. Some of the details of that period had grown hazy, but the emotion of the time burned bright. Whatever the glowering young men on the corners thought of them, few St. Paul cops at the time thought of themselves as "enemy soldiers." Shaking his head, Corcoran said, "I just couldn't believe that people in this town would kill us."

At the memorial services that took place over the next forty years, it was sometimes said from the podium that "Patrolman Sackett was a hero because of how he lived, not because of how he died." In truth, it's unlikely that Sackett, a modest man according to those who knew him best, would have thought of himself as a hero in death *or* life. A typical cop, he was at his core an ordinary guy, a working man from a working-class family, a husband and a father, a taxpayer, homeowner, and congenial neighbor, a guy who loved his job until the moment he died doing it.

Sackett was the youngest of three siblings and attended Johnson High School on Arcade Street. He grew up eating his mother's big breakfasts, and as an adult loved steak any way his wife prepared it. He drank beer when that's what he could afford at the air base enlisted men's club but preferred Scotch when he could afford it as a civilian. He smoked Camel cigarettes and was in the habit of field-stripping the butts long after he had left the service. He had a panther encircled by a snake tattooed above the elbow of his left arm.

He was an enthusiastic archer, proud of the double recurve bow he had purchased during a trip to Europe while in the Air Force, and he taught Jeanette how to shoot at the Keller Park range near their house. He liked to play golf and to hunt—deer with a rifle and grouse with a shotgun—though he did less of that as his young family grew. He loved tinkering with cars and carefully maintained the Chevy Impala that he and Jeanette bought not long after they moved into their house. He and several of his police buddies—Kothe, Montbriand, Winger, and Pelton—were dedicated weightlifters. He worked out in the basement of his house and was said by friends to be able to bench-press 250 pounds. He was a well-developed man who measured about five-eight and weighed approximately two hundred pounds when he died—"a young muscular adult male," according to his autopsy report. "One strong dude," according to his pal Montbriand.

"Jim was a funny guy," Jeanette told a journalist. "He loved life and was the life of the party. It didn't matter where he went—people were drawn to him and would want to talk to him. He liked parties. He was a very good dancer. He had a gift for gab. He had done some sales work while working at Pepsi. His boss told me that he could sell you anything."

"He was an extrovert," Montbriand said, "a guy who would organize things and take the initiative. He was ambitious, a go-getter." Montbriand could not recall his friend expressing either the objective of becoming police chief or the premonition of an early death—perhaps no one except Jeanette could—but then, as Kothe observed, neither idea was something a young cop was likely to tell his partner on the power shift. Montbriand did say, "He definitely had a future in the department. No doubt he would have been a lieutenant or captain some day."

"His family was the biggest thing in his life," said Winger. He spent a great deal of time with his kids. "Sometimes he would go off with them and give me a break—he was considerate that way," Jeanette said. "But he was no disciplinarian. He thought everything the kids did was cute. *I* was the tough cop in the family. He would never spank them, would never lay a hand on them. Jim Jr. and Jennifer remember wrestling on the floor with him, but Julie was only fifteen months when he was killed and Jerel was twenty days old. That breaks my heart, their never knowing firsthand what a good father they had."

"He was a fanatical family man who insisted on rounding up and kissing each of his kids before he went off to work," said Montbriand. "'You never know,' he used to say."

Sackett was easygoing and loved to joke. If he got uptight about anything, his friends say, it was his uniform. You wouldn't want to step on his spit-shined shoes or smudge the patent-leather brim of his cap. One of his partners told Jeanette about the time a guy Jim had arrested knocked the cap off his head. Jim picked the guy up, slammed him against the wall, and told him, "You *never* touch my cap." Jeanette said that despite his generally relaxed personality, the moment he put on that blue uniform he was "a different man."

"All cop" was the way Montbriand put it.

After nearly a year and a half on the job, Sackett was considered by his superiors hard-working, dependable, and productive. Besides responding to calls and working traffic details, he and Kothe were often given outstanding warrants to serve. Of course, they had to find the person before they could serve the warrant, and that, for the two of them, became a sport they relished.

"At the time we were on the power shift, which started at seven or eight in the evening and went till three or four the next morning," Kothe recalled decades later. "But there were all these old warrants—for burglary, fraud, forgery, robbery, stuff like that, some of them two or three years old. We decided to see how many of those guys we could find. We did it on our own time. During the day sometimes Jim and I would go around in our street clothes and badge our way into places looking for names on the list. We'd go to the driver's license office, insurance commission, and Selective Service board, looking for addresses. We found one guy who'd gone into the Navy, another guy who was living in Kansas. Once we went down to St. Paul–Ramsey [Hospital], went through their records, and found out that a guy we were looking for had an appointment the next morning. We showed up in the morning, waited for them to call his name, and arrested him. We ended up making about eighteen arrests off that list.

"You couldn't do that sort of thing today, what with the data-privacy laws and so forth, but in those days you could. Bostrom and Dexter put us in for commendations for all the extra warrant work we did. But we weren't trying to make names for ourselves. It was just fun. It was police work, and police work was fun."

"Jim loved being a cop," Winger said. "There were very few of us back then who didn't."

James Sackett was buried on Monday, May 25, three days after his murder. A thousand officers, representing jurisdictions around the country—Chicago, Detroit, Milwaukee, Kansas City—filed past his open casket at Wolff Crestwood Park Chapel, then stood in ranks outside and listened via loudspeakers to the Reverend George Voeks conduct the Lutheran rites for the dead. Family, friends, and dignitaries that included former Vice President Hubert Humphrey and St. Paul's incoming mayor, Charles McCarty, filled the room.

It was a brisk, breezy spring afternoon with dry but tempestuous skies that turned sunny when the coffin was carried from the chapel to the hearse, then driven through the heart of the East Side toward downtown and the freeway and the rest of the ten-mile route to Fort Snelling National Cemetery on the southwest edge of town. The hearse was followed by nearly two hundred squad cars and more than fifty private vehicles that created a procession almost two miles long. Six-year-old James Sackett Jr. would remember little about that day except, he said much later, "the cars, the cars, the cars."

"There were school kids lined up along the curb, holding flags and saluting as the procession worked its way down White Bear Avenue," Stuart Montbriand recalled. Decades later, Fred Kaphingst, another young patrolman at the time, could still picture the flag outside the public library at White Bear and Arlington snapping in the breeze. "When the procession passed the old fire station at Seventh and Flandreau, the fire rig was out on the apron and the firefighters were standing at attention," Kaphingst, who had been a Johnson High School classmate of Jim Sackett, said. "When we got into downtown, at Wacouta or Sibley, I saw an elderly black man standing on the corner, and I wondered how he was going to react. The man took off his cap and held it over his heart as we passed."

Kothe, Winger, Pelton, and Bostrom, joined by fellow officers Dennis Wilkes and Jon Markuson, bore the flag-draped coffin between the lines of saluting officers to the grave site on the west side of the sprawling burial ground. Aircraft taking off and landing at Minneapolis–St. Paul International Airport, which abuts the cemetery, drowned out some of what Pastor Voeks said by way of comfort and benediction, but the short, sad ceremony was familiar even to those who had never witnessed a police officer's interment. An honor guard fired three volleys into the noisy sky, a bugler played "Taps," and the tightly folded flag from the coffin was presented to the devastated widow.

Forty years later, Kothe said a police officer's funeral was intended to send a message to the greater community. "All the cars and red lights and ceremony—it's like we're telling everybody, 'One of ours went down, but the rest of us are still here. And we will never forget.'"

3

For a week after James Sackett's murder, the department blanketed the Hill with rolling patrols—often four officers armed with shotguns to a car and sometimes a patrol car shadowed by an unmarked squad as backup. "Think about a bee hive that got hit with a stick" was how a young man who lived in the neighborhood described the police activity at the time.

On May 28, six days after the shooting, deputy chief Richard Rowan told the *St. Paul Dispatch* the department was attempting "to verify every call for police aid in the Summit-University area before officers actually arrived at the scene." Two squad cars were directed to respond to every call "whenever possible." On the positive side, Rowan (who would be sworn in as chief the following month) said his officers were reporting a "noticeable decrease" in burglaries, robberies, and other crimes in the neighborhood. Unfortunately, in the same story, homicide commander Ernest Williams reported no new leads in the Sackett investigation, much less the identity of a suspect or suspects and an imminent arrest.

Williams's investigators had begun talking to Hague Avenue residents and other sources on the Hill within minutes of the shooting. The city's street cops, especially those who regularly patrolled the Hill, talked to their "friendlies" and kept their eyes and ears open. The uniformed officers watched their backs and the backs of their comrades. There had been no specific threat of another assassination attempt, but then there hadn't been a specific threat preceding Sackett's murder, either. There was, though, a near-unanimous sense within the department that they were facing a heightened danger—possibly from outsiders, meaning people they didn't know, but in any case from shooters who, if they weren't professionals, were proficient enough to kill from a distance.

The department's homicide detectives, now in charge of the investigation, had all but eliminated as suspects the residents of 859 Hague: seventy-year-old Frank Lopez; his daughters Bridget Wyzykowski, twenty-two, and Christine, seventeen; Christine's nineteen-year-old husband, Roger Egge (the young man who called the police immediately after the shooting); and Lopez's son Ernesto, who was fourteen. Christine, who said she had been sleeping in the basement, was the pregnant woman Sergeant Dexter nearly fired on when the officers charged through the Lopezes' back door. Frank Lopez's wife, Mary, was working the midnight shift at a home for mentally handicapped children when the shooting took place.

Egge, who was probably in the best position to see what happened when the shooting started and had a chance to calm down after he was grilled by the first responders, told the *St. Paul Pioneer Press* on Saturday that he and Ernesto Lopez had been watching TV in the darkened living room when they heard someone rattling the aluminum porch door out front. (The door had been wired shut, he explained, because the porch was used for storage. The family entered and exited the house via the back door.) When he went to investigate, Egge said, he heard a shot and "saw the officer fall" in front of the stoop. Stepping onto the porch, he saw through the glass in the front door the officer lying on his "back or side," bleeding profusely and weakly calling for help. Egge said he saw another officer in a "red" car parked at the curb talking into his radio. When he spotted Egge, the second officer ran back toward the house with his pistol drawn. "He looked angry and very frightened," Egge told the reporter. The cop fired his gun twice, but Egge had run back into the living room, dropped to the floor, and called the police. Before he could hang up, other cops burst through the back door.

When Earl Miels interviewed Egge on June 5, the young man said that he heard Sackett yell "God help me!" as he fell, that he did not know Kothe had actually fired at him, and that he had no idea who might have wanted to use their house as a "setup," though because he and his wife spent a lot of time in the yard, people in the neighborhood would have known she was pregnant. Egge, who had lived his entire life on the Hill, said he knew of (in Miels's words) "any number of young militant Negroes that would be mentally capable [of shooting] a policeman" and mentioned a half-dozen names.

Egge's account as recorded by Miels differed from other early reports in certain details—the young man's position when the police burst into the house, for instance. Kothe had stated, and would continue to state, that he fired his gun toward the movement in the house *before* running to the car and calling for assistance; Kothe, for that matter, always mentioned the "flash" that accompanied the sniper's shot and did not recall Sackett saying anything when he was on the ground. But none of those points, which probably only reflected the confusion typical of witnesses to traumatic events, was deemed crucial to the investigation. Then, and again decades later, Egge was considered a credible witness. In August, he agreed at Captain Williams's request to take a polygraph examination, though there is no record in the case files that he ever did.

Meantime, law enforcement agencies and media outlets throughout the Twin Cities received hundreds of calls and letters. The proffered information ranged from a mere nickname or two to interminable shaggy-dog stories—most of which, if remotely credible and sometimes even if not, were followed up by investigators.

An anonymous caller contacted the state Bureau of Criminal Apprehension in St. Paul, revealing both the identity of Sackett's killer and the immediate disposition of the murder weapon. Neither half of the tip proved helpful. The same day, police in Minneapolis were contacted by a nameless caller who said he had heard a man in a North Side pool hall either boasting of or confessing to the Sackett murder. The caller provided not only the man's name and home address but his race, height, weight, hair color, make and color of car, and its license-plate number. When checked out, the man was revealed to be a prisoner in the Hennepin County jail, awaiting trial on simple assault charges. He was summarily dismissed as a suspect in the Sackett case.

A woman having her hair done at a local salon was heard talking about her ex-husband, who she said had been talking about two men known as "Big Bruce" and "Calvin" who had in turn been talking about "how they got someone from Detroit to kill Sackett and how they got [the killer] on the freeway and out of town fast and [how] they were planning something else." A neighborhood restaurateur told Cecil Westphall that he had heard one young man tell another that he had killed Sackett. According to the detective's report, the speaker "went on to say that he made a living killing policemen" and had killed "one or two" in Illinois and the Dakotas since killing Sackett. The young man said he lured his victims with an emergency call regarding a woman about to deliver a baby and used a "collapsible rifle" for the hit. Unfortunately, the restaurateur would probably not be able to identify the killer because he had not personally seen him but only heard his comments through a vent in the wall.

There were the so-called "copy-cat" situations that invariably follow a high-profile crime. The Minneapolis Police Department received a spate of calls, all of them anonymous, in which snipers were reported waiting to shoot a policeman at the corner of Thirteenth Street and Hennepin Avenue. (The caller sounded like a young man, "possibly drinking.") Twenty minutes later, a caller told the Hennepin County sheriff's office that he was going to shoot a cop either at the Dutchman's Bar or in the parking lot of the Chestnut Tree Tavern. A third caller informed the local FBI office of his intention to shoot an officer at the White Castle at Grant and Nicollet in downtown Minneapolis. The caller said he was an escapee from a nearby state hospital for the insane and had killed the cop in St. Paul.

Detective Carolen Bailey listened patiently to the theories of a decidedly unconventional middle-aged St. Paul couple who told her, "We don't actually know anything, but we got some ideas." Their suspicions fell on "militants," "Commies," "drug addicts," and "the policeman's teenage sons." While they were at it, the couple expressed their displeasure with recently retired Chief Justice Earl Warren and the local Veterans Administration hospital.

A caller to the FBI said he had talked to a man who said Sackett's killer was a "Negro man who lives on Hague Avenue in a white house with pink shutters." A pair of St. Paul detectives dutifully cruised the nine-block length of Hague between Lexington and Dale, only to report that while there were many white houses on that street, none had pink shutters.

Then, as in most investigations, there were reports of odd occurrences and unexplained sightings that may—or may not—have been related to the main event.

A city bus traveling west on Selby was struck by a light-blue sedan entering the intersection at Victoria at 12:22 AM on May 22—roughly ten minutes after the Sackett ambush. According to the bus company's records, the car, which was coming from the south (from the direction of Hague Avenue), failed to stop after the collision, despite sustaining what a witness described as significant damage. (Curiously, the bus was not damaged, according to the police report, and no one aboard was injured.) The bus driver, who believed the car was a Mercury, Ford, or Plymouth of mid-sixties vintage, said he saw two white men in the front seat. The bus driver had seen the busy police presence at Hague and Victoria, but apparently none of those officers noticed or paid any attention to the bus stopped at the intersection a short block away. In any event, the blue sedan was never located, nor were its driver and passenger ever identified.

There were, inevitably, callers suggesting that Sackett had been the assassin's target all along. Someone posited that the killer had been having "a love affair" with Sackett's wife. Another source, without providing substantiation, described Sackett as a "thumper" and said his murder was payback for rough treatment he had meted out on the street. One said the shooter was the brother of a man killed by Sackett during a burglary. Sackett had in fact shot a burglar, but the man had been wounded, not killed. Police department files revealed, moreover, that Sackett had not been involved in the shooting described by the tipster.

The fact that Sackett was not—*could not have been,* given the known circumstances of the setup and shooting—the sniper's intended victim did not rule out revenge as a possible motive. But the revenge would have been directed against the police, not a specific officer.

The problem was, a lot of people were angry at the police and the "establishment" or "power structure" for whom the cops, in their eyes, did the dirty work. Citizens have always had grievances against the police, and those grievances have often been justified, but the historical anger had by the late 1960s risen to the level of rage. America's military involvement in Vietnam had much to do with that rage, because it was the cops who were called out first to deal with the protesters in the streets and the "radicals" who took over the administration buildings on college campuses. As for the African Americans, American Indians, and Latinos marching, sitting in, and sometimes setting their neighborhoods ablaze, it was the police who turned dogs and fire hoses on marchers, clubbed and dragged demonstrators out of lunchrooms, and opened fire on rioters. The discontent and response that lit up America during the late sixties and early seventies cast a harsh light on the fault lines separating generations, the sexes, social and economic classes, and races.

On May 4, eighteen days before Sackett was murdered, Ohio national guardsmen shot and killed four students during antiwar skirmishes at Kent State University. A week before Sackett's murder, police shot and killed two black students and injured a dozen others at Jackson State College in Mississippi. In St. Paul, black citizens were talking about a pair of separate incidents that took place three months earlier.

Shortly before midnight on February 7, a white officer named Ronald Olson shot and killed Keith Barnes, a twenty-year-old black man, during a scuffle outside the Factory, a popular lounge at University near Lexington. Olson said he was attacked by Barnes while he and his partner checked the bar for suspects in another matter. Barnes's family and friends insisted the victim was trying to defend himself and his brothers against the officers, who they said had initiated the altercation. The shooting quickly drew a crowd, and several squad cars, including one manned by Kothe and Sackett, responded to the urgent call for backup. Three days later a Ramsey County grand jury declined to return an indictment against Olson, declaring, according to the *Pioneer Press,* the officer had acted "reasonably under the circumstances." A small crowd protesting police brutality at a Concordia Avenue playground burned an effigy of a police officer.

Then, on the evening of February 25, two young men walked into the Muntz stereo shop on University Avenue between Victoria and Milton, pulled out guns, and demanded cash from the store's clerk and customers. But St. Paul's intelligence unit had been tipped off about a possible robbery attempt at the store, and four plainclothes officers had staked out the site. When the robbers emerged, the cops were waiting.

According to police reports, Sergeant Paul Paulos stood up behind a retaining wall and shouted, "Stop! Police!"

"Fuck you!" one of the young men shouted back, and fired his pistol at Paulos.

Unhurt, Paulos took down both men with three blasts from his shotgun.

Wayne Massie, who was three months shy of his twentieth birthday, died of his wounds a short time later. Eighteen-year-old Byrd Douglas was hospitalized with buckshot wounds in both legs.

The news of the Muntz shooting electrified the neighborhood. Minutes later, a black man walked up to one of the patrolmen protecting the crime scene and said he'd heard a "nigger" had been shot. "You killed my brother last week," the man went on, and identified his brother as Keith Barnes. "You guys are in for it now," he told the officer before walking away.

Massie and Barnes were sons of well-known local families, and their funerals were attended by hundreds of friends and neighbors. Both incidents, neighborhood residents argued, exposed the readiness of white cops to use deadly force against blacks. In the Massie case, they asked why, if the police knew in advance of the robbery, the robbers weren't stopped on the way in, reducing at least the potential threat to the store's employees and customers. If the department officially responded to that question, the response was not recorded. Some citizens believed the two youths had been set up.

In fact, the consensus among St. Paul cops was from the beginning that Sackett's killer and whoever helped him were black. That's because the shooting took place on the Hill, where most of the city's African Americans lived, and because an unknown number of young black men had sporadically though ineffectually exchanged gunfire with officers over the past couple of years. In the wake of the Barnes and Massie shootings, officers had to be aware that there were blacks on the Hill who were angry enough to want to kill them.

Few if any in the department expected a blowup such as they had seen in Detroit, Chicago, Newark, Washington, DC, and other cities during the previous few years. They could tell themselves that St. Paul's black population, though it had grown substantially during the previous decade with the influx of newcomers from Chicago, Gary, and the Deep South, was still small and "manageable"—scarcely more than 3 percent of the city's total. St. Paul, moreover, had a hundred-year tradition of law-abiding middle-class African Americans who made respectable livings as railroad porters, stockyard workers, and entrepreneurs, who owned barbershops and beauty parlors, small law offices, insurance agencies, and other storefront businesses, who maintained comfortable homes, and who attended services at one of several vibrant churches. People watched out for each other and for each other's children, and with a few notable exceptions kept the neighborhood's kids on the straight and narrow. St. Paul's blacks had been energized by the civil rights movement that had taken root in the South after World War II and spread northward during the 1960s. There was reason for them to believe that with the wider equality and expanded opportunity promised by the movement and the politicians who belatedly supported it, the lives of African Americans everywhere would improve.

But nobody with even a passing familiarity with the neighborhood could overlook the devastation wrought by the imposition of Interstate 94 during the previous decade. Hundreds of homes had been removed and families displaced during the freeway's construction, and many of the small businesses owned by African Americans were shuttered or torn down. Selby Avenue and other Summit-University thoroughfares had grown seedy, pocked with vacant lots, boarded-up storefronts, and a slew of bars, pool halls, after-hour drinking and gambling establishments, and other sites that both the police and law-abiding residents—always the vast majority on the Hill—considered problems. The local black population was younger and poorer than it had been a few years earlier, less rooted in the community's historic values and less likely to have a good job or any job at all. Street crime frightened everyone except the muggers and car thieves themselves. African Americans from bigger cities with larger black populations scoffed when they heard the area described as a "ghetto," but there were few persons who would deny the fact that stretches of Summit-University had become slums.

Life in the black community could be—and often was—dangerous, especially for young men who "might get caught up in something," said Nathaniel ("Nick") Abdul Khaliq, who was Nick Davis back in the day, got in trouble with the police himself, and much later became president of the National Association for the Advancement of Colored People's St. Paul chapter. Khaliq, who also served the community as a firefighter, added that the rest of the city did not seem to mind what was happening in the neighborhood so long as it was only blacks getting shot, stabbed, and robbed.

"Those were wayward times," an elderly African American who lived in the area recalled forty years later.

Relations between the neighborhood and the police, meanwhile, were historically uneven. Though St. Paul had hired its first black police officer, Louis Thomas, in 1881, there were, by the late 1960s, only four black officers in the department. Few white cops lived on the Hill anymore, even if, like Glen Kothe, they had grown up there. Local blacks spoke affectionately of Patrolman William Skally, a gangly Ichabod Crane lookalike who, for much of his thirty-two-year career, walked the neighborhood beat, knew everybody black and white, and was renowned for providing winter boots for chilly school patrols and for returning errant teens to grateful parents before the kids could get into serious trouble. Skally was "a true community policeman before community policing had a name," said one African American admirer, Deborah Gilbreath Montgomery, who as a child had been a beneficiary of Skally's kindness. But Skally, who retired in 1973, was considered an exception among the white cops who patrolled the area, and even the department's few black cops were often viewed suspiciously by residents as "spies" or, worse, traitors to their kind. They were called, in the parlance of the times, "Oreos"—black on the outside but white inside.

Most African Americans on the Hill had been as shocked by Sackett's murder as their white neighbors, and some had been shamed as well, suspecting, or maybe knowing, that the killer was one of their own. "We were upset about a lot of things," one long-time resident recalled, "but we weren't about to kill anybody over it." William Finney, who lived on Rondo Avenue as a kid during the fifties and sixties and decades later became St. Paul's first African American chief of police, pointed out that St. Paul's black middle class was in many ways, including their view of law and order, as conservative as their white counterparts. At the same time, African Americans were fed up with justice unequally applied, which, in the eyes of many citizens and police officers alike, was all too common in Summit-University. Indeed, it was a rare black family anywhere in America that didn't have stories of mistreatment at the hands of the police and/or the courts dating back to the end of slavery. Black Americans in St. Paul and elsewhere grew up distrusting and fearing the police, while most whites did not and have had difficulty understanding, much less sympathizing with, the black perspective on the issue. As the African American writer James Baldwin noted at the time, "[W]hite people seem affronted by the black distrust of white policemen, and appear to be astonished that a black man, woman, or child can have any reason to fear a white cop." Too many white people were either ignorant of or indifferent to the history of blacks in America.

While even black cops could insist the Sackett case was about a murdered police officer, not about race, for many Summit-University residents race was always part of the conversation when the police were involved. Just a year earlier, a thirty-five-year-old African American, Luther Fulford, was convicted of second-degree murder in the death of a white St. Paul officer named Richard Younghans. The veteran cop had been off duty and, according to Fulford's trial testimony, had badgered Fulford with racial and sexual slurs before the two of them tangled in a downtown hotel and Younghans was fatally stabbed. Local blacks insisted that Younghans had a history of race-baiting and that Fulford, who was reportedly about sixty pounds lighter than the burly officer, had only been defending himself. Whatever the truth, many African Americans were convinced that if Fulford were white and Younghans black, Fulford would never have been arrested in the case, let alone tried and convicted.* Thus, when the Sackett investigators came knocking on their doors in 1970—and would again decades later—it was for many African Americans a matter of choosing sides. You were either with the white cops or you were with the black suspects—either with "the man" or with "the brothers." For many African Americans it was and would forever be a troubling but certain choice.

In 1970 African Americans complained about frequent harassment at the hands of police. One white officer was known to break the taillights of black persons' cars to give him a pretext to stop the drivers and nose around in their cars. Others groused about cops planting dope and other contraband in their cars during traffic

---

*Younghans has not been included among the fallen officers honored during the St. Paul department's annual Memorial Day Service.

stops. Some citizens considered the police department's purchase of AR-15 semi-automatic assault rifles during the late 1960s a blatant provocation. The use of the word "nigger" was common among police addressing blacks long before cops were called "pigs." Cops, meanwhile, were frequently "rough with their hands," in the words of an African American man who came of age during the sixties. "The cops could do whatever they wanted" when dealing with blacks they suspected of violating "white rules," he said, his youthful anger still simmering decades later.

Many residents recalled the shooting death of Oliver Crutcher, a thirty-year-old African American, on September 10, 1949, if not necessarily the shooting death of Allan Lee, a white St. Paul detective, that immediately preceded it. Shortly after four o'clock that Saturday afternoon, Crutcher held up Janssen's Liquor Store on University Avenue just west of the Capitol. Two uniformed officers responded and exchanged shots with Crutcher, who ran south on Virginia Street in the direction of Rondo Avenue. Sergeant Lee was one of dozens of cops who flooded the area and joined in the manhunt, which, a couple of hours later, centered on a house on St. Anthony. According to police and news reports, Lee confronted the fugitive near the front door and was fatally shot in the head and stomach. Crutcher leapt over Lee's body and escaped.

Three hours later, police converged on a small apartment building at Rondo and Louis. This time a young African American officer named James Griffin, who lived nearby, and two white officers caught up with Crutcher hiding under a bed in an upstairs room. The officers opened fire. Crutcher was killed—reportedly struck by a dozen bullets without firing a shot himself. Some African Americans insisted the police were out for blood that evening, had declared "martial law" in the neighborhood, and were determined to kill Crutcher. Passing time, failing memories, and the vagaries of urban mythology sometimes garbled later recountings—confusing Lee, for instance, with the officers who killed Crutcher. But what the neighborhood knew for certain was that a black man had been shot to death by the police.

Paul Paulos, a Greek immigrant's son who had lived in the neighborhood since the early 1950s, conceded the point decades later. There was a great deal of racial resentment among the blacks on the Hill, he said. "They felt the cops were picking on them—and, it was true, some of them were. Traffic stops, harassment, all kinds of things. Some cops went overboard." Paulos himself maintained a stable of informants, people for whom he would tear up a traffic ticket and who would be encouraged to call him at home if they had something important to share, but he admitted that he had enemies in the neighborhood, too. It's not a coincidence that in the aftermath of the Barnes and Massie killings, both he and Ronald Olson had been rumored to be on a hit list.

Some cops looked back beyond the Barnes and Massie incidents to what they believed might be the true harbinger of the Sackett assassination—the so-called Stem Hall riots that took place during the Labor Day weekend of 1968, when young African Americans clashed with police following a concert and dance downtown. The police say the crowd became unruly after an officer confronted a young man armed with a gun in a restroom. Community sources said the cops locked the crowd inside the hall, then tossed in tear gas. At any rate, the melee spilled into the street and expanded into a ragged running battle back up to the Hill. Police and civilians exchanged gunshots, and passersby and reporters were roughed up. Businesses were torched, cars trashed, and countless windows broken, resulting in thousands of dollars in property damage. According to a report produced by the St. Paul Urban Coalition, four policemen had been shot (none fatally) and twenty more suffered non-gunshot injuries; hundreds of young persons were "tear gassed," and twenty-six persons were arrested. (How many civilians suffered minor injuries—luckily, there were no fatalities—was not recorded.) Mayor Thomas Byrne told reporters he saw "neither rhyme nor reason" for the violence. But, in the eyes of the coalition and others, the riots revealed an understaffed and inadequately funded police department ill-prepared to handle a major disturbance of this kind and insufficient black representation on the police force as well as a plethora of larger, societal problems, ranging from lack of living-wage jobs and affordable housing to a heritage of bigotry and discrimination.

To many unnerved St. Paul citizens, the coalition's assessment, which was controversial, echoed the federal Kerner Commission report, issued in early 1968, that warned of worsening, apartheid-like conditions in many American communities and future racial violence if "separate and unequal" conditions were not addressed and improved. "A new mood has sprung up among Negroes," the Kerner report noted, "particularly among the young, in which self-esteem and enhanced racial pride are replacing apathy and submission to 'the system.' The police are not merely a 'spark' factor. To some Negroes, police have come to symbolize white power, white racism, and white repression." To St. Paul's cops, the Stem Hall eruption demonstrated that significant numbers of young blacks were willing to take them on in the streets.

St. Paul was hardly unique. By late 1968, police officers in cities from New York to Oakland had been fired upon, sometimes lethally, by both individual blacks and members of defiantly armed organizations such as the Black Panthers. In those cities, cops and many blacks alike were convinced the other side was out to kill them. In early 1970, however, St. Paul cops were still leading a charmed life. In the year and a half since the riots, neither conditions in Summit-University nor relations between police and the black community had improved—if anything, they had worsened. Yet the fact that since Stem Hall it was the police who had done most of the shooting—*all* of the deadly shooting on the Hill—had doubtless stoked the anger among many blacks while possibly lessening the sense of danger in the minds of many officers.

In the three months between the Barnes and Massie shootings and the Sackett ambush, there had in fact been sundry rumors and at least one outright warning. Olson's and Paulos's names came up in the chatter, but not Sackett's or Kothe's—at least nothing that survives in the department's files. Most of the noise was coming from the streets, overheard in bars and pool halls and passed along by confidential informants or disclosed in exchange for a pass on some minor offense. Much of it had to do with the Oakland, California, based Black Panther Party—"those fearsome, frightening, arms-bearing black men, with their paratroop berets, and swagger, and revolutionary rhetoric," in the words of journalist Michael Arlen—which, since its founding in 1966 by Huey Newton and Bobby Seale, had achieved mythic status among young African Americans. A large part of the organization's appeal lay in the members' ability, as black men with guns, to scare the wits out of white people, especially white governors, mayors, and law enforcement officials. Ever since FBI director J. Edgar Hoover declared, in late 1968, that the Panthers were the single greatest threat to the nation's internal security, authorities everywhere had been intently—in some places obsessively—monitoring Panther activity.

A few days before Sackett's murder, for instance, Captain Williams received word that a group of Twin Cities youths had traveled to Des Moines and then to Kansas City where, in Williams's notes, "they are alleged to have formed a group to be called the Sons of Malcombs [sic]." The youths' contact was a man "alleged to be with the Black Panthers," and the "Sons of Malcomb are believed to be assigned to the Midwestern states with the intent of creating terror." By "Malcomb," Williams's informants were presumably referring to Malcolm X, the charismatic black leader who had been assassinated in New York in 1965. At any rate, no further mention of the group can be found in the department's files.

In retrospect, one comment proved decidedly significant and would resonate for decades to come.

Exactly one week before Sackett was murdered, patrolmen James Jerylo and Laverne Lee stopped a blue Cadillac driven by a young Vietnam War veteran named Joseph Edward Garrett, known in the neighborhood as "Eddie." The officers, according to Jerylo's report, didn't specify why they stopped Garrett but said that while checking his car they "turned up" a .22-caliber revolver locked in the glove compartment. Jerylo and Lee confiscated the pistol but chose not to arrest Garrett on a firearms charge. By way of returning "the favor"—that was Jerylo's interpretation—Garrett, "in an unsolicited statement," told them to "watch the rooftops." Garrett would say no more on the subject, but the cops, who in recent days had heard their share of angry blather and vaguely worded threats in the dives along Selby Avenue, took Garrett's comment as a warning and passed it along to their superiors.

Garrett's words were surely on the officers' minds seven days later when they arrived at 859 Hague, saw Sackett's blood on the sidewalk, and within minutes spotted Garrett approaching the gathering crowd. Even before they saw Garrett, in fact, Lee had called headquarters and requested a "pick up" order for the young man ("male negro about 22 yrs"), albeit "for information only." When, a few minutes later, Lee and Jerylo spotted Garrett standing around near the crime scene with "other young negroes," they hustled him into the back seat of their squad car. Lee asked him, as they had asked him a week earlier, where he had gotten the "rooftops" information. This time Garrett was slightly more forthcoming. He said he'd heard talk at Cotton's, a pool hall on Selby. Pressed for further detail, he said the "threats" had been voiced by several of the pool hall's patrons, none of whom he could, or would, name. He also said he had seen several "new faces" in the neighborhood—individuals from other parts of the country (Los Angeles, Chicago, Milwaukee) who might have been Black Panthers operating "under cover."

"Again we pressured [Garrett] for some names," Lee wrote in a subsequent report, "but again he stated that was just what he had overheard in the area. When asked if he knew of any persons who he thought might have done the [Sackett] shooting, he stated no."

Eddie Garrett's was not the only familiar face among the rubberneckers standing under the street lamps at Hague and Victoria that night. Lee, Jerylo, and other officers jotted down the names of several other young men with whom they had some experience, including one Kelly Day and a youth whose name was mistakenly recorded as "Randal Reed."

On June 3, Sergeant James Hedman, while knocking on doors in the neighborhood, talked to a woman who lived in a fourplex at 869 Hague, across Victoria and three houses west of the crime scene. Edith Carroll told Hedman that the night before the shooting two policemen had come to the back door of her apartment and said they were responding to a call about a sick child. Carroll said she told the officers she knew nothing about a sick child and had not made the call.

Back at headquarters, Hedman checked the records and discovered that the sick-child call, phoned in by a man who identified himself as "John Anderson," had actually been received two minutes before midnight on May 19 and that a car had been dispatched moments after midnight on May 20. Squad 315—patrolmen Thomas Owens and Tony Bennett—responded to the location and reported back that the call was "unfounded." Like the bogus O.B. call two nights later, the May 19 call had been recorded.

Hedman's report raised several questions. Presuming this wasn't a coincidence, had the sniper intended the first call to be a test of the police response and serve as a dry run for the assassination? Or had the call been the real thing, and the sniper for some reason did not like his chances or lost his nerve? Or, as seemed most likely, had the call been for real, but foiled by Squad 315's decision to park in the alley, out of the sniper's sight? There were other questions as well. False alarms and prank calls to the police and fire departments were common and quickly forgotten; still, given the rumors and tensions in the neighborhood, why had no one mentioned the May 19 call at subsequent roll calls? (Apparently, if the memories of a few long-retired officers could be trusted, there had been some roll-call chatter about Eddie Garrett's warning to Jerylo and Lee in the days prior to Sackett's murder.) Why had the "unfounded" sick-child call not been brought to investigators' attention until Edith Carroll mentioned it to Hedman nearly two weeks after Sackett's murder?

No certain answers survive, but it has become an article of faith among two generations of St. Paul cops that Owens and Bennett had almost literally dodged a bullet because, unable to find space to park in front of Carroll's fourplex, they pulled into the alley behind it. A corollary holds that 859 Hague was chosen two nights later because there was no alley on that block, so whether the responding squad parked in front or on the side of that house, the officers would be in the sniper's field of fire.

The thought and planning implied by the last conclusion pointed to a particularly dangerous assailant, not merely someone with a grudge or an impulsive nature and a high-powered rifle. Just as vexing, Ernest Williams's detectives believed from the beginning of their investigation that people on the Hill knew who was involved in Sackett's murder. Even if an outsider had pulled the trigger, *someone* in the neighborhood knew the shooter's name and the names of others involved. But paradoxically in light of the deluge of calls and letters, few of the people who might actually know something were talking to the police. St. Paul's investigators were dealing with a hard reality built on the fear and distrust of the police among many young people and persons of color. It was a new era in the neighborhood. Many of its citizens believed the police were there not to serve and protect the community but to oppress it. "It wasn't like the old days when people felt obligated to tell us things," a veteran cop lamented. "Now there was a code of silence. *You do not talk to the pigs.*"

The police had to deal with internal communication problems as well. A wall built of status and tradition separated the detectives from the uniformed cops, and that wall often impeded the sharing of important information. The detectives, who had come up through the ranks, were what most street cops aspired to be, and homicide investigators were the elite of the elite. Tough, demanding, and fastidious, a handsome fashion plate with a curious mind and varied interests, Williams personified the superior image of his small, select unit. For fear of jeopardizing a developing case or exposing a confidential informant, or simply because information was the gold they mined and hoarded, his detectives were ill disposed to share what they knew. A callow patrolman, at the entry level of the departmental hierarchy, wouldn't think of approaching a homicide investigator and asking him or her for an update on a case, even when it was a case in which they both had a life-and-death stake.

At that time, moreover, another crew—the small, innocuously named Law Enforcement Aid Unit, under the command of a flamboyant lieutenant, Jack O'Neill—was busily gathering intelligence, mainly from their own informants as well as via surveillance of neighborhood hot spots ("hiding in plain sight," in the words of the omnipresent Paul Paulos, who, as part of the LEAU, was legendary for his ability to sit silent and immobile for hours at a time while on a stakeout, like a cat watching a mouse hole). On paper, the LEAU provided information to the homicide squad and other units, but, according to several officers who were active in 1970, the group operated with a great deal of autonomy. "The LEAU had contacts, snitches, all this information, but they kept it to themselves," said Glen Kothe, from the perspective of the street cop he was at the time.

Even before the Sackett shooting, the LEAU and other local law enforcement groups had been keeping an eye on an organization called the Inner City Youth League, which was located in an inconspicuous, two-story brick building at the corner of Selby and Victoria. Established in 1968, the ICYL was one of a handful of storefront organizations in St. Paul and Minneapolis whose self-proclaimed objective was to provide educational and recreational opportunities not otherwise available to kids in poorer neighborhoods. Like other groups at the time, the ICYL was funded at least in part by local philanthropies such as the Hill Family and Amherst Wilder foundations and corporate grants from the likes of the 3M Company. It reportedly paid one dollar rent to the building's owner, Edward Hamm, scion of a local brewing family. Despite the high-minded mission and well-known underwriters, however, the police believed the ICYL was doing more than offering film-making classes and boxing instruction; they had come to view it as a gathering spot for "radicals," "militants," and "Panther wannabes" as well as for petty criminals and other bad actors. At some point, a rumor began circulating that armed men were taking target practice in the ICYL's basement.

Following the Sackett murder—which, coincidentally or not, occurred only a short block away—the St. Paul police and the FBI watched the ICYL more closely than ever. People were photographed coming and going, and a multitasking businessman named Harold Mordh provided a form of freelance electronic surveillance. (The owner of several nursing homes and the longtime director of the Union Gospel Mission downtown, Mordh, who had connections in both the police department and city hall, was listed on FBI rolls as a "ghetto informant." He had provided agents with confidential information about several young African Americans at least since the beginning of 1970.) Detectives interviewed, without much enlightenment, the organization's leaders, at the time the brothers Robert and Jackie Hickman, and duly noted the names of many of the regulars, including a pair of recent Central High School classmates named Ronald Reed and Larry Clark. If not officially Panthers, Reed and Clark were said to be talking the Panther line during meetings at the ICYL and in other venues in the neighborhood.

Reed was becoming important to investigators working the Sackett case. The code of silence was very much in effect on the Hill. No eyewitnesses to the murder had come forward, and despite a dragnet of the neighborhood and beyond no one had come up with anything that might link Reed (or anyone else) to the murder. Reed had been in minor trouble with the law and had spent a few months at Totem Town, a reformatory for boys. In January 1969, he was one of a group of mostly African American students who occupied offices in the administration building at the University of Minnesota, demanding a black studies program, greater opportunities for black students (of approximately forty thousand persons enrolled at the university, fewer than a hundred were African Americans), and other reforms. Reed was a member of a well-known, church-going Summit-University family. Now nineteen, he had a steady girlfriend and a baby daughter.

But Ronnie Reed apparently liked to talk, and what he talked about, investigators were hearing, was revolution and striking back against "police repression," violently if necessary—the kind of incendiary rhetoric favored by the Black Panthers. It was the kind of talk that made the authorities nervous and, in the wake of Sackett's assassination, highly suspicious as well.

As far as homicide detective Carolen Bailey was concerned, Ronald Reed was a suspect almost from the start of the Sackett investigation. Reports from the period indicate his name was among those of a dozen or so young men the police and FBI were keeping tabs on beginning in 1969. St. Paul detectives did not *know* that Reed was involved in Sackett's assassination, but early in the investigation many of them began having reasons to *believe* that he might have been.

On the night of June 22, 1970, Jim Jerylo and another officer, Dennis Klinge, spotted a blue 1960 Chevrolet parked on Kent Street near Iglehart. Two young men were sitting in the front seat. The patrolmen had been on the lookout for such a car after a blue Chevy was reportedly involved in the robbery of a Clark service station on West Seventh Street early that morning. While talking to the car's driver, who identified himself as Ronald Reed, Jerylo noticed a baby-food jar containing, oddly enough, pennies and bullets, as well as a length of cable wrapped with tape on one end. After putting Reed in the back seat of their squad car, Jerylo found a nine-millimeter automatic pistol in the Chevrolet's glove compartment. In the car's trunk, besides several articles of clothing and a rubber glove whose twin had been found in the front seat, was a .22-caliber rifle equipped with a scope. Reed, who wouldn't admit to owning the car or even having a Minnesota driver's license, was taken downtown, where he finally produced a driver's license and was booked on charges of possession of a dangerous weapon and illegal transportation of a firearm.

Jerylo's report included nothing to suggest that he, Klinge, or anyone downtown asked Reed about the Sackett shooting on that occasion, which happened to be a month to the day after the murder. In fact, if surviving records and the memories of elderly cops can be trusted, Reed was questioned about Sackett's murder only once that summer. In surely one of the unlikeliest confrontations during the forty-year Sackett narrative, Carolen Bailey called on Reed at a Summit-University residence where he was hanging out with friends. A county social worker before she became a cop and the department's first female homicide investigator, Bailey was an attractive, self-assured white woman in her middle thirties who was comfortable walking into illegal Selby Avenue establishments or portraying a hooker in a blond wig and red miniskirt on the corner of Selby and Western at two in the morning. "I had a huge advantage being a woman," she said of her experience. "I was still fairly young at the time, and I didn't threaten people." Though she didn't have backup when she approached Reed that summer afternoon, she carried both her service revolver and a two-way radio. She said that she and Captain Williams, who had asked her to try to talk to Reed, simply figured she would have a better chance of getting information than her male colleagues and would be perceived as less a threat if she was by herself.

"There were five young guys in the living room, and three of them were sitting on a long sofa against the wall," Bailey recalled decades later. "There were posters on the wall behind the sofa—Panther stuff, 'Kill the pigs!'—and they were smoking pot, which I could smell when I walked in the door. I didn't know any of them, so I showed them my badge and said I wanted to talk to Ronnie Reed. Reed was sitting on the sofa. He stood up, held his hands out like he was going to be handcuffed, and said, 'Hey, baby, you can arrest me anytime.'"

Bailey didn't arrest Reed but asked him to step outside. "We just chatted," as she remembered the conversation. "He wasn't nasty or cocky. He was flirtatious—and I was a young chick back then. I asked him what he knew about Sackett. I asked him if he *killed* Sackett. Though I was pretty confident he had, I didn't expect him to confess to it, and he didn't. Mainly, I wanted to find out something about his girlfriend. I wanted to know if Connie Trimble was his old lady." And that much, Bailey said, Reed confirmed that afternoon.

It was no secret among their friends that Reed and Trimble were a couple. They had been going together for several years and had a daughter named Cherra who, in the early summer of 1970, was about six months old. Connie was a slender, attractive girl in her late teens, with mocha-colored skin and thick dark hair that she liked to pile high on her head or wear in an Afro. Some people in the neighborhood said she fancied herself looking like Angela Davis, the telegenic California radical who was often on the evening news. Trimble had moved to St. Paul from Denver with her family when she was fourteen and met Reed while hanging out at the Oxford playground near the high school.

But Trimble was of interest to investigators because they thought there was a chance she herself was involved in the Sackett murder—specifically, that she might have made the O.B. call on May 22. That fifty-nine-second call, recorded on magnetic tape, was, besides the misshapen piece of lead that had passed through Sackett's body, the only meaningful evidence the police had been able to collect after the murder. They believed, though, that that brief recording could be the key that provided entrée to the plot. The caller and the shooter, if not one and the same person, most certainly knew each other.

Unlike DNA analysis, voice-print technology was available to investigators in 1970. It was new enough, however, that even major-city detectives such as Williams, Miels, and Bailey had not yet used it. One of the recognized experts in the emerging field was a Michigan State Police detective named Ernest Nash. On June 1, St. Paul investigators mailed Nash, in East Lansing, the tape of the May 22 call, followed within the week by reels containing the voice of the May 19 "sick-child" caller who had identified himself as "John Anderson" and the voices of six individuals ("possible suspects") recorded by the police for purposes of comparison. Four of the voices belonged to residents of 859 Hague and two were those of neighborhood women, one of whom was named Brown. On June 15, Nash wrote back: "After comparing the spectrograms of the voice of the unknown caller with spectrograms of the suspects' voices it is the opinion of the undersigned that none of them made the call for assistance." Furthermore, Nash's analysis showed, not surprisingly, that the May 19 and May 22 calls had not been made by the same person.

Because Ronald Reed was by that time a prominent blip on the detectives' radar, Connie Trimble's voice print was of interest. The problem was, the apartment where Trimble and Reed were living at the time had no phone. Bailey felt the nature of the crime justified subterfuge. Trimble, she learned, was enrolled in a government program known as Aid for Dependent Children, and Bailey asked a supervisor from her former job in the county welfare department to bring Trimble on an unrelated pretext into his office, where Bailey would call and record her voice.

The report that Bailey made at the time was lost, and four decades later she couldn't recall how she identified herself—"I'm sure

I told her I was a police officer," she said—and what exactly she induced Trimble to say, though the words, per Ernest Nash's instructions, included much if not all of the language from the May 22 call. Bailey managed to get her to use the specific words she wanted.

Bailey's ploy, when it became part of the public story, infuriated civil libertarians and welfare-rights activists and resulted in someone printing up "Wanted" posters with a price on the detective's head. It was not the only time Bailey was threatened, and she would always insist that the posters didn't faze her. She could not recall if any attempt was ever made to record Ronald Reed's voice and compare it with "John Anderson's." At any rate, she had managed to record Connie Trimble and presently sent the tape off to Michigan for analysis.

4

The torrent of calls, letters, and tips on the street during the first few weeks following Sackett's murder thinned during the summer of 1970. In the wake of even spectacular crimes such as this one, both the quantity and quality of information almost always fall off within a week or two of the event, and weeks had become months without a breakthrough or arrest in the Sackett case. Many if not most of the leads the St. Paul police were picking up were not, in any event, coming from sources on the Hill, where people were keeping their mouths shut, and what the investigators were hearing was not very helpful. Typical was the call, in late September, from the Holy Spirit Catholic School on Randolph Avenue, where a "boastful" young teacher reportedly told his students he was tight with the Black Panthers and knew who killed Sackett. When questioned by Earl Miels, however, the teacher conceded that while he did believe certain (unnamed) Panthers had been involved, he personally knew nothing about the shooting.

Meantime, tensions remained high in the area. Flashing red lights drew unfriendly crowds. Squads responding to calls in Summit-University made quick work of their responses, getting in and out in a hurry, often with a second squad backing them up. Ed Steenberg and John LaBossiere, back walking a beat on the Hill (foot patrols had been suspended for a couple of weeks after the Sackett murder), were told that certain individuals had gotten their hands on a number of cut-down .30-caliber carbines and that officers "should be careful" in the area of Cotton's pool hall and the apartment buildings between St. Albans and Grotto. Informants told their police and FBI contacts about late-night gatherings at which "black nationalist activities" were discussed and about "informal meetings" where "individuals discussed how to make bombs." Ronald Reed, Eddie Garrett, and Kelly Day, another young man well known to police at the time, were among those mentioned in the reports.

Then, just before suppertime on Saturday, August 22, a two-pound stick of dynamite planted in a wastebasket and activated by a timer blew the door off a women's restroom on the main floor of the Dayton's department store in downtown St. Paul. The restroom's sole occupant at that moment was a forty-seven-year-old high school English teacher and Democratic Party activist named Mary Peek, who was combing her hair when the dynamite exploded and who was critically injured in the blast. Police and firefighters responding to the explosion discovered, moreover, a timer and twenty pounds of dynamite in a coin-operated locker outside the restroom; the second, much more powerful bomb, if it had exploded, would doubtless have caused dozens of casualties, mostly among the cops and firefighters. Witnesses reported seeing an African American boy or young man, wearing a woman's wig and dress, running from a door near the restroom and locker area shortly before the explosion.

Within the next two weeks St. Paul police and local FBI agents responded to bombings or attempted bombings at a Union 76 storage tank, the Midway National Bank, the Burlington Northern Railroad Building, and a Gulf Oil facility. Near the Wabasha Street Bridge, a small, soft-spoken fifteen-year-old Central High School student was slightly injured in a small explosion. His name was Gary Hogan. A wig, woman's dress, and bomb-making instructions were reportedly found in his possession, and, despite his age, he was reported to have ties with the Panthers and other militant groups. He was soon charged with attempted first-degree murder in the Dayton's bombing.

On September 12, acting on an informant's tip, police found a dozen cases of dynamite in a car parked in a garage behind a Dayton Avenue apartment rented by Kelly Day.

The bombings were part of a wave of terroristic explosions throughout the United States and Europe at the time. Two days before the St. Paul Dayton's explosion, a bomb caused a half-million dollars in damages (but no serious injuries) at the Federal Building in downtown Minneapolis. Two days after the Dayton's blast, a massive bomb detonated in the early hours of the morning killed a graduate student at the Army Mathematics Research Center on the University of Wisconsin's Madison campus. Antiwar activists were blamed for both the Minneapolis and the Madison blasts.

No one had forgotten about Sackett during the stretch of explosions, but the bombs reminded edgy cops and nervous civilians alike that snipers were not the only threat in those perilous times.

Considering the level of mayhem in their own backyard, it's unlikely the St. Paul police noticed or paid much immediate attention to a botched bank robbery 380 miles away, in an Omaha, Nebraska, strip mall, on the evening of October 20.

According to witnesses, about five minutes before the eight o'clock closing time, three young men wearing military attire entered the Ames Plaza Bank and pulled weapons from under their coats and jackets. One of the robbers, a teller told a reporter, shouted, "Hit the floor, this is for real!" Everybody, with the exception of bank guard William Tate, a middle-aged off-duty sergeant with the Omaha Police Department, complied. Tate drew his revolver and exchanged fire with the robbers. He was hit in the shoulder but believed he had shot one of the gunmen before the trio bolted out the door and into the parking lot, where at least two of the three reportedly got into a waiting car and sped away. No money had been taken. And amazingly, in light of the dozen-plus bullets and shotgun blasts that gouged the bank's walls and floor, no one besides the moonlighting cop and possibly one of the frustrated robbers had been injured in the fray.

Omaha police told the media they were looking for "three Negro men in their early 20s. One is short and the other two [are] of average height." Witnesses said a fourth person drove the getaway car, described as a white 1962 Chevrolet, but they couldn't agree whether the driver was a man or a woman.

Within a week, however, police and FBI agents in the Twin Cities were looking with intense interest at the Omaha incident. At the request of their Omaha counterparts who were acting on tips from informants, St. Paul detectives sent mug shots and background information regarding thirteen local robbery suspects to Nebraska. Sergeant Tate and Ames Plaza Bank employees and customers subsequently identified two men from the photos: *Reed, Ronald Lesley, Negro/male, DOB 31 Aug 50* as "being similar to the party that entered the bank armed with a carbine . . . covered by a trench coat," and *Clark, Larry Larue, Negro/male, DOB 9 Feb 51.* Additional witnesses looking at the photos identified both men as two of the three would-be robbers.

Investigators had quickly gotten their hands on a receipt for the aforementioned trench coat, which one of the robbers had dropped on the bank floor. According to the receipt, the coat—Glen Eagle brand, size thirty-six—had been purchased at Liemandt's clothing store in Minneapolis three days before the robbery by a Ronald L. Reed of Fuller Avenue in St. Paul. The FBI also determined that Reed had purchased, in St. Paul, two .30-caliber carbines similar to the guns used at the Ames Plaza Bank. University of Minnesota records indicated, moreover, that Reed had been issued a size thirty-six Army uniform when he was briefly a cadet in the school's Reserve Officers' Training Corps.

Omaha police reports noted Reed's arrest in St. Paul the previous June on charges of possession of a dangerous weapon, illegal transportation of a firearm, and suspicion of robbery, though the robbery charge had been almost immediately dismissed because of insufficient evidence and the other two charges had been dropped within a month. The only other arrests on Reed's record—for aggravated assault and burglary—had occurred in 1966, when he was fifteen and sixteen, with no disposition. Larry Clark's rap sheet, according to the Omaha reports, revealed arrests for theft and burglary in 1966 and 1967, with no disposition. Both Reed and Clark, however, were suspected of having participated, along with a third man, in the September 4, 1970, robbery of the First Grand Avenue State Bank in St. Paul. Confidential informants said Reed had "planned and engineered" that job. The reports went on to say, apparently based on additional confidential information, that both Reed and Clark were "known as militants" who "have caused much trouble and refer to teachers and police as fascists and pigs."

According to the reports, both men were wanted for questioning in the murder of St. Paul patrolman James Sackett.

*   *   *

All of a sudden, or so it must have seemed to frustrated investigators as the dangerous summer of 1970 melted into an uncertain fall, the Sackett case was about to break.

On September 29, Michigan State Police voice-print specialist Ernest Nash sent a brief message to homicide commander Ernest Williams in St. Paul: "After comparing spectrograms of the voice of Connie Trimble with spectrograms of the unknown [May 22] caller . . . it is the opinion of the undersigned that Connie Trimble's voice and the voice of the unknown caller are one and the same."

Why it took a month for St. Paul investigators to act on Nash's report is not part of the record; presumably investigators were digging for additional information to tie Trimble to the murder. But by the last week of October her fugitive boyfriend was a suspect in two attempted armed robberies, and they no doubt figured they had better move before Trimble went on the lam as well.

Late in the afternoon of October 30, homicide unit and LEAU detectives, following the issuance of a first-degree murder warrant by municipal court judge J. Clifford Janes, converged on Fuller Avenue near Oxford Street. Trimble and her baby were living at the time in a duplex at 1027 Fuller. Detectives Leroy Thielen and Russell Bovee, in an unmarked car, spotted a woman walking in their direction on Fuller, carrying a child. The woman fit Trimble's description so they turned the car around and watched her enter a house up the block. They knew the house: Ronald Reed's parents lived there. When Lillian Reed, Ronald's mother, answered the detectives' knock, they could see Trimble sitting on a sofa in the living room. Then Reed's father, Walter, appeared and blocked the door. Unwilling to force the issue, the detectives directed a squad to watch the back door, then called for the officers who carried the actual warrant. When detectives arrived a few minutes later with the paperwork, Walter Reed went back inside the house and spoke to Trimble. Moments later, Trimble appeared at the door, and the detectives arrested her. Earl Miels read Trimble her Miranda rights against self-incrimination, and Trimble asked Lillian Reed to call an attorney. Then, with ten-month-old Cherra in her arms, the teenage mother left for downtown with her escort of detectives.

An hour later, Bovee and Thielen saw Larry Clark driving a blue Mustang on Hague Avenue. When Clark got out of his car in front of 882 Hague—a half-block west of the Sackett murder scene—the detectives identified themselves and arrested him on an outstanding illegitimacy warrant. Strangely enough, Miels and the other detectives looking for Trimble had stopped Clark in the Mustang that afternoon and inquired whether one of the two young women in the car with him was Trimble. Those detectives must have either been unaware of the outstanding warrant or believed their first priority was apprehending Trimble. In any event, it was not until the following day that the St. Paul police learned Omaha authorities had filed three felony charges against Clark: entering a bank with unlawful intent, use of firearms in commission of a felony, and shooting with intent to kill, wound, or maim.

The same charges had been filed against Ronald Reed, but his whereabouts (as well as the whereabouts of the third alleged Ames Plaza Bank gunman, Horace Myles) remained unknown, at least to the authorities. The communication prepared by the Omaha police on November 2 included Reed's correct middle name—it was Lindsey, not Lesley—and noted that he was "usually neat in appearance and well dressed," "has used drugs in the past," and should be considered "armed and dangerous." The accompanying mug shot—taken following Reed's June 22 arrest in St. Paul—showed a lean young man in a rugby-style shirt, with a moderate Afro haircut and a Fu Manchu mustache. He looked bored, or perhaps disdainful, more than dangerous.

At 5:45 PM on the day she was arrested, Constance Louise Trimble was shown to a chair in Ernest Williams's office at police headquarters. Williams, too, read Trimble her Miranda rights, then asked her to read them herself on a printed form and sign it. She read the information and told Williams she understood what she had read but refused to sign the piece of paper.

Williams's impressions of the composed young woman were not recorded or, if they were, have not survived. He would have known, or learned eventually, thanks to his investigators' research, that Trimble had been born on March 4, 1952, in Denver, that her father, Sherman, was a welder at American Hoist and Derrick in St. Paul, and that she had three brothers, two of whom were older and one of whom was serving time in Colorado. Connie had lived in two different apartments in St. Paul before renting half of the duplex on Fuller, where the landlord knew her and her boyfriend as "Mr. and Mrs. Ronald Reed." A Ramsey County case worker told Carolen Bailey she had seen anti-police posters ("'Kill the pigs!' et cetera") hanging in one of Trimble's apartments. Trimble had graduated from Central High School only the previous June. Her high school record revealed both an indifferent student who was twice suspended for smoking in the lavatory and missed a lot of class (blaming her attendance problems on the need to help care for a sickly mother) and a lively girl who typed sixty words a minute, held a summer job as a clerk-typist at a federal government office downtown, and liked to sew, cook, dance, and hang out at the Inner City Youth League. Trimble was said to have tried unspecified "narcotics."

That evening in his office, Williams wanted to know if Trimble had called the police on May 22, seeking help for a pregnant woman at 859 Hague. Trimble at first denied making the call, then moments later admitted that she had. According to Williams (and other detectives in the room at the time), Trimble proceeded to tell a long story by way of explanation. She said she had been following a set of unsigned instructions she had found in her mailbox in order to get a man named Gerald Starling in trouble with the police. Starling was supposedly having a "pot party" at the Hague address that night; the officers arriving there on the bogus O.B. call would discover the illegal activity and arrest Starling, against whom, Trimble said, she held a grudge because he had threatened members of her family. She had no idea, she told Williams, that an officer was going to be killed and she felt terrible when she heard about the murder the next day. She insisted she didn't know who had instructed her to make the call.

When Williams asked why she hadn't come to the police with her story, Trimble replied, "Who would believe it?"

When asked what she did with the letter, Trimble said she tore it up and burned the scraps.

While Williams was out of the office for a few minutes, other members of the homicide unit chatted with Trimble. One of the detectives eventually left the room and told his boss Trimble wanted to tell him "the whole truth on this murder." But when Williams returned, Trimble said she wanted to speak to her lawyer, a Twin Cities criminal attorney named Neil Dieterich, who arrived a short time later and conferred with her privately. After talking to Dieterich,

Trimble told Williams she didn't want to resume their conversation and from that point forward she would not to talk to investigators unless Dieterich was present. During a restroom break, however, Trimble told Bailey she was afraid of reprisals against her and her baby by "those involved in the killing" (Bailey's words). She did not say who she thought those persons were but "volunteered that they were not related to her or her baby."

Trimble was fingerprinted, booked, and assigned a cell in the Ramsey County jail adjacent to police headquarters. Her baby was sent, at her request, to the home of Walter and Lillian Reed, whom she described as the child's natural grandparents.

The next day, Trimble talked to homicide detectives Thomas Opheim and Edward Fitzgerald; Dieterich apparently wasn't in the building. She told them that Ronald Reed was baby Cherra's father but that she didn't know where he was. She expressed concern about Cherra and said she hoped the child was getting enough to eat. Opheim asked if she wanted to discuss anything else with them, and she told him she only wished they would believe what she told Williams the previous evening. Opheim said he didn't think anyone was going to believe the story about the unsigned instructions. He also said it would be in her best interest to tell them the "whole story." She then asked them, Opheim wrote in his report, "what would happen if she told us what we wanted to know." Opheim replied that the police would tell the "proper authorities" she was cooperating with the investigation and, when the case went to trial, a jury would likely "show leniency in her particular situation." But at that point, according to Opheim, she asked to speak to her lawyer and their conversation ended. Opheim and Fitzgerald later that day tracked down Gerald Starling at an apartment on Carroll Avenue, but Starling refused to answer their questions.

Trimble was charged with first-degree murder on November 2. Bail was set at fifty thousand dollars, a very large amount at the time. On November 12, she was indicted by a Ramsey County grand jury following the testimony of seven witnesses, most of whom were police officers. The indictment was the first definitive step in a long and tortuous legal journey, the actual length and tortuousness of which no one could have possibly imagined.

*   *   *

Ronald Reed, meanwhile, had finally been found. The circumstances of which he was instantly at the center could hardly have been more spectacular, at least on paper.

On November 12, St. Paul detectives were told by Kelly Day—who was, it turned out, both a closely watched suspect in a number of local cases (including the discovery of that automobile trunk full of dynamite behind his apartment) and a "reliable" confidential informant—that he, Reed, and another man were planning to hijack an airliner at Minneapolis–St. Paul International Airport. The hijackers, Day told the cops, would kidnap city councilwoman Rosalie Butler and hold her hostage, fly the commandeered airplane to Canada, and there demand the release of Larry Clark, Connie Trimble, and Gary Hogan, the accused Dayton's department store bomber. The hijacking, originally scheduled for that day, had for some reason been rescheduled for the next.

Preposterous as it seemed, Day's report was taken seriously. Security at the airport was placed on high alert. In addition to law enforcement agencies representing state and local jurisdictions, the FBI, Secret Service, and Federal Aviation Administration sprang into action. Everybody was looking for Ronald Reed, the peripatetic fugitive whose apprehension now seemed to be a matter of national security.

Additional tips to the police the afternoon and evening of November 12 placed Reed at two different addresses on Franklin Avenue in south Minneapolis. At the second site, a fourth-floor apartment at 402 West Franklin, officers appeared to be only minutes behind him—the door was unlocked and the TV was on when they arrived. Then an informant told St. Paul police that Reed had holed up in a second-floor apartment on Washington Avenue in southeast Minneapolis, near the University of Minnesota's football stadium. (The informant said he had just left the apartment and could vouch for Reed's presence.) Shortly before 4 AM on Friday, November 13, shotgun-toting raiders from the St. Paul, Minneapolis, and university police departments as well as the FBI were poised to take a prisoner.

Accounts differ as to the details of the raid. Three young women (one on crutches, nursing a broken leg, and at least one of them a U of M student) either lived or were staying at the Washington Avenue address, and the officers either knocked on the door and were admitted by one of the occupants or they barged in, waving their guns and terrifying the women. Not in dispute was the fact that Reed was on the premises and neither resisted arrest nor attempted to flee. He was, according to police reports, wearing a red sleeveless T-shirt and brown corduroy pants when the police arrived and seemed to have been sleeping.

Decades later, lawyers would argue about whether the police had the proper paperwork in hand and whether the women consented to a search of the apartment, which consisted of several small rooms. That search turned up, under a mattress in one room, a loaded .38-caliber snub-nose revolver. A sawed-off 12-gauge shotgun, a handful of shotgun shells, a red safety flare that could have been mistaken for a stick of dynamite, and a pair of walkie-talkies "still in the box" were discovered in another. On the suspect himself police found, according to their reports, a Social Security card, a Nebraska driver's license, and a Braniff Youth Air Fare ID all bearing the name "Dana W. Hudson." Also confiscated was a black leather bag containing a shirt, a pair of bell-bottom jeans, and other articles of clothing, a North Central Airlines ticket dated October 7, 1970, for Flight 744 to Omaha, a matchbook from the Imperial Hotel in Omaha, a small book comprising the quotations of Mao Tse-tung, and twenty-three dollars in cash.

At least as significant given the immediate threat were several pieces of paper that seemed to belong to Reed. One, which the raiders said was removed from Reed's pants pocket, was a handwritten note, laced with crossed-out words, misspellings, and eccentric punctuation, addressed to "control tower to be relayed to Governor [Harold] LeVander, police, FBI or any agents of the government concern."

The note began, "We our revolutionary, take heed to our first and last warning. If there is any attempt to interfere or stop us, we will blow this airplane up and everybody on it.

"We our well arm and we our carrying explosives. The plane & hostages will be held until our demand our met." The demands included the release of Clark, Trimble, and Hogan, ("brought to the airport and allow to bored the plane unescorted"), fifty thousand dollars in gold, and national television time for the Black Panthers.

"The fate of these hostages will be determined by the United States government," the note continued. "Will they live or die?

"We will not hesitate to kill or die for our freedom. We have nothing to lose and everything to gain.

"For the benifit, comfort & safety of the hostage, it would be best for you to be exspeedeant."

The note was signed, "All power to the people. Seize the times." Instead of a period or exclamation point, the last sentence ended with a colon.

Besides the note, police confiscated a to-do list that included the notations "kidnap governor"* and "liberate prisoner" as well as reminders to "contact United [Airlines]—make reservation—purchase tickets:" Another scrap bore the names Angeles (presumably meaning Angela) Davis, Bobby Seale, and other "revolutionaries" in custody. Yet another was a short grocery list that specified Dutch cleanser, milk, bread, soap, and toilet tissue. There was also a three-page letter addressed to Connie Trimble. The letter, which was more carefully written than the notes but similarly distinguished by the peculiar use of colons in place of periods, acknowledged Trimble's legal bind ("the trick bag that you're in"), the writer's own difficulties with the "pigs" ("they our trying to murder me or railroad me off to jail for the rest of my life"), and the need for her to remain patient and steadfast. "I love you and miss you and I will be waiting for you. Please remain beautiful and I will write you everyday:" Undated and containing no mention of the supposedly imminent airplane hijacking, the letter closed with "All power to the people" and was signed "Ronnie Reed."

The front-page story in the November 13 *Dispatch* quoted Minneapolis's deputy chief Joseph Rusinko saying that an informant had told police that Reed had "planned to board the plane disguised as a woman at about 8:45" that morning, though there was nothing in the confiscated papers, Reed's travel bag, or relevant police reports that indicated a disguise or a specific boarding time. There was no mention in the confiscated notes, for that matter, of any conspirators or other "revolutionary" action.

So, nearly six months after James Sackett's murder, St. Paul investigators finally had their men—or the persons they believed to be their men—in addition to their woman. But from a prosecutor's

*Coincidentally or not, Councilwoman Butler and Governor LeVander were neighbors on Summit Avenue.

point of view on that chilly autumn morning, the case against Reed in both the Sackett murder and the alleged hijacking plot would seem problematic at best: no eyewitnesses or physical evidence in the first instance, no actual crime committed (with the possible exception of weapons violations) in the second. Thus, when Reed appeared in front of St. Paul municipal judge James Lynch later on November 13, he, like Clark, would be arraigned on charges relating to the Omaha bank case, in which there were eyewitnesses and evidence (Reed's trench coat, the Liemandt's receipt, shell casings, et cetera). Assistant Ramsey County Attorney Paul Lindholm asked that Reed's bond be set at $150,000, the highest to date in Minnesota history.

Reed said little during the formalities and admitted nothing. With no hope of making bail, he joined Clark and Trimble in separate cells at the Ramsey County jail.

The *Disptach*'s headline trumpeting Reed's arrest that day said an "Alleged 'Panther'" had been seized. But at the end of its top-of-the-front-page story that jumped to page four a smaller headline read, "Panthers Disclaim Connection."

The story that followed quoted a spokesman for a Black Panther Party delegation that happened to be in the Twin Cities for a series of college lectures saying the group had "no knowledge" of Ronald Reed.

Emory Douglass, described in the story as the Panthers' "culture minister," who headed the touring group, was not available for further comment.

5

A few days before Christmas, Ronald Reed and Larry Clark appeared in front of a police line-up in St. Paul and were identified by William Tate, the wounded Omaha police officer, as two of the three men who attempted to rob the Ames Plaza Bank in October. At the request of Nebraska governor Norbert Tiemann, and with the subsequent approval of Governor LeVander, the two suspects were formally extradited to the Cornhusker State to stand trial on three felony charges related to the Omaha case. Their joint trial, in Omaha's Douglas County district court, began on August 9, 1971.

Despite the evidence and eyewitnesses, there were enough inconsistencies in the testimony to make the outcome not quite the sure thing that local authorities might have hoped. The most interesting discrepancy was the testimony of Sergeant Tate, who said that during the brief shootout with the would-be robbers he had fired his .38-caliber revolver at one of the gunmen from six inches away and was sure he had wounded the man, whom he and other witnesses had identified as Reed. Reed, however, bore no signs of a "penetrating-type wound." Prosecutor Sam Cooper conceded that Tate had not in fact shot Reed, though Tate "very honestly believed" that he had, but whether he did or did not was irrelevant in any event and did not lessen Tate's credibility as a witness. Cooper also dismissed the testimony of Alex King, identified as an acquaintance of Reed's from St. Paul, who testified that *he* had purchased the trench coat dropped at the bank using Reed's identification and that the coat had later been stolen.

And in a statement that would echo in another courtroom thirty-five years later, Cooper acknowledged there was "more evidence pointing at Reed than at Clark"—but there was enough, he added, to place the latter in the Ames Plaza Bank with Reed and Horace Myles. The sole witness speaking on Clark's defense, according to the *Omaha World-Telegram,* was his mother, Alma Porter of St. Paul, who told the jury her son had never been charged with a felony until the Omaha case.

After five hours of deliberation, the jury of seven women and five men—one of whom was an African American—voted to convict Reed and Clark on all three counts: entering a bank with unlawful intent, use of firearms in commission of a felony, and shooting with intent to kill, wound, or maim. Judge C. Thomas White sentenced both men to ten to twenty-five years in prison. (Myles was tried separately and convicted.) Reed and Clark were transferred to the Nebraska Penal Complex in Lincoln on September 11, 1971, to begin serving their terms.

Investigators in the Twin Cities no doubt felt some satisfaction knowing the men they believed had been involved in James Sackett's murder were behind bars for a substantial stretch of time. If they thought they had the Sackett suspects by the short hairs, however, and could leverage those long sentences into accusations and confessions, they were seriously mistaken. Indeed, the mixed emotions that arose from "knowing" who murdered Jim Sackett but not being able to prove it would gnaw at the case's original investigators for years to come. In a brief 1972 report, Earl Miels wrote a melancholy postmortem: "The arrest and conviction of Ronald Reed and Larry Clark in Omaha . . . are to the benefit of society even though they apparently cannot be tried here for their part in the murder of Officer Sackett."

During visits to their Nebraska prison by St. Paul detectives over the next several years, neither Reed nor Clark was willing to listen to offers of reduced hard time in exchange for information implicating themselves, one another, or others, or to appeals to conscience and common sense. Decades later, Russ Bovee recalled observing the two men through a window in the penitentiary at Lincoln. Informed they had a visitor from Minnesota, the inmates literally turned their backs on the detective. The code of silence that had frustrated the police at home extended beyond state lines. (Myles, too, refused to have anything to do with the Sackett investigators. After serving his time he changed his name and reportedly relocated in the Pacific Northwest.)

Neither Reed nor any of his alleged co-conspirators was ever charged in connection with the hijack scheme. Reed's conviction in Omaha may have been deemed sufficient by prosecutors in the Twin Cities, or perhaps they didn't believe they had a case, since the plot existed only in Kelly Day's statement to police and in the note seized by police during their November 13 raid. Reed, for his part, denied any knowledge of a plot. When his November 13 arrest was brought up during the Omaha trial, he said the pants in which the note was found belonged to another man, whose full name and current whereabouts he didn't know.

But, of course, Reed and Clark were only two of the three Sackett suspects in custody. Connie Trimble was in the Ramsey County jail awaiting trial for first-degree murder. Beginning in November 1970, she and her counsel—Neil Dieterich, Donald Wiese, and eventually Douglas Thomson, one of the Twin Cities' best-known defense attorneys—proceeded through a series of pretrial hearings, focused on matters ranging from the admissibility of her statements to the conduct of investigators Williams, Bailey, and Opheim following her arrest to the credibility of the voice-print technology that led to her arrest in the first place. Prosecutors stood by their witnesses and evidence.

On December 16, for instance, Ernest Nash, who compared Trimble's voice print with the May 22 caller's, was questioned in St. Paul by Wiese and Paul Lindholm, the assistant county attorney, before a Ramsey County judge.

"In my opinion," Nash said, "the voice of Connie Trimble and the voice that made the call . . . are one and the same and could be no other."

"What is your degree of certainty in your expression of this opinion?" Lindholm asked Nash for the record.

"Beyond any doubt," Nash replied.

But, no matter how assured expert opinion may be in court, citizens have their own—not necessarily expert but definitely assured. Not long after Trimble's arrest, a series of broadsides appeared in the neighborhood. One, typed, mimeographed, and unsigned, bore the headline "Sister Connie Kidnapped!" and urged not only Trimble's release but the release of "all political prisoners." Crackling with the overheated rhetoric of the time, it began by accusing the St. Paul "pig department" of attempting to "railroad" Trimble "for the revolutionary justice which was dealt to a pig policeman last Spring." It dismissed the spectrogram evidence, insisting there was "no accurate way" to compare voices, and described the process under way in the courts as a "legal lynching" consistent with the government's "fascist actions against the people." Complicit in those actions were "the racist news media of St. Paul and Minneapolis."

Another notice, this one printed and signed by the Minneapolis-based Women's Action Committee, challenged the credibility of voice-print evidence, called out Carolen Bailey for her welfare-office ruse, and declared the police action part of a concerted attempt to "target . . . a group of people working for human liberation." It was no coincidence, according to the committee, that Ronald Reed and Gary Hogan had also been arrested in recent months, "nor . . . that the charges should be similar to those being brought against others in other parts of the country."

At least one local organization began a grassroots effort to raise funds on the defendants' behalf. The Black Legal Defense Committee, whose rather more temperate appeal listed eighteen community residents, including the Reverend Denzil Carty, rector of St. Philip's Episcopal Church, Robert Hickman, director of the Inner City Youth League, and Connie Trimble's brother Herman, soberly referred to "the very serious situation involving several of our young people." The appeal's language was calm and measured, and, though it did not name names nor cite the specifics of the "situation," the objective was clear. "The young people presently in trouble are ours, whether we know them personally or not. . . . They need the help of the total community."

In the winter of 1970–71, *Free Connie Trimble!* became a rallying cry in the black community. If it didn't have the nationwide appeal of *Free Angela Davis!*, it was very much in tune with the angry, insistent times in the Twin Cities, and it reminded locals that there were not only varying opinions on matters of crime and justice but divergent realities as well.

During the protracted wait for Connie Trimble's trial to begin, there were no more arrests in the Sackett case. Unable to make her fifty thousand–dollar bail (even with the community's help), Trimble bided her time in the Ramsey County jail, reading and writing letters and chatting with a series of female cellmates. She saw her daughter, who remained in the care of family and friends, at least once a week. Well coached by her lawyers, she did not speak about the Sackett case with investigators, not even to the personable and persistent Carolen Bailey.

Officers patrolling the Hill occasionally reported gunshots fired in their direction. Tensions remained high, and officers exercised a caution that had not been thought necessary until Sackett's murder, and that caution further inflamed many residents, more and more of whom were by this time referring to the cops with their four-man squads, riot gear, and military-style, semi-automatic rifles as an occupying force.

The officers' major concern, at least for the time being, was less gunfire than explosives, in part because bombs were jangling nerves, damaging property, and sometimes killing people around the country and in part because Gary Hogan's trial began, in January 1971, in Ramsey County district court. That trial, which centered on graphic testimony about the bomb blast that nearly killed Mary Peek in the Dayton's restroom, ran seven weeks. At least as chilling as the description of the first bomb and its victim was the potential horror of the second charge, found in the locker outside the restroom door. Prosecution witnesses said the second bomb would have killed "everyone there." Tried as an adult, Hogan, now sixteen, was convicted in March of attempted first-degree murder and aggravated arson and sentenced to twenty years in prison. At the time, and for the rest of his life, Hogan denied any involvement in the crime.

But St. Paul had not experienced the last of the bombs.

At 5:10 PM on July 27, 1971, more than five pounds of dynamite blew off doors, shattered windows, and damaged cars behind a shuttered bar at Selby and Dale. Immediately adjacent to the erstwhile Frank's Regal Lounge was a house that at the time served as the police department's recently opened Summit-University community-relations office. No one was injured in the blast, but the three officers who happened to be inside the house were knocked off their chairs. One of them, James Mann, told reporters he didn't think the bomb was intended to injure any cops—if it were, it would have been placed directly behind their office, not behind the vacant building next door—but was probably intended as a "scare tactic." Mann was one of the department's four black officers at the time. Though popular in the African American community, he was distrusted by many white cops, and his comment reminded some of them of remarks attributed to him following the Sackett murder. At that time, he was quoted by the *Minneapolis Tribune* saying, "If we get emotional and sympathetic when an officer gets hurt, we must also get emotional and sympathetic when anyone gets hurt"—which, though reasonable enough on the face of it, did not endear him to fellow officers who believed themselves targeted for assassination. No one was arrested in the community-relations office bombing, but police had several familiar suspects under surveillance—among them the ubiquitous Kelly Day and a friend of Day's named John Griffin.

On the legal front, the case against Trimble moved slowly forward. Her attorneys' challenge of the voice-print evidence as the basis of her arrest and its admissibility during the upcoming trial was knocked down, in February 1971, by a Ramsey County district court judge and then, the following November, by the state supreme court. The high court also ruled that while Carolen Bailey's voice-print deception may have been ethically questionable, it had not violated Trimble's constitutional rights.

Two months later, Trimble's lawyers petitioned the court for a change of venue, arguing that the extensive publicity as well as a local fund-raising campaign on behalf of the Sackett family jeopardized the defendant's ability to get a fair trial in St. Paul. The venue-change request was duly granted, but the case was transferred only across the river, to the Hennepin County Courthouse in downtown Minneapolis. Considering that the Minneapolis papers covered the case almost as closely as their St. Paul counterparts and that local radio and television stations saturated the entire metro area, the change seemed inconsequential if not laughable. The trial, scheduled to begin February 7, was then again re-sited, this time to Rochester, about eighty miles away, which made more sense. Ramsey County judge David Marsden, who would preside wherever the trial took place, ordered the change at least in part because of the sale in the Twin Cities of large lapel buttons reading *Connie Trimble Not Guilty.* Reportedly, the Inner City Youth League had ordered 2,500 buttons (or 5,000, depending on the report), to be sold for a dollar apiece. Nobody could remember when a venue change had been granted twice in Minnesota.

On Friday afternoon, February 18, a large explosion tore through a wall of the State Office Building across the street from the Capitol, injuring a half-dozen employees and causing extensive damage. The blast was described by investigators as "well planned [and] very strong." Despite investigators' interest in the usual suspects, no one was ever charged in the case.

When her trial got under way on February 22, 1972, a year and nine months since Sackett's murder, Trimble had been incarcerated for sixteen months. Even so, seated at the defense table in the Olmsted County Courthouse in downtown Rochester, the defendant, in her carefully coiffed Afro and modish miniskirts, struck observers as remarkably poised and self-possessed. The same could hardly be said for Olmsted County authorities, who installed metal detectors and assigned sheriff's deputies to pat down everybody passing through the courtroom doors. At the prosecution's request, nobody wearing a *Connie Trimble Not Guilty* button would be admitted. Nevertheless, the courtroom's 110-seat gallery was full of Trimble supporters, almost all of them African American and some of them, in the opinion of prosecutor Theodore Collins, willfully intimidating in their oversized hairdos, leather jackets, and almost tangible solidarity. (Collins later referred to the men as the "drill team" and said their intent was to frighten both the jury and the defendant. Collins asked the judge to restrict the men's access to the courtroom, but his request was denied. He would later concede that fearsome as they might have appeared, the men did not disrupt the trial proceedings.) Jury selection, true to expectations, moved slowly, going through forty-six of the fifty-four prospective jurors before six men and six women—one of them black—were seated on February 29.

On March 2, Collins outlined the state's case before the Rochester jury. An experienced St. Paul lawyer who had been hired to run the prosecution for an understaffed Ramsey County Attorney's office, Collins had successfully prosecuted Gary Hogan the previous year. He said the testimony would show that Trimble made the call that lured Patrolman Sackett into the ambush and that Trimble knew the officer would be murdered. In chambers, the famously aggressive Doug Thomson, now Trimble's lead attorney, argued that the prosecution could not prove first-degree murder and asked Judge Marsden for a directed verdict of not guilty. But Marsden denied Thomson's motion—the first of several before the trial's end—and, back in front of the jury, the testimony began. The prosecution's initial witnesses included six residents of 859 Hague Avenue as well as Glen Kothe and five other police officers, all of whom testified about the events of May 22, 1970. The next day, Saturday, March 4, there was no trial, and Connie Trimble celebrated her twentieth birthday in her Olmsted County jail cell.

When the trial resumed on Monday, a prosecution witness named Vera Washington described hearing voices and footsteps moments after being awakened by a loud noise on the night of the Sackett murder. Sitting up in her first-floor bedroom, she told the court, she heard "someone running—it sounded like boys running" between her house and the house immediately to the east. "I didn't see anything, but just heard their voices." (The woman, who lived at 878 Hague, said she told officers what she had heard when they came down the street looking for information shortly after the shooting. She apparently had not told homicide investigators her story until they spoke with her in December, almost seven months later; the reason for the delay was not given.)

Later that day, Jeanette Sackett, who had been present in the Rochester courtroom from the beginning, took the stand and described her family life before and after her husband's murder. Jim Sackett's father and mother listened intently from the gallery.

Collins asked the widow if she knew anyone who had reason to kill her husband.

She said she did not.

Was she aware of any threats against her husband?

She was not.

"Did he ever tell you he had any fear for his safety?"

"No," she said.

Thomson chose not to cross-examine.

After testimony regarding the path of the sniper's bullet and other crime-scene matters—criminalist Harold Alfultis described the fatal bullet as a steel-core copper jacketed projectile fired from a .30-caliber or larger rifle, most likely from between the third and fourth houses on the south side of Hague west of the Hague-Victoria intersection—jurors listened to the single piece of evidence that linked Connie Trimble to the shooting: the fifty-nine-second telephone conversation with police operator John Kinderman. The jury actually heard two recordings, the first one almost incomprehensible owing to background noise and the second filtered free of most of the extraneous racket. A third tape was also played. On this one Trimble, taking Carolen Bailey's call in the welfare office, repeated many of the words on the May 22 recording. Analyst Ernest Nash then repeated his opinion that Trimble and the May 22 caller were one and the same. Nash was followed by Dr. Oscar Tosi, a professor of audiology and speech sciences at Michigan State University, who spent more than two hours explaining voice-print technology itself and testified to Nash's expertise in the nascent field.

Collins called still more witnesses, including two women in their early twenties, Sandra Webb and Diane Hutchinson, who were acquaintances of Trimble's. Webb said that during the summer of 1970 Trimble told her she had made the May 22 phone call but "had no idea what was going to happen." Hutchinson, who lived at 882 Hague, said Trimble had never said anything to her about the call, nor had she (Hutchinson) witnessed the shooting, nor did she know the identity of the shooter. When queried by Collins, however, Webb said she knew Ronald Reed; Hutchinson said she knew both Reed and Larry Clark. (Hutchinson was living with Clark at the Hague address in May 1970.) It was the first time the two men, who had begun serving their time in Nebraska, were mentioned during the trial.

Detectives Williams, Opheim, and Bailey recounted Trimble's statements about the mysterious written instructions she described during her first evening in custody and her stated fear of reprisals if she told investigators the "whole truth." But the state was foiled when a secret witness, whose name—Kelly Day—had been kept off Collins's witness list for "reasons of personal safety," according to Collins, failed to appear. When St. Paul officers brought the fugitive witness into court the next day, he told Judge Marsden that he had changed his mind and did not want to testify. Collins asked that Day be cited for contempt and his bail be increased (Day was facing an aggravated forgery charge in Ramsey County), requests that Marsden, no doubt as frustrated as Collins, took under advisement.

Thomson began the defense's case by calling to the stand, to nearly everyone's surprise, the defendant herself. No longer able to challenge the voice-print evidence, the defense would argue that while Trimble did in fact make the May 22 phone call, she did not know or anticipate the outcome. And while Trimble could not credibly deny knowing who told her to make the call, she could refuse to name him. Now, on the stand, she denied a social worker's allegations that she was a militant "Black Muslim" with Black Panther posters festooning her apartment walls—she was a Baptist, she said, who had been studying the Muslim religion. She reiterated her fear of reprisal against her and her baby.

Under Collins's ninety-minute cross-examination, the witness described her personal history and her relationship with Ronald Reed. She coolly conceded that she had lied to Williams and his detectives about the anonymous letter she said directed her to make the call but insisted that she believed the intent of the call was to sic the police on Gerald Starling.

"There is no doubt that you made the call, is there?" Collins said, in an exchange reported by the *Pioneer Press.*

"No. I made it," she agreed.

"Where did you make it from?"

"From a telephone booth at Selby and Victoria."

"How did you get there?"

"In a car."

"Whose car was it?"

"I do not wish to answer."

When Trimble continued to refuse to answer questions about her companion that night, Marsden told her she *had* to reply. After a pause, however, she said, "I refuse to answer that question."

Following a recess, she was asked the same question, which she again refused to answer, despite Marsden's insistence.

"It is a proper question and I order you to answer it," the judge told her.

"I'm afraid to answer it," she said.

Trying a new tack, Collins asked her about Reed's whereabouts the night of the murder. Trimble said she did not know where he was when she made the call, but when she returned to their apartment at about half-past midnight, she found him there, asleep.

"Do you tell lies whenever it suits you?" Collins asked her.

"I'm not a habitual liar, if that's what you mean," the witness replied with her customary aplomb.

Whereupon the prosecutor produced St. Paul patrolman Laverne Lee, who testified that he saw Reed—supposedly at home in bed—among the crowd that had gathered at Hague and Victoria shortly after the murder.

Late on March 15, the case finally went to the jury, which was charged by Judge Marsden with deciding whether the defendant was guilty of first-degree murder and nothing less, meaning a guilty verdict would result in a mandatory life sentence. After only three ballots and six hours of deliberation the jurors, on March 16, decided the defendant was not guilty. Trimble's friends in the courtroom erupted, her mother, Dorothy, fell to her knees and loudly praised God, and the defendant, according to the *Pioneer Press*, "threw herself into the arms" of attorney Neil Dieterich, sobbing.

"It's a victory, that's all," the paper quoted her as saying. "I can only thank God."

Reporters quoted jurors saying the state hadn't proved beyond a reasonable doubt that Trimble had intended to commit murder.

Trimble was not yet, though, a free woman. Before the verdict, Marsden had cited her for contempt and imposed a thirty-day sentence to be served in St. Paul. Theoretically, if she continued to refuse to name the person who directed her to make the May 22 phone call, she could have been jailed indefinitely. But after thirty days Ramsey County Attorney William Randall decided enough was enough, and early in the morning of April 7, 1972, a cool spring day, she was for the first time in more than seventeen months free to enjoy the fresh air.

Perhaps because of the fury manifested by the calls and letters that followed the verdict, or as a continuing show of solidarity by her supporters, or for other reasons possibly unfathomable to the city's white majority, a group of six young African Americans, at least one of whom wore a *Connie Trimble Not Guilty* button on his leather jacket, formed a tight human shield around her when she emerged from the county jail and walked her to a waiting car.

Then, at least as far as that white majority was concerned, Connie Trimble disappeared.

*   *   *

One night during the spring of 1972, about the time of Trimble's acquittal or possibly a few weeks later, a squad car drew up in front of 859 Hague. The driver, Patrolman Glen Kothe, turned off the car's engine, pointed at the two-story frame house with the enclosed front porch and short front sidewalk, and said simply, "Right there."

Kothe's partner that night, William Scott Duff, was a tall, skinny, twenty-one-year-old rookie from the Minneapolis suburb of Robbinsdale. Duff had enrolled at the University of Minnesota intending to be a wildlife biologist, then taken the St. Paul Police Department exam on a whim. He was a member of the department's class of 1971, which also included a hot-shot East Sider named Thomas Dunaski, and was a few months ahead of a brash product of the Summit-University community, William Finney; all three would have illustrious careers as St. Paul cops. Though Duff was too new on the job to have known James Sackett, he knew Sackett's story, or at least the terrible end of it, and he knew this was where it happened and it happened on a spring night possibly not much different from this one.

"It was late," Duff would remember almost forty years later. "The streetlights were on, but it was foggy. There was mist in the air. Kothe said, 'Right there' and explained the whole thing—where he walked around to the back of the house and where Jim was, where the flash occurred, and where he believed the shot came from." Sackett's story had been discussed at length in the academy, a powerful cautionary tale for young officers preparing to work in a dangerous environment. But that night in the misty dark of Hague Avenue the murder seemed real in a way that it hadn't in class. "It was emotional," Duff recalled. "You could hear it in Kothe's voice. Only two years had passed, and you could tell he was still hurting."

Kothe had returned to work after taking three or four days off to collect himself, which was all that was believed necessary in those days, even after an officer's partner had been killed and even though the fatal bullet, or a second one, might have killed him. St. Paul cops weren't used to being shot at—certainly weren't used to one of their own getting killed—and post-trauma therapy, support groups, and grief counselors were still, in the early 1970s, several years away. So within a few days of his partner's murder Kothe went out on patrol and with a new partner responded to a call about a car sitting in a vacant lot. Approaching the car, he felt the hairs standing up on the back of his neck. He called for backup, and three or four squads raced to the site. But the abandoned car turned out to be nothing more than an abandoned car, and Kothe felt like a fool.

Then and for years to come Kothe spent a lot of time second-guessing himself. *I virtually witnessed a friend of mine, my partner, get murdered,* he would think. *Did I do something wrong? Should I have done something differently to prevent it? Maybe I shouldn't have gone around to the back.* All of that was running through his mind, and he was afraid he was driving himself nuts. And, as if the self-interrogations weren't bad enough, there were the dreams. For many years after the murder he would dream about walking into a robbery and being unable to pull the gun out of his holster or about seeing a bullet coming at him and not being able to move.

Later in 1972 Kothe got himself transferred to the department's K-9 unit, where his partner was a dog. He preferred that to working with another human being. He had reached the point where he didn't want to work with anybody. He didn't want to feel responsible.

Kothe's brief stop there with Patrolman Duff was not his first visit to 859 Hague since the murder. That had occurred three months after Jim Sackett's assassination. Kothe drove there with Jeanette Sackett, at her request and in her car. It was warm and sticky, a typical late-August day. When they reached the site, Jeanette took photographs of the house and the intersection and then turned on a small tape recorder. She told Kothe she wanted to be able to explain to her kids, as truthfully and completely as possible, when they were old enough to understand and started asking questions, what had happened to their dad at that spot on May 22, 1970.

The intersection was quiet, and the house on the northeast corner looked like dozens of others in the neighborhood, except for the broken glass in the front door. Jeanette could tell it was difficult for Kothe to go back there. But she told him, "You're the only one who can answer my questions. Please explain things to me." Kothe answered her questions but was careful about what he told her. He didn't tell her about Jim's scream or the blood staining the sidewalk, figuring neither she nor her kids needed to know that, or if they did, they could find it out on their own, when they were ready. And that would be the last time Jim Sackett's widow and his final patrol partner would speak for thirty-five years.

Kothe would come to believe that Jeanette blamed him for Jim's death.

Jeanette denied that, blaming Kothe's "survivor's guilt" for the subsequent lack of contact and communication while acknowledging her own struggle following her husband's death. For several days, she recalled decades later, she could hardly move. "I couldn't nurse my baby, couldn't even give him a bottle. I was so distraught I don't think I was all there. I just couldn't accept that Jim was gone. I'd wake up in the middle of the night and think I heard a car door close and expect him to come walking in. For a long time I'd be in a crowd and expect to see him. Or I'd be driving to the grocery store and look into the car next to mine and think, *What if it was Jim?*"

The police department wasn't any better prepared to deal with a murdered officer's widow than it was to deal with a murdered officer's partner, offering neither psychiatric care nor financial or legal counseling to help cope in the aftermath. For the first couple of weeks, officers' wives would come by the house with hot dishes and other food. But that stopped after a while, and it seemed to Jeanette that many of the cops and their wives and some of their other friends didn't know what to say or do so they kept their distance. Jim's parents and siblings did their best to help, but they were struggling with their own grief. Jeanette's blood kin had returned to Louisiana after the funeral, and though she went back for a few days herself and briefly wondered if she should relocate, she decided St. Paul was the only home her kids knew, so St. Paul was where they were going to stay.

Money was a problem, then and for years to come. She received Social Security payments for herself and the kids as well as Jim's police department pension (if memory served, less than four hundred dollars a month), but that and the proceeds from a trust fund established for the family at a downtown bank barely covered the family's needs. She would eventually go back to work, but for a few years, while the kids were little, she stayed at home and made do with what she had. There was more to deal with, after all, than the mortgage. The two oldest children, Jim Jr. and Jennifer, were old enough to have an inchoate sense of what had happened to their father, and they were not only heartbroken, they were terrified, knowing before they had the means to deal with such knowledge that there were people in the world who might hurt them. That fear eventually solidified into a wariness and mistrust of others that would last a lifetime. For the children's sake as well as her own, when Jeanette went somewhere, whether it was to the supermarket or the doctor's office, she took all four along.

At least once a week for the first several months, she would pile her kids into the car and drive to the cemetery at Fort Snelling. "I would look at the long lines of graves and think, *What do I have here? I have this headstone,*" she said. "But it would give me peace, going to the cemetery and saying my prayers. I'd buy flowers on the way or take them from our yard, and we'd put them on Jim's grave."

Sometimes, though, the challenges of everyday life seemed too much to bear alone. Almost forty years later she recalled an incident in the parking lot of a Woolworth's five-and-dime store near their home. She had tears in her eyes when she mentioned it, yet she was laughing at herself, too, embarrassed by the memory.

"It was the first Christmas Jim was gone," she said. "I'd taken the kids to the store because the older two wanted to buy me a present. Well, when we came out of the store, the car had a flat tire. Jim had taught me how to change a tire, but that day I thought, *I can't do this.* So, if you can believe it, I called the police. They sent out a squad, and the guys changed my tire while I sat there with my children and cried."

Part Two

A Very Cold Case

"Is it solvable?"
"Sure. Then we'll find Jimmy Hoffa."

1

This time there was no middle-of-the-night call for assistance, no counterfeit concern expressed about a sick child or a pregnant woman, no apparent need to hurry. Not at first.

Rookie St. Paul officer Ronald Ryan Jr. was responding to a call about a "slumper"—in police lingo somebody sleeping or passed out in a car—in this instance a red Plymouth Sundance parked outside the Sacred Heart Church at East Sixth and Hope streets. It was seven o'clock on August 26, 1994, a bright, late-summer morning with a high blue sky, for tens of thousands of Minnesotans a perfect day for the state fair situated only a few miles away. According to one witness, who happened to be looking out her apartment window across the street at the time, Ryan spoke to the car's occupant, then walked back to his squad car, at which point the other man got out of his car and shot him multiple times. All at once there were several urgent calls, from witnesses to the shooting or the immediate aftermath, to the 911 emergency-response number, which the public in St. Paul and virtually everywhere else in the United States had been using for more than a decade to summon help in a crisis.

On this day the calls would continue all morning, as Twin Citians watched live television coverage of the manhunt that swept across St. Paul's East Side and called to report sightings of the fugitive shooter. By about ten o'clock, the focus had shifted three-quarters of a mile to the southeast of Sacred Heart Church, to a nondescript house on Conway Street, where Ryan's killer—the twenty-six-year-old patrolman had been pronounced dead two hours earlier—was holed up in a backyard fish house and where he shot and mortally wounded K-9 unit officer Timothy Jones and Jones's German shepherd, Laser. In another two hours, heavily armed and armored teams from several jurisdictions finally ran the killer to ground, dressed in camouflage and cowering beneath a sheet of plywood outside a house on Euclid Street, a block from the Conway address. The pistol apparently used in both shootings, as well as the service weapons taken off the fallen officers, were found nearby.

The killer, who suffered only bruises and a dog bite, was identified as Guy Harvey Baker, a twenty-six-year-old Persian Gulf War veteran from Mason City, Iowa, who was wanted for a parole violation following his conviction on illegal firearms possession charges. His reason for firing on Jones and the dog was apparent—he was trying to avoid capture. Why he shot Ryan was not immediately clear.

Not that it mattered, at least at the moment. The city was shocked and sickened, the horror of the first killing compounded by the horror of the second. The beauty of the summer morning and the homely ordinariness of the crime scenes made the event seem especially surreal. Within the department, the rage and grief were beyond words. Ryan was not only a husband and father, he was the much-loved son of a longtime St. Paul cop, Ron Ryan Sr. Jones, also a husband and father, was a popular sixteen-year veteran who, with Laser and another dog, had won several national K-9 honors. Their funerals, on successive days the following week, were attended by thousands of cops from around the country and observed, in person or via live TV, by tens of thousands of citizens.

St. Paul had not suffered a cop-killing since James Sackett's, twenty-four years earlier. In 1974, Patrolman John Larson died following a traffic accident while responding to an emergency call, and, seven years later, Patrolman John O'Brien was fatally injured when a driver fleeing police collided with his squad car, but none since Sackett had been murdered in the capital city. Minneapolis had experienced a more recent atrocity. Shortly after midnight on September 25, 1992, a veteran Minneapolis officer, fifty-three-year-old Jerome Haaf, was shot in the back while he sipped coffee in an East Lake Street pizza joint by a pair of Vice Lord members during a particularly volatile stretch between police and mainly black gangs. The Haaf murder was clearly an assassination: a cop was the designated target. Four men were later arrested, tried, and convicted on charges connected with the crime.

Haaf's murder may or may not have been "political," depending on a citizen's definition of the term and maybe on which side of the color line he or she stood. But, unlike Sackett's, the case did not have the opportunity to grow cold.

More than twenty-two years had passed since Connie Trimble's acquittal in Sackett's death. Ronald Reed and Larry Clark had each served more than ten years in Nebraska following their conviction in the Ames Plaza Bank case, had been paroled, then discharged from parole several years earlier, and, like Trimble, had fallen off the St. Paul department's radar.

Times had changed. Weakened by government prosecutions, internecine feuds, and violent death, the Black Panther Party, whose hard-core membership may never have exceeded a few thousand persons nationwide, was in terminal decline by the mid-1970s. (The Panthers' self-declared archenemy, J. Edgar Hoover, had himself died, of natural causes, in 1972.) But America's inner cities, if they had changed at all, had grown more desolate, desperate, and dangerous. Street gangs had replaced revolutionaries, semi-automatic weapons had supplanted bolt-action rifles and homemade bombs, and crack cocaine and other illicit drugs, not radical ideologies, fueled most of the carnage. Murder rates soared in many American cities, including St. Paul and Minneapolis ("Murderapolis" in the national media during the middle nineties), mainly attributable to power struggles and turf wars between the gangs. Homicide investigators struggled to keep up with the fresh corpses.

Though there had been no arrests or significant developments in the Sackett case since the Trimble trial, the case had not been forgotten. Jeanette Sackett had never stopped thinking about it, nor had Glen Kothe and his contemporaries who patrolled the Hill during the early seventies, nor had former investigators such as Earl Miels and Carolen Bailey, who had retired without having shared the satisfaction of closing the notorious case.

Joe Corcoran, who spent his first night with the department's crime lab at the Sackett murder site, would be forever haunted by the memory of the young officer's blood on the Hague Avenue sidewalk. Rising through departmental ranks and seeing his share of brutality, he would never shake the sense of wonder and despair he experienced in the murder's immediate aftermath, realizing, first, that some citizens hated the police so much they were willing to kill them and, second, that even greater numbers either hated the police or were so frightened of their neighbors that they would not tell the authorities what they knew about Sackett's killers.

As it happened, in the late summer of 1994, Lieutenant Joe Corcoran was running the department's overtaxed homicide unit. When he took the job in 1990, the case load was already bulging, with almost twenty murders a year. Gang violence had erupted. Heavily armed drug dealers were moving in from Chicago, Detroit, and Gary, and in 1992 the number of homicides in St. Paul—thirty-three—hit an all-time high. On February 28, 1994, in a case that should probably not be called typical of that or any other period, yet could surely stand as a marker of the viciousness of criminal activity in the city at the time, five children between the ages of two and eleven perished in an East Side house fire set by gang members striking back at the kids' older brother, whom the gangsters believed (erroneously, it turned out) had broken their version of *omerta*. The Coppage murders, and the murders of officers Ryan and Jones six months later, accounted for seven of the city's twenty-nine homicides that year.

In the two days following the Ryan and Jones murders, two of Corcoran's investigators, Neil Nelson and Gerard Bohlig, extracted a detailed, videotaped confession from Guy Harvey Baker (who claimed to be suffering from Gulf War syndrome) that guaranteed a double life sentence without the chance for parole. But the case, not surprisingly, drained the homicide squad and the rest of the department emotionally. Years later, Corcoran would remember August 26, 1994, as "the day from hell—for me, for my unit, for everyone." The cops wept and hugged each other at the funerals and then, as was their primal custom, sang, caroused, and drank themselves blind at the wakes that followed the services.

After Ron Ryan's funeral, Russ Bovee, one of the original Sackett investigators and more recently the homicide unit's commander, approached Corcoran, his successor.

"Joe, you got yours," Bovee told him, referring to Baker. "I didn't get mine." There was no need for Bovee to explain who he meant by "mine."

"We're going to get yours, too, Russ," Corcoran said.

Corcoran made the same promise to Jeanette Sackett.

How Corcoran's team would make good on that promise remained to be seen. They didn't know the whereabouts of their suspects, much less the availability of possible witnesses. There was still no sign of the murder weapon, and no one besides the persons interviewed during the nearly two years between Sackett's murder and Trimble's acquittal had come forward or been identified.

Then, three months after the Ryan and Jones murders, Corcoran got a call from a reporter at KSTP-TV, the local ABC affiliate. Tom Hauser was one of the several local journalists whom Corcoran had made a point to befriend when he became St. Paul's homicide commander, believing that a well-informed media would give him much-needed allies in the struggle against the rising murder numbers. ("Joe, you're using us," a Minneapolis newspaperman complained at the time. To which Corcoran replied, "We're using each other.")

"Joe," Hauser said, "do you have twenty minutes to look at something?" He didn't say to look at what, but Corcoran, who had learned to trust the young, baby-faced journalist, drove the few miles to the Channel Five studios on the St. Paul–Minneapolis border anyway.

"We found Connie Trimble," Hauser told Corcoran when he arrived. Hauser declined to say *where* they had found the woman, only that she was driving a bus for a living. "We found her and interviewed her, and I thought you might want to see the video."

Corcoran sat down and watched a pretty, cigarette-smoking, sometimes tearful, middle-aged woman wearing what appeared to be a municipal transit company uniform respond to a half-hour's worth of questions from Hauser, sitting on the other side of her kitchen table. Sometimes succinct, sometimes rambling, and occasionally getting up to answer her telephone, Trimble expressed surprise at the appearance of someone asking questions about her past. She nonetheless reiterated her story about making the May 22 phone call as part of a plan to exact revenge on an individual who had abused her family, spoke of her sympathy for the Sackett family

("May God be with them and bless them all of the time"), and described her fear then and now of the people "behind" the officer's murder, though she insisted she didn't know who they were. She said she had been thinking about writing a book recounting her experience—"a real ordeal in my life, you know."

When Hauser asked what she would tell the police if they came to her door and posed the same questions, she replied, "I don't know. I need to talk to my Maker about this, you know. Maybe it's time. I don't know, you know. Maybe it's time."

When Hauser brought up Ronald Reed and Larry Clark, Trimble denied that the men had been involved in the murder. She said she had not seen or talked to Reed since her mother died three years earlier and couldn't remember the last time she had seen Clark.

Hauser pressed on.

—Do you believe in your heart that [Reed] had nothing to do with this?

—Yes, I do. . . . I know he didn't kill the police. I know that. I do know that. It's impossible to be in two places at one time.

—Where was he?

—He was with me, you know. Right there when I made the call. . . .

—So he was with you when you made the call, and then you both went home?

—Yeah. Both went home. It was raining. I'll never forget that night. It was real bad.

Trimble said Reed was with her, in Hauser's words, "when the shooting happened, but he was also there when the phone call was made."

"That's right," she said. "He was right there."

A few moments later, Trimble said she couldn't remember word for word her message to the police operator—"something about my sister, Mrs. Brown, or something, is having a baby"—but said again that "Ron was at the phone booth with me," that he "knew what I knew" about the call's intent ("like we were trying to get even with this creep"), and that neither she nor Reed knew that an officer was going to be shot.

"Holy Christ!" Corcoran exclaimed, watching Hauser's video. The tape continued for another few minutes, but he had already heard an earful. For the first time, Trimble had publicly acknowledged Reed's presence with her at the phone booth on the night of the murder.

Corcoran again asked where Hauser had located Trimble, but Hauser wouldn't say. Hauser did give the investigator a copy of the interview tape—a tightly edited version of which aired on Channel Five's 10 PM newscast on November 18. Most of the dramatic, ten-minute-long report was devoted to a graphic reprise of the murder and the initial, 1970 investigation. Jeanette Sackett was shown turning the pages of a scrapbook filled with newspaper clippings, and Sergeant Glen Kothe, silver-haired and thicker around the middle than he had been twenty-four years earlier, appeared with Hauser at the Hague Avenue site. Then Hauser confronted a surprised Connie Trimble as she stood alongside a black-and-white SUV in a parking lot, and excerpts of their subsequent conversation, taped in her apartment, followed. (There was snow on the ground, but Hauser offered viewers no clue as to the location, presumably to keep a source to himself in his highly competitive industry.) Finally, Corcoran appeared on camera, telling the reporter the investigation was still open.

Corcoran quickly received Chief William Finney's approval to pursue the Trimble lead. Finney, the department's first African American leader, had grown up on the Hill, attended Central High, and knew many of the people whose names had appeared during the first Sackett investigation. A large, powerful man now in his middle forties, he was still known throughout the black community as "Corky," his childhood nickname. Finney had been a student at nearby Mankato State College—and president of MSC's Black Student Union—when Sackett was murdered. Inspired by the few black officers who patrolled the neighborhood when he was a kid, he had already decided to become a cop himself. Because of a chesty self-confidence and career ambitions that he didn't bother to conceal, he had enemies among his colleagues from the beginning. As chief, Finney was disliked by many of the department's ranking officers because of an alleged inclination to play favorites and no doubt by some because of his color. He enjoyed, however, Corcoran's confidence—and vice-versa. The chief insisted that Corcoran brief him on every new homicide and that he call him, day or night, when a homicide arrest had been made.

Corcoran assigned Neil Nelson and Gerry Bohlig to find and interview Trimble. Both men were seasoned investigators known for their ability to pry information out of reluctant sources. They had gotten Baker to confess to the Ryan and Jones murders after convincing the intelligent but egotistical gunman he would be starring in a police training video. (The tape was a highly charged topic within the department; a rumor made the rounds that Baker's vainglorious account would indeed be used as a training video and officers would be required to watch it. Finney kept the tape in a safe, and it was seen by few people. One person who saw it, according to Corcoran, was Baker's court-appointed attorney, who consequently decided that a guilty plea was Baker's only practical option.)

Nelson had joined the department in 1977, after working in sales for a vending-machine company. He was a buttoned-down erstwhile narcotics division detective who was becoming a nationally recognized expert on criminal interview technique. Recently transferred to homicide, he had been enjoying a precious day off, en route with his wife and kids to the state fairgrounds, when he heard the news about Ryan's murder on the car radio. Bohlig, a twenty-seven-year department veteran who had worked in a suburban Mendota bar and dug graves at Resurrection Cemetery before becoming a cop, was a notorious eccentric and sharp-tongued loner in a group of detectives known for eccentrics and lone wolves, respected more than loved by his colleagues. ("Every one of my guys was an individual," Corcoran once acknowledged. "Trying to pair them up was like herding cats.") After splitting ten years between vice and narcotics investigations—"That's where I learned how to work with assholes," he said later—Bohlig had been a homicide investigator for four years. Neither he nor Nelson had known Jim Sackett personally, nor had they ever spoken to Jeanette Sackett about the case. They were familiar, nonetheless, with the Sackett story and eager to have a chance to talk to Connie Trimble.

First they had to find her. The detectives went back to KSTP-TV and watched the unedited tape, but they were no more successful than their boss in getting Hauser to divulge Trimble's location. They could not see her SUV's license plate on the tape or read the logo on her ball cap. The only visible clue was the snow in the outside pictures. Back at headquarters, Bohlig called the department's communications center and asked a staffer to run a driver's license check on Trimble in every state where there was likely to be snow on the ground. Fifteen minutes later, the woman called back and said, "Here's the address. It's in Wheat Ridge, Colorado." The information

made sense, considering the fact that Trimble had spent her childhood in Denver.

When Bohlig told his boss, Corcoran said, "You gotta get out
there right away."

The detectives knew there were three means by which to solve a
homicide: physical evidence that connected the killer with the crime,
witnesses who were able and willing to provide the same connection, and/or a confession by the killer or killers.

Reviewing their prospects for solving the Sackett case in November 1994, Corcoran, Bohlig, and Nelson were reasonably certain
the possibility of claiming either the first or third of those necessities was slim to none. The rifle used to kill the officer was not likely
to magically reappear almost twenty-five years after the fact. Nor
were Reed and Clark—still presumed to be the killers—likely to
speak to investigators, much less confess to the crime; they hadn't
talked in any meaningful way as teenagers in 1970, and, as middle-
aged men hardened by lengthy prison time, they weren't going to
talk now. Nelson believed this was a "witness case" the day it happened and a "witness case" still. Given the political environment and
the animosity toward the police at the time of the crime, the possibility of witnesses coming forward was remote. In the intervening
years, somebody had to get religion or somehow be motivated to
share what he or she knew.

One obvious "somebody" was, of course, Connie Trimble.

After contacting a local detective to make sure Trimble still re-
sided at the Wheat Ridge address, Bohlig and Nelson, with special
funds approved by Finney, flew to Denver in early December. They
didn't call first. They would confront Trimble unannounced, lest she
try to avoid them or seek outside counsel who would probably tell
her to keep quiet. They knew from long experience it was almost
always advantageous to catch a potential witness unawares, before
she or he had a chance to prepare, rehearse, or duck out of sight.

Trimble was living in a second-floor unit of her building, acces-
sible by an exterior stairway. At the top of the steps a small landing
provided barely enough space for two people to stand. As they were
knocking on the door, Bohlig muttered to Nelson, "Boy, if this turns
bad, we're both dead."

Trimble eventually responded. From behind the closed door, she shouted, "Who is it?"

Bohlig shouted back, "Police! We're from St. Paul, and we'd like to talk to you."

"Go away!" Trimble replied. "I don't want to talk to the police!"

"She knew right away we were there about Sackett," Bohlig said several years later. "We said that yes, we were looking at that homicide, but we only wanted to talk. We told her we had seen her on TV. We stood there at her door for maybe twenty minutes. I don't remember everything we said—it was the stuff we often said to a witness, knock 'n' talk stuff, tricks of the detective's trade, trying to make her feel good, getting her to believe we had her best interests at heart. Well, pretty soon we were sitting on her couch and she was making us coffee."

The apartment building was in a working-class section of metropolitan Denver. "The place is a mess," Trimble complained, blaming a pair of rambunctious grandchildren as she let the detectives inside. Nelson said, "I got three kids, Gerry's got three kids—this place looks just like ours." Everybody laughed.

Trimble, approaching her forty-third birthday, was not the sleek, modishly done-up teen she had been in 1970. She seemed to have difficulty breathing, and she told the detectives about a series of medical issues and surgeries, including a struggle with cancer, as well as "problems" with drugs and alcohol.

The detectives decided to move slowly, allowing her to warm up to them, putting her at ease, trying as hard as two white cops could to identify common ground. Nelson told her that he, too, was a Central High alum—he was, he said, the only white guy on the school's track team one year. When she asked if she was in trouble, they quickly said no, that she'd already been tried and acquitted in the Sackett case, and "legally there's nothing anybody can do to you." Neither cop was armed. Nelson had switched on a tiny tape recorder in his jacket, but after about an hour of small talk, he went into the bathroom and turned off the device. "I figured she'd have to be in for a penny, in for a pound," he explained years later, meaning it wouldn't matter what she told them in Colorado if she wouldn't be willing to say the same thing to a jury in Minnesota. "She had to want to help." Furthermore, he was quite sure that if she had gotten wise to the surreptitious taping, she would have stopped talking then and there. Wary of spooking their witness, the cops didn't even take notes.

The detectives spent three days courting Trimble in Denver. They would visit her for two or three hours, then excuse themselves and return the next day. Most of the conversations took place at Trimble's kitchen table, where she kept her Bible and photos of her deceased mother and the two grandsons she helped care for. She said she had lived in Texas for a while with her husband, a man named Smith, who was not around at the time, then moved back to Denver, where she was employed by the municipal bus company. She was currently on sick leave, she said, and was drawing disability payments for a back injury she had suffered on the job. Cherra, her now twenty-four-year-old daughter by Ronald Reed, stopped by, as did her grandsons and one of her brothers. Trimble politely introduced the detectives to each of the family members, who did not come across as either helpful or hostile. As her kin came and went, Trimble—a good cook—prepared food for the cops.

"We tried hard to get her to talk about a lot of things, but all she would do is basically acknowledge what she told Hauser in the video—that Reed had been with her at the phone booth," Nelson said. Curiously, she seemed to believe that was old news. "She was extremely surprised when we told her that she hadn't said that during her trial or told anybody else about it before telling Hauser. She seemed absolutely convinced she had said it before."

"I think she enjoyed talking about the past—except she wouldn't go to that one spot," said Bohlig. "We figured it out the first day: she had a child by Ronnie Reed, and it's tough to get a woman to give up the father of her child."

On and off for those three days, the detectives nevertheless worked the obvious angles. "We tried to portray her as a victim, but a victim with some responsibility," Nelson said. "We tried to convince her that Reed had victimized her as well, and she needed to set this right. We harped on honor, pride, reputation. We talked about the Sackett family, and how this wasn't about politics but about the death of a husband and father and about bringing some closure to a mother like herself. We tried to make it very much a personal thing and about doing the right thing. I think we were close a couple of times. But then she'd back away. I can't recall how often she said she just couldn't do it, on account of her daughter or Ronnie's mother, whom she said she was still very close to.

"We tried to steer her toward a religious reason to put this away when she talked about her cancer, like, 'You don't want to die with this on you.' Another time, we suggested that her mother would want her to tell us what she knew—but that backfired. She straightened up and said, 'If my mother was here right now, she'd tell me to keep my mouth shut!'"

The detectives arranged to have Finney call her from St. Paul. Trimble was one of the few neighborhood people Finney did not know personally, but the fact that the chief was an African American only a few years older than she, had also attended Central, and was familiar with many people she knew would be enough to get her talking. "We thought, whatever St. Paul was like back then, and whatever deep-seated hatred of the police remained, talking to a black police chief might convince her that we were different now, that times had changed," said Nelson. "My guess, though, was that she wasn't a true believer back in 1970. She was at the phone booth because her boyfriend was there, and she was doing what he asked her to." At any rate, Finney and Trimble chatted on the phone for almost an hour, reminiscing about the neighborhood and the folks they knew back in the day, but when they had finished, she had told him no more than she had told his detectives.

Bohlig and Nelson decided they had to get Trimble out of the apartment, away from the kitchen table with her mother's portrait and away from the family members coming in and out and, in the detectives' opinion, verbally or otherwise dissuading her from telling what she knew. They had gleaned from their conversation that Trimble enjoyed listening to jazz and told her they would like to take her to a downtown jazz club they had heard about and have dinner, just the three of them. She said dinner out sounded good and agreed to go.

"We were *psyched,*" Nelson said later. "We figured we're finally going to get her away from that kitchen table and out where we could forge a stronger relationship. So that evening Gerry and I are in the car going to pick her up when she calls us on a cell phone we'd rented at the airport and says, 'I fixed you guys dinner. We don't have to go out.' We hang up and we're like, *'Son of a bitch!'* We couldn't believe it. She would *not* leave that apartment."

"We'd have had her if we'd gotten her out of the house," Bohlig grumbled.

As they were leaving her apartment for the last time, they asked Trimble if she needed money for medications and other expenses, which they strongly believed she did, but she declined to accept anything from them.

The investigators departed Denver convinced that Trimble knew far more than she had divulged. They believed that she had not only been following Reed's instructions at the phone booth but that she knew the real purpose of the call—to draw a police officer into an ambush. But in terms of testimony that could someday put Reed and whomever else might be involved behind bars for good, they returned to St. Paul with no more in hand than Trimble's assertion on Tom Hauser's videotape, plus an uncertain relationship with a dubious witness.

"That had been our goal—getting to Connie," Joe Corcoran said. "That would be the starting point for reinvestigating that case. We wanted to see what kind of pressure we could put on her, and to see what might have changed. Because things *do* change. Relationships change. Maybe she wasn't so loyal anymore. Maybe she would be willing to talk to us now."

Corcoran, with Finney's continued encouragement, told the investigators to call Trimble once a week. "I told them to go back to the religious side of things, to tell her she needs to get her life together before she goes. Her cancer, if that's really what she had, could go quick. Like, 'Now's the time to come clean with it so you won't have to worry when you get upstairs.' Well, they made the calls, but by that time her daughter and maybe other people were putting pressure on her not to talk. Then it got hard to get hold of her."

When they did speak on the phone, Trimble seemed uncertain and confused. She complained of various ailments. Nelson or Bohlig—or both at the same time, though for some reason she seemed to prefer talking to Bohlig—listened sympathetically and assured her she was in their thoughts and prayers. When she would muse about maybe getting out of Denver and "starting all over," they made commensurately vague offers of support—always on the condition of her continuing cooperation. Telling *them* what she knew

would not be enough, they reminded her. She would have to be willing to tell her story to a jury.

"You're the only hope for us now, Constance," Bohlig told her at
one point. "We're up against a wall."

Trimble agreed only to stay in touch.

One Monday morning in August 1995, returning to work after a
rare weekend away, Bohlig found a call slip on his desk. Trimble had
phoned from a hospital in Denver the previous Friday night. "I think
she thought she was dying," he said later. "I called back right away,
but it's Monday now and she's clearly feeling better. I thought, *Shit!
She was willing to tell all then, but she wasn't now.* When they rang
her room, I got one of the kids, and I could hear him say, 'Oh, it's that
cop.' I knew I didn't have a chance." That would be the last contact
either Bohlig or Nelson had with her. They sent her birthday cards
over the next few years, and at one point asked Jeanette Sackett to
write her directly, mother to mother, urging her cooperation, which
the widow did—but the communication moved in only one direction. For a while, the investigators lost track of her entirely.

The detectives had other cases to work. St. Paul's homicide unit
was dealing with the city's peak murder years during the mid- and
late 1990s. Corcoran's crew—who, despite their individual idiosyncra-
sies and personal rivalries, were required to share information at the
commander's frequent "murder meetings"—worked hard and were
remarkably successful; they boasted one of the best rates in the nation,
closing, in that especially deadly year of 1994, all twenty-nine of their
cases. But, operating with tight budgets and hiring constraints, the investigators often worked seven days a week for weeks at a stretch.
Investigations were only part of the job; many additional hours were
spent preparing for and appearing in court. There were no cold-case
specialists and nobody who could be spared to work full-time on a
cold case, even if the case involved the murder of one of their own.

When Bohlig retired in July 1999, Nelson was the lone investigator working on Sackett, and he worked on Sackett only when he
could take time from his current case load, which wasn't often. After
the short-lived excitement following Hauser's discovery of Trimble
in Colorado, the investigators found themselves, for all intents and
purposes, back at square one. Neither Bohlig nor Nelson believed
there was much they could do to get more information out of Trimble under the prevailing circumstances. And they didn't like their

odds of bearding either Reed or Clark. "If we were going to confront a guy who had everything to lose, I needed to have more than Connie saying he put her up to making the call," Nelson explained. "We had no reason to arrest Reed and nothing new to offer him. If we'd have had something to bluff with, or some new information we could ask him to respond to—but we didn't. We might have even lost ground, hurting our chances for a more substantive interview in the future. It's sometimes better to stir the pot from the outside."

Tom Hauser did speak to Reed. He contacted him at his home in Chicago, invited him to stop by the station the next time he was in town (several of Reed's family members, including his mother, still lived in the Twin Cities), and offered to show him the interview with Trimble. Reed eventually met with Hauser and watched the video, but he didn't make a statement or submit to an interview with Hauser or with anyone else.

As time allowed, Nelson returned to the Sackett files and tried to track down other witnesses who, in his words, "might be motivated to talk to us after all these years." After Reed, Clark, and Trimble, the name that jumped out of the reports most frequently was Kelly Day.

Kelly Fernando Day was last seen in connection with the Sackett case in March 1972, when St. Paul detectives escorted him into a Rochester courtroom as the prosecution's secret—but suddenly uncooperative—witness. The files showed that up until then he had been willing to share information with both the police and the FBI, including, in November 1970, the intelligence that his pal Ronald Reed was planning to hijack an airliner. Day and another man had been arrested but never charged in connection with the alleged hijack plot.

In February 1972, Day, who was twenty-one at the time, sat down with homicide detective Cecil Westphall and, in a nine-page signed statement, said that the morning after the Sackett murder Reed told him confidentially, while standing outside the Inner City Youth League a block from the crime scene, that Larry Clark had shot the officer. According to Day, Reed let him in on the secret because Reed thought Day might know if the police could trace phone calls and match recorded voices. When Day asked who made the O.B. call the night before, Reed indicated Trimble. Day said Reed also asked him if he knew how to "cut up a gun." Day told Westphall he himself knew nothing about the murder plan but had "first-hand knowledge of it after it occurred," and he assured the detective he would be willing to testify in court. His unwillingness to tell his story in front of the Trimble jury the following month, however, was blamed by many for the subsequent not-guilty verdict. Still, Day's relationships with the Sackett suspects and his knowledge of their activities in 1970 made him a source with tantalizing potential thirty years later.

"Reading the files," Nelson said later, "I figured the two people who, if they ever got religion, could solve that case were Connie Trimble and Kelly Day."

Day had had several run-ins with the police and was reported to have both used and sold narcotics, though when Nelson tracked him down he was gainfully employed as a counselor of some kind at a YMCA branch in south Minneapolis. Nelson showed up there around lunchtime one day in 2000.

Day was now a heavyset, middle-aged man with a calm and confident manner. Though Nelson had appeared unannounced, Day, sitting behind a desk in an office, did not seem surprised to see him. Day was no doubt aware of Trimble's appearance on the evening news and had probably heard about the cops' visit to her apartment in Colorado. More than five years had passed, but he likely figured it would be only a matter of time before a detective showed up on his doorstep, too.

Leading with a bluff, Nelson told Day the Sackett case had been retooled and was moving forward and Day would be either a witness or a suspect in the new investigation. If Day was rattled by Nelson's statement, he didn't show it. "He just sat back and listened to me make my pitch and then said without hesitation, 'Yeah, I know what happened, but I'm never going to testify about it.'" When Nelson raised the possibility of a sizable reward (which did not yet exist), Day held his hand over the top of his desk and said, "You can stack the money to the ceiling, but I'm never going to testify."

"He was a street-savvy guy," Nelson said. "A cop could bluff all he wanted. He wasn't going to play the game, and he knew it wasn't going to cost him anything."

A few months later, Nelson called Day and told him the case was gathering steam. But Day was no more impressed than he'd been the first time they talked.

"Basically, he blew me off," said Nelson. "He wasn't rude, but he made it very clear he wasn't going to talk to me."

Neil Nelson returned to the Sackett files every so often, seeking both fresh information and renewed enthusiasm for a case that seemed frozen as a Minnesota lake in deep winter. Trimble had slipped out of touch, and Day wasn't interested in speaking with him further. He worked a few other, more tenuous connections that led nowhere. In 2003 he produced a short local-access television spot about the case, standing in front of 859 Hague, displaying photos of James Sackett and his family, and pleading for new information. But there was no meaningful public response.

Bill Finney was still running the department, but Joe Corcoran, the Sackett case's in-house champion, had retired in 1998 and was succeeded by a younger man, John Vomastek. Before he transferred out of homicide in 2004, Nelson told Nancy DiPerna—who in turn succeeded Vomastek and became St. Paul's first female homicide commander—that despite the fact that the Sackett case was now more than thirty years old, "I think this is solvable, I really do." But, he added, "it's going to take a full-time commitment."

2

Jeanette Sackett knew little about the start-and-stop investigation. As time passed, she had less and less contact with the department and with individual officers, including Jim's old partners and friends, many of whom were beginning to retire and live off their pensions and relocate to lake places up north. She knew she could count on the department and whatever acquaintances remained if she got in a bind, but, all things considered, she could not escape the fact that her husband's murder was for many people, if not for her and her children, becoming a remnant of distant history.

In May she would attend the department's annual Memorial Day Service, when she and her kids gathered with other police families, department officials, and city dignitaries, and listen with shining eyes as Jim's name was read aloud from the list of St. Paul officers who had died in the line of duty. Jim's name was listed with the "Sr." attached, to distinguish the father from Jim Jr., who by the mid-1990s had already lived longer than his dad. By May 1995, with the addition of John O'Brien, Ronald Ryan Jr., and Timothy Jones, the roster of St. Paul's "fallen" had reached twenty-nine, and Sackett's murder was the only one that was not closed. Before and after the ceremony, which was replete with bagpipes, a bugle, and the dolorous tolling of a ceremonial bell, old friends in their dress uniforms and black-banded shields would come by, offer hugs and handshakes, and inquire about the family. Someone might remark on how much Jim Jr. looked like his dad, depending on how Jim Jr. was wearing his hair. Once in a while someone would whisper something to Jeanette about a possible lead in the case, but not often. Officially, there was nothing new to report.

A few years after Jim's death, Jeanette had married another St. Paul officer, but the marriage did not last long. When the kids were old enough to go to school, she took a part-time job at a downtown bank, applying the bookkeeping skills she'd learned in a Louisiana business school and enhanced with a refresher course in St. Paul. She always did her best, when the kids would ask, to explain what happened to their father on May 22, 1970. She would play the audio tape she recorded on Hague Avenue with Glen Kothe and open the scrapbook full of newspaper clippings about the murder and its investigation, though the dates on those clippings extended no further than the spring of 1972.

When Ryan and Jones were gunned down on that sparkling August morning in 1994, Jeanette was riven by a familiar shock, anger, and heartache, but she neither contacted nor was contacted by the new widows. She had been befriended by the wife of a Minnesota State Patrol officer who had been murdered during a traffic stop a few years before Jim was killed, and the two remained close for several years before the woman remarried and began a new life in Wisconsin. She had also enjoyed a friendship for a while with Joan O'Brien, John's widow, after his death in the car wreck in 1981. But Jeanette was, or had become, a loner, focused on her kids and the bountiful garden behind the house. As far as the investigation was concerned, she heard little and didn't demand to know more, believing if the department had significant news, the department would tell her. Looking back, she wondered if she should have "pushed the issue." She also wondered if during those first several years after the murder the department had done enough. Everybody seemed to know who killed Jim. So why couldn't they make the arrests and secure the convictions and put that part of their lives to rest?

One day in late 1994, Tom Hauser from Channel Five showed up at her door. He told Jeanette about locating Connie Trimble, then videotaped Jeanette paging through her scrapbook and asking for closure. "He brought the story alive," she said later about Hauser's telecast, "and we had high hopes." But then weeks passed and stretched into years, and the terrible month of May would come and go again with nothing new to report.

Glen Kothe was a forty-eight-year-old street sergeant when Ryan and Jones were killed. Both officers had worked for him. He and Ryan's father went way back, and when Jones was having problems with one of his canines, Kothe's second wife, Susan, who trained dogs for a living, helped him out. That August morning, Kothe was a leader of the posse that arrived at the fish shack shortly after Jones and Laser were gunned down, and he watched as members of the Critical Incident Response Team shredded the flimsy structure with automatic weapons fire, unaware that the killer had slipped away and would elude them for another several minutes.

Later that day, following Guy Baker's capture, Kothe happened to step out of a men's room at St. Paul–Ramsey Hospital just as the bruised and bitten gunman was wheeled past on a gurney. Everybody froze. For a split second Kothe stared into the face of the presumed cop-killer while Baker's escorts, a phalanx of St. Paul officers and sheriff's deputies, stared at Kothe. Baker did not know Kothe, let alone his story, but the other cops did. "You could see it on their faces," Kothe said later. "They had no idea what I might do. *I* had no idea what I might do. I had two dead friends because of that dirtbag." Before anyone had a chance to find out, his fellow officers moved swiftly around the gurney and backed Kothe away from the prisoner.

Twenty-four years after his partner's murder, Kothe was still feeling the terror and stress of that night, though less and less with the passing of time. He had been one of the St. Paul officers who testified at Connie Trimble's trial in 1972, reliving the event for the Rochester jury. Now the Ryan and Jones murders brought it all back again in a rush, as had, and would for as long as he lived, every news account of another murdered officer from around the country.

Kothe had gone back to work, transferred to K-9 duty, and eventually returned to regular patrol and a series of assignments. Fifteen years after his hire, he passed the sergeant's exam with flying colors and would be number two on the lieutenant's list when he retired in 1997. Some of his colleagues grumbled that because he had been Sackett's partner he could do "pretty much what he wanted," and Kothe would concede that at least for a while after the murder the administration handled him with care. But whatever he did, it would take him a long time to shake the worst of his demons.

He believed Jeanette Sackett, who was avoiding him at memorial services and on other occasions that put them in the same room, blamed him for Jim's death, which he said he accepted as "only natural." "I could understand that," he said. "'Why my husband, and not you?'" (Though she insisted she never thought that.) In the absence of any formal counseling or guidance, Kothe would occasionally talk to a few of his buddies in the department about personal matters, though "sharing feelings" was not something men of his generation, let alone men of stout "German-Bohunk stock," as he described his pedigree, were comfortable doing. "Men don't cry," he explained. "That's the way I was brought up." Meantime, he had developed a reputation among his colleagues because of the risks he was taking on the job. He refused to wear a protective vest when kicking down a suspect's door, and he would join in car chases with the recklessness of a terrier on a squirrel.

"I'd go out of my way to get in the middle of something," he said. "Somebody would give me lip, I'd knock them on their ass. There were some complaints, the usual stuff, but I never went too far. Obviously, though, I became a little bit nuts. Actually, a whole hell-of-a-lot nuts. Which I kind of promoted up to a point, figuring the brass would leave me alone. Like, 'Don't fuck with him. He's crazy.'"

In the early seventies a Los Angeles cop, Joseph Wambaugh, wrote a best-selling book called *The Onion Field* about the 1963 murder of an LAPD officer named Ian Campbell by a couple of small-time thugs. Kothe identified, at least in part, with Karl Hettinger, Campbell's partner, who couldn't deal with the guilt and blame he experienced as the murder's survivor and who eventually left the department. Kothe never considered quitting, though he was not entirely sure why not. He drank too much. His wife divorced him. And there were times when his dark thoughts sought extreme remedies. One night, maybe ten years after Sackett's murder, he sat in his truck and stared down the barrel of his pistol before finally deciding not to pull the trigger. After the Ryan and Jones murders, the department brought in a psychologist to debrief the shaken troops. Kothe was also asked to speak to his colleagues from the perspective of his own experience. At lunch, the psychologist asked how he was dealing with his past. Kothe told the man that, among other things, he thought and dreamed about his partner's murder only in black and white. The psychologist told him that was not unusual after such a trauma, but that in the cases with which he was familiar the condition lasted only a few years, not almost twenty-five as it had with Kothe. The two continued to talk, and Kothe sat down with the man for two or three one-on-one sessions, which Kothe believed were helpful.

Beyond his conversations with detectives immediately following the murder, Kothe played no formal role in the Sackett investigation, at the time or later. When asked about the ambush, he would consistently recount the basics: their arrival in front of 859 Hague, the lack of response at the front door, his attempt to get an answer at the back door, the barking dog, the shouted warning to Sackett, the flash and explosion, Jim's scream. He continued to believe the shot originated near the Hague and Victoria intersection (as opposed to some point down the block), which was where he placed the blast in the neat schematic he sketched for his supervisors the night of the murder.

As the years passed and his dreams and recollections regained their color, Kothe never added to or subtracted from his account, at least not when anyone was recording it. No suspect or witness ever emerged from a suppressed memory—though he would swear he saw Connie Trimble standing alongside a man who might have been Ronald Reed in the crowd that gathered across the street after the shooting. That, of course, contradicted Trimble's trial testimony and was never corroborated by any other officer at the scene.

Tom Dunaski was a year older than Glen Kothe but four years behind him in department seniority. He was still a year and a half away from his first police academy class when Jim Sackett was murdered. He didn't know Sackett and would learn only later that they were shirttail relatives and that Sackett had sat behind his sister in one of their classes at Johnson High.

Rare among St. Paul cops, Dunaski had neither a father, brother, nor cousin in the police department, past or present. Like many city cops, however, Dunaski was a bred-in-the-bone East Sider, and, when he was a kid, he looked up to an officer, George St. Sauver, who lived in the neighborhood. Dunaski's father was for most of his working life a foreman at Minnesota Box and Lumber, a respected and resource-ful man who could do almost anything with his hands; his mother worked at the Emporium department store downtown, raised Tom and his sister, and cooked big dinners after Mass on Sunday. After graduating from Hill (now Hill-Murray) Catholic High School in 1962, Dunaski served three years in the Army, then returned home and became an apprentice in the sheet-metal trade.

Five years later Dunaski achieved journeyman's status, upon which, to his parents' surprise, he decided to become a cop. He had become a competent "tinner" and enjoyed the work, but he had mar-ried and become a father and, like many of his contemporaries, was attracted by the kind of job security and insurance benefits the po-lice department offered, plus the opportunity to do something inter-esting and important with his life. He drew on the positive example of Officer St. Sauver and the encouragement of a couple of cops who provided security and traffic control at St. Casimir's Catholic Church, where he'd worked part-time as a janitor while apprentic-ing. "They were nice guys," he recalled years later. "They'd say, 'Go ahead, take the test. You'd make a good cop.'" The clincher was the robust endorsement of his next-door neighbor, an officer named Bill MacDonald, who had been a cop in Duluth and White Bear Lake be-fore joining the St. Paul force (and serving with Jim Sackett). With all that wind at his back, he passed the department's entrance exam and became a proud part of the class of 1971.

Decades later, Dunaski laughed when he thought about the reas-suring words he had heard from the cops at St. Casimir's. "They'd say, 'Yeah, I didn't have to take my gun out more than once or twice in twenty years.' Well, when *my* class came on, guys were work-ing twelve-hour days, wearing helmets, and sitting behind plastic shields, sometimes riding four to a car." The St. Casimir cops had spent most of their careers in the traffic unit and administration. Dunaski's class was facing riotous antiwar demonstrations at the University of Minnesota and the constant churn among disaffected youth on the Hill.

A beat cop named Fred Leske ("a roofer originally") showed the young officers around and introduced them to the denizens of the Hill. The East Side could count the number of African Americans on one hand when Dunaski was growing up, but he had gotten to know black soldiers in the Army and black business people while doing metalwork in the Summit-University neighborhood. "You learned how to deal with the people up there," he said. "You learned how to be civil, to be respectful." He knew that every cop didn't share that approach, that there were racists, bullies, and just plain bad apples in St. Paul's department as in every police department, and that even in St. Paul there had been enough of them and enough history going way back to help explain the distrust and hatred that made conditions dangerous for everyone.

Dunaski, like every other cop in the city, knew the story of the Sackett assassination, and because of revised department procedures and his own developing street sense was careful not only to get to know the Hill but to watch his back when he was up there.

In 1989, after fifteen years on the job, Dunaski, now a sergeant, was assigned to the joint FBI-police task force created to combat the alarming growth of local gangs, the organized drug trade, and the violent crime that accompanied it. He had already distinguished himself as a particularly able detective in the department's vice and special investigations units, with what would become a near-legendary reputation for tenacity and an ability to get people to talk.

Now in his middle forties, Dunaski was a rugged-looking man of average size, with a pink prizefighter's face, a toothy grin, and the raw, raspy voice of a longtime cigarette smoker, though Dunaski hadn't smoked much since he was in the service. He talked loud, fast, and often, in the funny, coarse, sometimes jumbled syntax of the East Side tinner he used to be. He smiled a lot and loved to laugh, but he was not, by the look and sound of him, the kind of guy a miscreant would want to cross. He was, conversely, the kind of guy a great number of miscreants decided they wanted to please.

Married and the father of three children, including a mentally disabled daughter, Dunaski had developed a sprawling extended family of sorts during his years as a vice squad investigator, dealing with prostitutes, drug users, and assorted sketchy characters. He loved working on the street, with one of a handful of partners over the years, more or less (as he chose to see it) his own boss. He made plenty of busts, but just as assiduously he made friends, many of whom became trusted informants and the core of his "intelligence base." He became famous, in the process, for kindnesses that often transcended the possibility of a practical payoff. He and his partners would buy Santa Bears and Cabbage Patch Dolls for the children of young hookers. When a prostitute they knew was murdered, he and partner Gary Bohn bought a dress for her funeral. He was known to bring confidential informants over to his house before his wife, Charlene, would open a garage sale to the public so the CI's could get first pick of the toys for their kids and take what they wanted for nothing.

Once he brought leftovers from his mother's Thanksgiving dinner to a contact who was working outdoors as a private security guard on a brutally cold night. The young man, who was selling drugs when Dunaski first met him, had only a flimsy jacket and nowhere to warm up, so Dunaski and his brother-in-law drove back in separate cars with a snowmobile suit, heavy gloves, and a pair of Sorel boots for his shivering friend. He even left his car so the young man would have a place to sit down and warm up. Making a point of noting the mileage on the odometer, he said, only partly joking, "I better not find out tomorrow that this car was involved in a drug deal or a stickup." Many years later, the young man, who had apparently turned his life around, was still checking in with Dunaski, always making sure to call and say hello on Thanksgiving.

On another occasion, a young woman Dunaski was working with told him she was afraid that her abusive boyfriend would track her down in the hospital, where she had just given birth, and try to snatch their newborn baby. With the woman's permission, Dunaski took the baby back to his house, where he and Charlene looked after it for a few days, and in the meantime had what he ominously called a "little chitchat" with the boyfriend, "just to let him know what the situation was."

"You work with people over the years, you develop a trust and a relationship, and they'll do anything for you," Dunaski once explained. "The books say that's taboo—you don't get that close to your CI's. But sometimes you *do*." Not all of the hundreds of such relationships lasted or bore investigative fruit, but many did. Even after his retirement in 2009, Dunaski was still talking to sources he had known for decades, "some [of whom] are now quite old."

A high-profile case that began with an execution-style murder in June 1990 relied on informants of another kind, who were equally valuable to Dunaski and his colleagues.

The smoldering body of a twenty-six-year-old Los Angeles drug dealer named Duon Walker was found in an alley behind Iglehart Avenue near I-94. Walker had been shot three times in the head, then set on fire. It took St. Paul police two weeks just to identify the body, which had been moved to the Iglehart location from an unknown site. Though Joe Corcoran's homicide crew soon established connections between Walker and two other men, including St. Paul businessman Kenneth Jones, who was known to deal cocaine, no one was talking and the investigation hit a dead end. A year after Walker's murder, the Organized Crime–Drug Task Force working out of the FBI's St. Paul office took over the case. Dunaski, John Culhane, and FBI agent Grant Beise—with access to the feds' deep pockets and state-of-the-art surveillance resources—began their own probe.

It took five years, the work of scores of support staff, and hundreds of thousands of dollars, but the task force detectives finally secured the arrests of Jones and suspected hit man Jeffrey Barnes. Wiretaps and other electronic surveillance provided some of the evidence, but the key was the testimony of several difficult individuals who had been snared on federal drug charges and turned into informants and cooperative witnesses. Convicted in 1996 of "murder in furtherance of a continuing criminal enterprise" (Jones's cocaine trade), Jones and Barnes were both sentenced to life in federal prison. As a bonus, the investigation resulted in dozens of other narcotics-related arrests and convictions.

The long and expensive case was groundbreaking for several reasons, not least because it was the first time the U.S. Attorney's office in Minneapolis had successfully prosecuted a continuing criminal enterprise murder and because it made ad hoc teammates of Tom Dunaski and Assistant U.S. Attorney Jeffrey Paulsen.

The tenacious detective and the fastidious prosecutor collaborated on several of the most infamous local cold cases of the 1990s. At the time, the concept of the cold case was novel. Most murders were solved quickly, within a few weeks if not days or hours, or they were not solved at all. Evidence disappeared and witnesses forgot what they saw, were scared silent, moved away, or died. Budgets were tight, and there were only so many hours in a detective's day. Unsolved murders were abandoned for fresher cases where evidence, witnesses, often even the murderer himself were there on the premises when the police arrived. With more elastic criminal stat-

utes and the introduction of DNA technology and other advanced forensic tools, however, the cold case had become solvable, or at least
somewhat more likely to be solved than it used to be.

When the five Coppage children were murdered in February
1994, St. Paul investigators swiftly identified members of the 6–0 Tre
Crips gang as likely suspects. But witnesses were intimidated, hard
evidence was nonexistent, and the case seemed likely to languish,
despite public outrage. But over the next few years, Dunaski and his
team, again using the looming sword of federal drug charges, per-
suaded several witnesses to testify against two gang leaders, Robert
G. ("Buster") and Robert J. ("Duddy") Jefferson, and Paulsen secured
indictments of the half-brothers on federal racketeering charges. All
told, twenty-two persons associated with the 6–0 Tre Crips were
indicted on charges ranging from criminal conspiracy to attempted
murder, with the prospect of long federal prison terms. All but six
pleaded guilty and many agreed to testify for the prosecution. Both
Jeffersons received life sentences in late 1998.

In July 1996, four-year-old Davisha Brantley-Gillum was shot
while sitting in the back seat of a car parked at a gas station off
I-94. She died of her wounds, and her pregnant mother and another
woman were injured. Once more, it didn't take investigators long to
figure out what happened. Davisha and her mother had been caught
in the line of fire when members of one gang attempted to ambush
members of another. But again authorities were stymied by the
unwillingness of witnesses to break the gangsters' code of silence.
And again Dunaski and his colleagues worked their contacts on the
street, then leveraged federal drug charges to draw out crucial information and essential testimony from gang members. In late 2002,
three men—Timothy McGruder, Kamil Johnson, and Keith Cren-
shaw—were sentenced to life terms without the chance of parole. As
it did against the 6–0 Tre Crips, the prosecution also brought the federal Racketeer Influenced and Corrupt Organizations (RICO) statute
to bear against the Rolling 60s gang, empowering the government to
seize assets illegally acquired by the defendants.

Years later, Paulsen gave Dunaski, who had become a close
friend, the lion's share of the credit for breaking those cases. "He's
rough and tough on the outside, but he really has a heart of gold,"
Paulsen said. "That's one of the reasons he'd get through to people
who ordinarily don't trust cops. Early on, when I first knew him, he

called me—it was a Saturday—and said we couldn't meet as we had planned because he had this informant whose car he was going to help fix. How many cops will spend their weekend helping an informant fix his car? And not because it's for some quid pro quo, but because he has a relationship with the guy and actually cares about him. He told me, 'I'd like to see the guy be able to drive to work so he doesn't have to rob a liquor store.'

"Any witness who was worried about his safety or whatever, Tom was there for him," Paulsen continued. "That's how you get people to come forward. It's about taking care of them in the big sense of the word. Even in the cases where we used the stick more than the carrot—the Coppage fire-bombing, for instance. Those people were really ruthless, and nobody was going to tell us what happened because nobody wanted to be the next Andre Coppage, whose house they burned down. So we decided early on the only way we were going to solve that one was to wrap up the whole gang, indict the whole gang, get them all in the same boat where they've got no choice but to give it up. It won't be just one person going out on a limb, it will be nine or ten. The bad guys will be locked up federally and they're not getting out.

"But even when we got to the point where we could bring those guys in—a guy like Frank Adams, the enforcer, as tough a gangster as you'll ever meet—breaking through his armor could not have been done by the average detective, certainly not by the prosecutor. It had to be done by Dunaski going over [to the Ramsey County jail], spending time with him, and finally pushing through that hard exterior."

Racial differences were usually not a barrier, Paulsen said. "Somehow Tom was able to talk to people of different backgrounds and races on their level."

Tom Dunaski was tying up loose ends on the Davisha Gillum case—helping Jeff Paulsen build the case for trial, writing thank-you notes and letters of commendation for persons who had assisted with the investigation—when someone brought up the coldest of local cold cases: the assassination of Patrolman Sackett. It's impossible to know who first mentioned the case to whom in the wake of the successful cold-case prosecutions that would conclude with the Gillum convictions. Neil Nelson, who was planning to leave the homicide squad when he assured unit commander Nancy DiPerna that the Sackett case was "solvable," albeit requiring a "full-time commitment," might be as good a guess as any.

DiPerna was reviewing a number of cold cases for possible investigation. Deciding which of several possibilities to pursue was a dicey occupation in its own right. Cold cases were by definition extremely difficult, demanding big-time allocations of money and manpower, so the odds of actually solving one had to be better than nil. Raw sentiment—as in the case of a murdered police officer—was not enough to justify reopening an investigation, though it doubtless helped; there must be sound reasons why seasoned investigators believe they can succeed where their predecessors failed. It wouldn't hurt, of course, to have the wealth and reach of the federal government involved, too.

In a meeting on July 1, 2002, DiPerna brought up the Sackett case with Dunaski and two other members of the FBI-police task force, Jane Mead and Robert Kosloske. When DiPerna asked them if *they* thought the case was solvable, Dunaski said, "Sure." And with his barking laugh, he added, "Then we'll find Jimmy Hoffa."

Ignoring the reference to the long-missing Teamster boss, DiPerna asked what it would take for the task force to go after Sackett's killers. She and Dunaski were longtime colleagues and friends; they both knew that departmental bureaucracy had a way of bogging down investigations. "Not being called in every week to find out where we're at and what we're doing," he replied to her question. The state Bureau of Criminal Apprehension had recently established a hundred-thousand-dollar "Spotlight on Crime" fund (supported in part by Minneapolis-based Target Corporation and other companies). With that money in mind, Dunaski also said he wanted enough cash for confidential informants "so we don't have to go through five different channels to pay off a CI."

The FBI's approval was required, as well as Chief Finney's, both of which were quickly forthcoming. Finney's go-ahead was, typical of his twelve-year administration, a source of contention. Some in the department said he was pushing for a solution to the Sackett case so he could share in the credit before he retired (he planned to step down in 2004). Members of the African American community, including many of Finney's lifelong friends and supporters, reacted with dismay, wondering why, after nearly thirty-five years and a trial that ended in an acquittal, the chief would want to open old wounds. Summit-University was not the place it was in 1970, but the chasm between black residents and the still predominantly white police department remained deep and perilous. As self-assured and combative as ever, Finney—who had been chief when officers Ryan and Jones were killed—emphatically rejected the criticism of both sides, telling a journalist a few years later, "It was about solving the case of a St. Paul police officer who had been assassinated. I said, 'We know who did it. Let's bring them to trial. And let's do it right, so they don't get away this time.' [The critics] never understood that about me. It wasn't about credit or politics or the racial stuff. We had a dead cop here."

Dunaski, for his part, had reservations, at least momentarily. What were his chances of solving the case if Neil Nelson and Gerry Bohlig, two of the finest investigators he knew, not to mention Earl Miels, Cecil Westphall, Tom Opheim, Carolen Bailey, Russ Bovee, and the other detectives at the time of the murder, hadn't been able to crack it? Sackett would surely be the most challenging investigation of a career filled with challenging investigations. But whatever his incentives for taking on Sackett, one would undoubtedly be exactly that: the greatest challenge of his professional life. Nelson said, "Tom, I'm telling you, even though this is ancient history, it's solvable. There are people out there who know what happened." Whether Dunaski really believed the "solvable" part at the time is debatable.

Dunaski's team at the moment comprised only one other investigator, Sergeant Jane Mead, who was also on loan from the St. Paul department and designated a Special Federal Officer. Their "case," so far as they could actually put their hands on it, consisted of a couple of cardboard boxes full of scribbled notes, typewritten reports, and newspaper clippings, plus a few reel-to-reel recording tapes and an ancient Dictabelt in a manila evidence envelope.

But that would have to be enough to get them started.

3

After several years as an investigator (sex crimes, homicide, special investigations, and the joint task force), Jane Mead was familiar enough with large boxes full of paper but not so sure about the Dictabelt. When she checked with the department's communications center, she confirmed it was the recording medium for a machine called the Dictaphone, which was once as common as typewriters and rotary telephones in American offices. "That's what we used to record our [radio] calls on," she was told. "Be careful with it. It's probably pretty fragile." She was given the name of a man who could transfer data from brittle Dictabelts to twenty-first-century audio disks.

Mead, who was fourteen years old when James Sackett was murdered, had been a St. Paul police officer since 1986, so she knew the broad outline of the case. She knew that Neil Nelson and Gerry Bohlig had spent time on it. She knew that there had been a trial and an acquittal more than thirty years earlier and that her predecessors "pretty much knew who the killers were—though that was true in a lot of cases," she said later. "You believe you know, but you can't prove it." Her experience working with Tom Dunaski on the Davisha Gillum homicide reinforced that point, only in that case they *were* able to prove the persons they suspected were in fact the killers. It just took a lot of time and effort. As for cop-killings, she had some personal experience with that as well, having been among the heavily armed officers closing in on Guy Baker after Ron Ryan's murder. She was close enough to have heard the shots that killed Tim Jones and Laser.

Mead had succeeded her close friend Sergeant Nancy Smolik on the task force after Smolik was diagnosed with breast cancer. Smolik's illness and eventual death were hard on both Mead and Dunaski, for whom partners and colleagues were, like his street people and confidential informants, branches of a large family. Physically, Mead was the unlikeliest of cops. Pretty and petite (she stood five-three), with reddish-blonde hair, delicate features, and a friendly smile, she could have passed for everybody's favorite third-grade teacher. When she was a patrol officer, she was hard put to sit down for a quick meal at Burger King without strangers sitting down beside her and pouring out their problems. That easy approachability helped make her an effective investigator, especially when she was paired with a tough-looking mug like Dunaski. More than once during an investigation, when the two of them walked into a room, a potential witness would tell her, "I ain't talking to him. But I will talk to you." Among her other qualifications, Mead was one of the best pistol shots, male or female, in the department.

The third of five children, Mead grew up with two older brothers, one of whom served as an undersheriff of Ramsey County, and her father was a volunteer firefighter whose friends included several cops who frequently visited their Falcon Heights home—all of which helped explain her confidence operating in a predominantly male environment. She was an athletic kid, skating for the fun of it and cheerleading for the glory of Alexander Ramsey High School. A dozen years later, when her two children were old enough to go to school, she entered St. Paul's police academy, class of 1986.

Though the Gillum case was still inching toward trial in late 2002, Mead began to dig into the Sackett files. She would pore over them at her desk in the cramped task force conference room at the FBI's St. Paul headquarters and review documents when riding with Dunaski to a meeting. Every once in a while she would say, "Tom, you gotta listen to *this!*" And she would read something out loud. Much of the files consisted of reports by the case's original investigators, all of whom had retired and some of whom—including Ernest Williams, the homicide unit boss in 1970—had died. "They had interviewed tons of people," Mead said. She knew she and Dunaski would have to track down and reinterview as many of the same people as they could find nearly thirty-five years after the fact, and hope the memory of at least a few of them was still reasonably sound.

Missing from the hundreds of documents was the transcript of Connie Trimble's Rochester trial, which would have laid out the state's case in 1972 and identified dozens of witnesses. To their great disappointment, Mead and Dunaski soon learned that the trial's court reporter had destroyed her notes without ever transcribing them; because the case had ended in acquittal, there would be no appeal so there was no need to produce an expensive transcript. The case's latter-day investigators would have to rely on newspaper accounts of the trial, which fortunately were extensive, as well as the memories of surviving participants such as retired prosecutor Theodore Collins.

Mead took the reel-to-reel tapes she had found in the boxes to the Minnesota History Center, which owned equipment that could play them, and listened for the first time to Trimble's midnight phone call requesting help for her "sister." She listened to Carolen Bailey's voice as Bailey prompted an unsuspecting Trimble to repeat the key words of that call at the welfare office. Later, after the Dictabelt messages had been transferred to a disk, she and her colleagues listened for the first time to Glen Kothe's distress call moments after the shooting.

"Hair-raising" was how Mead described the scratchy reprise of the patrolman's voice that night.

Jeff Paulsen first learned about the Sackett murder when he was a twelve-year-old newspaper carrier, delivering the *Minneapolis Star* in that city's affluent Kenwood neighborhood on the afternoon of May 22, 1970. Little did he imagine that more than thirty years later he would see the same shocking headlines in a stack of reports and clippings that Tom Dunaski asked him to read. It was late 2002 or early 2003. The Gillum case was finally concluded, and Dunaski had called the U.S. Attorney's office to see if Paulsen might be interested in another, even colder case.

"I've got this new project I'm working on," Dunaski said innocently enough. "Do you want to get involved?"

Dunaski and Mead struck people as an odd couple, but Dunaski and Paulsen may have been an odder pairing yet. The prosecutor was a businessman's son who had grown up across the street from an esteemed Hennepin County district court judge named Lindsay Arthur, his first professional role model. He earned degrees from prestigious Carleton College and Stanford University's law school, then clerked for federal judge Harry McLaughlin before spending several years with the U.S. Justice Department in Washington. He had been an Assistant U.S. Attorney in his hometown since 1988. He was a trim, middle-aged man with a full head of neatly combed dark hair who favored well-fitted dark suits, crisp white shirts, and conservative neckties. He was a husband and father and, in his free time, a collector of antique furniture, several pieces of which graced his immaculate office looking out on the downtown skyline. But those were matters of background and appearances. Measured by resourcefulness and tenaciousness while making a case, not to mention a passion for professional autonomy and a needling sense of humor, the prosecutor and the cop actually had a great deal in common.

Paulsen knew as well as any homicide detective that the time to solve a murder was right after it happened. He knew that there had been earlier attempts to solve Sackett that had sputtered and run out of gas. He knew that a case without hard evidence or reliable witnesses wasn't likely to grow more solvable in thirty-plus years. When he told a colleague he was taking a look at the Sackett murder, the colleague laughed and said, "Good luck with that"—meaning, "You're never going to solve that one." On the other hand, Paulsen was as energized by a challenge as Dunaski was, and the fact that nobody expected them to solve Sackett would be part of its appeal. Still, if Sackett had been the first cold case Dunaski had brought to him, Paulsen, who was not wanting for business, might have passed. But there was that rich recent history: Jones-Barnes, Coppage, and Gillum—"unsolvable" cases all, and they had solved them.

"Count me in," he told Dunaski.

Paulsen drove across the river and sat by himself in the task force conference room, reading what Mead and Dunaski had read. The yellowed paper and quaint typewriter fonts reminded him they were dealing with a *very* cold case. The absence of a Trimble trial transcript was unfortunate to say the least, but there were plenty of other intriguing items, beginning with Trimble's recorded call for help and including photocopies of the hijack notes found on Ronald Reed when he was arrested in November 1970. Mead had indexed the entire collection.

Also reviewing the original Sackett files for the first time in 2003 was Assistant Ramsey County Attorney Susan Hudson, who had been introduced to the case by Neil Nelson, with whom she had worked on several narcotics and homicide prosecutions, following the Ryan and Jones murders. A plainspoken fifty-year-old woman with short gray hair and an animated, irreverent manner, Hudson had grown up in Aitkin, Minnesota, the daughter of a lawyer and district court judge. She graduated from the University of Minnesota's law school in 1982, served as an assistant county attorney in Crow Wing County near her hometown, then joined the Ramsey County Attorney's staff in 1989. Because most homicide prosecutions fall to the state courts and because the Minnesota Bureau of Criminal Apprehension had come forward with a hundred-thousand-dollar reward for information pertaining to Sackett and needed a prosecutor's name attached to the case, Ramsey County Attorney Susan Gaertner tapped Hudson, by then one of her most experienced lawyers, for the job. Though the objective all along was to get the case tried in federal court, Ramsey County (which had prosecuted Trimble) would be an active participant from the beginning.

"At the time I was assigned," Hudson said later, "I'm not sure anyone knew the case would actually go anywhere." She had learned enough going through those old files, however, to suspect that the case would be, if nothing else, "interesting and intellectually challenging."

In late March 2003, in a six-page report to Commander DiPerna, Dunaski and his team presented what amounted to a précis of the Sackett case history, a list of basic assumptions about the suspected perpetrators and their motivation, and a preliminary action plan for bringing them to justice. For all intents and purposes, the report answered DiPerna's question about the solvability of Sackett's murder with a definite yes.

Granted, the newly reopened investigation had already suffered a major setback. Kelly Day's name had been as obvious a red flag for Dunaski and Mead as it had been for Neil Nelson when he re-viewed the original files. Indeed, it was Day's vivid 1972 Q & A with Cecil Westphall that most clearly and unequivocally linked Connie Trimble with Ronald Reed and Larry Clark and connected all three to Sackett's murder. Dunaski and Mead also had Nelson's report quoting Day saying he knew "everything" about the murder, though he vowed he would never tell. Ted Collins, Trimble's prosecutor, had told Dunaski and Mead about Day's agreement and then his refusal to testify in Rochester.

Thus, in the fall of 2002, in one of their first initiatives after re-opening the case, the task force tracked down Day on the East Side. They staked out his Third Street residence, placed a pen register on his home phone to track the numbers of outgoing calls, and sur-reptitiously pawed through his trash. Informants had led them to believe that although Day had been in poor health in recent years—reportedly a diabetic, "he looked terrible," Mead recalled—he was still using illicit drugs and possibly selling them. If that was true, the detectives figured they could leverage narcotics charges against him to encourage his cooperation, as they had done with potential wit-nesses in the earlier cold cases.

Then one Sunday morning in December 2002 Mead was skim-ming the obituaries in the *Pioneer Press* when a familiar name caught her eye. Kelly Day was dead at fifty-two. Mead called Dunaski. "Are you sitting down?" she asked him.

"You gotta be shittin' me!" he roared when she told him the news. "Well, that knocks our solvability factor down to about 4 percent."

"We were blown away," Mead recalled. "We'd been told he was sick, but no one told us he was *that* sick."

Dunaski's people pulled surveillance at Day's funeral a few days later, videotaping mourners arriving at and departing from the Will-werscheid and Peters mortuary on Grand Avenue and jotting down license-plate numbers. But the effort yielded nothing of value—not even a sighting of Ronald Reed, one of Day's oldest friends, whom the detectives expected to be there.* Kelly Day was no more helpful to the investigators deceased than he had been to them alive, at least in his later years.

---

*Reed later told the author he had in fact paid his respects at the funeral home.

Still, as their report to DiPerna made clear, the detectives were optimistic about their chances. That is to say they were confident they knew who was responsible for Sackett's death: Reed, Clark, and Trimble, all of whom "were either members of the Black Panther organization or sympathetic to [its] revolutionary cause." That was what the original investigation led detectives to believe, the report said, and there was no reason to believe otherwise almost thirty-five years later. "It should be noted," the report said, that much of the information implicating Reed, Clark, and Trimble "came from Kelly Day, who was a close associate" and "a possible co-conspirator . . . who would later become a paid informant of the police." Among the questions that remained—besides, of course, how to prove the first assertion—were: who else might have conspired with the suspects, and who might the suspects have confided in after the fact?

The report went on to enumerate the steps taken so far to advance the new investigation. Those steps included, besides updating the locations of the three suspects, reviewing old police and FBI records, interviews with law enforcement officers "originally involved with this case," locating and interviewing when possible the "original confidential informants involved in this case," the identification of a "number of individuals" believed to have made up the suspects' "inner circle of friends and associates" in 1970 (who "will be interviewed when located"), contacting authorities in Nebraska regarding Reed's and Clark's prison records and associates, and "continuing surveillance" of pertinent characters.

Dunaski may not have taken kindly to superiors' queries about his investigations, but he worked hard to keep them informed of his team's activities. Over the next three years he would provide periodic written updates to his St. Paul and federal bosses.

In June 2003, for instance, in a detailed memo to the U.S. Attorney's office in Minneapolis, he reported that through police contacts around the country the three primary suspects had all been located. Reed was living in Chicago "and is an unemployed sprinkler fitter." Clark had recently returned to St. Paul (presumably from the Omaha area), had "no visible form of income," was "heavily addicted to crack cocaine," and talked "about wanting to rob banks." ("Larry was right here, but under the radar," Dunaski said later. "It took us a long time to find him.") Trimble was still living in suburban Denver, where she was on "medical retirement" from the bus company and "has had recent involvement with law enforcement for shoplifting." Having located the three suspects, Dunaski wrote, investigators were concentrating on finding "past friends and associates" who "may have information related to the Sackett murder." As always, the identity of the three core suspects was never in serious doubt. The issue was not *who,* but *who else?*

Over time, however, the reports occasionally reflected a revision of the case's history and context, or at least the investigators' understanding of it.

In a November 2003 memo, Dunaski wrote that the suspects' associates during the late sixties and early seventies, like the suspects themselves, had been "influenced by the Black Panther movement"—which was not the same as identifying them as Black Panthers. (Dunaski later referred to "aspiring" Panthers "fueled" by Panther philosophy, but that's not quite the same either, which may not have been especially relevant to the ultimate issue of innocence or guilt but would certainly be a point of discussion if the case returned to court.) In the same report, it was noted that, according to their sources in recent interviews, some of the property damage that was "blamed on the protests and riots related to the civil rights movement" was "in reality" criminal activity commissioned by unnamed "local businessmen to collect on insurance claims." "Whether fire or criminal damage," the report said, "crimes of opportunity were staged that . . . would be automatically blamed on civil rights activists."

That report reiterated earlier police beliefs that the 1968 Stem Hall disturbance was likely the "flash point" for the unrest and disorder of the following few years and that the Panthers' "influence" spread to groups such as the Inner City Youth League, where, "whether or not by chance . . . many criminal acts were planned."

Then, in an acknowledgment surprising in tone if not in content, Dunaski wrote: "Coming away from these interviews we were left with the knowledge that the violent memories from over thirty years ago have left an indelible mark on the lives of many who lived it. In speaking with some of these individuals, we saw in their eyes the hatred and lack of trust they had for police officers during that time, which has continued to live with them. It is troubling to hear that there were others besides Reed and Clark who either tried or planned to shoot police officers."

*   *   *

By the fall of 2003—roughly the first anniversary of the start of the latest Sackett investigation—Dunaski and Mead had identified about fifteen members of their suspects' "inner circle" in May 1970. About ten of them had been located and two had given statements "regarding admissions that were made by either Larry Clark or Ronald Reed that they killed the officer." The November 13 memo added, "No specifics, but we hope it is a start."

The task force's strategy was clear and not particularly subtle. It was based on the assumption that (a) Reed, Clark, and Trimble were complicit in Sackett's murder, though maybe as part of a larger conspiracy, (b) judging by more than thirty years of denial, silence, and noncooperation, Reed and Clark were neither going to confess nor implicate each other, and (c) while Trimble was far more likely than Reed or Clark to open up, for a number of reasons (health problems and addictions, family pressure, whatever influence Reed himself might still have with her) she couldn't be counted on. Therefore, the investigators would work from the outside in, speaking to as many family members, friends, and erstwhile associates as they could track down, appealing to middle-aged sensibilities and consciences, and using whatever leverage any criminal activity still actionable within the statutes of limitations might provide them. The outside-in approach, complemented by the muscular application of federal drug laws, had worked in the previous cold cases.

With his admitted inside knowledge, apparently failing health, and alleged drug-dealing activity, Kelly Day would have been the ideal candidate to squeeze: an ailing man in his fifties would presumably opt for cooperation over the prospect of ten years in prison. Without Day, and until other candidates could be identified, the investigation would require, as Dunaski put it, "old-fashioned, hit-the-bricks police work, where you go out and talk to a lot of people and see if you can get them to come over to your side."

The task force had added a third full-time detective, Sergeant Scott Duff, who, as a rookie patrolman, had memorably visited the crime scene with Glen Kothe two years after the murder. Duff and Dunaski had sat next to each other in the academy and become pals, their common interest in hunting and fishing trumping the differences in age and family status. (Dunaski, six-plus years Duff's senior, was a husband and father when Duff was still single.) The two had occasionally worked together—Duff had also been a member of the special-weapons squad that ran Guy Baker to ground and, more recently, pitched in on Coppage and Gillum—and Dunaski counted Duff among the smartest, hardest-working investigators he knew. When Dunaski looked at the daunting list of names and incidents he and Mead had pulled out of the old case files and their recent interviews, he knew they needed help and knew the person he believed could best help them.

To either Finney or DiPerna or maybe both, Dunaski said, "You got Jane and me, so now give us Scotty and we'll do this thing." Duff, who was with the department's Special Investigations Unit at the time, happily joined the team.

Duff brought an amalgam of skills and interests to the effort. He knew guns and ballistics, which would be important whether they ever located the Sackett murder weapon or not. (They still had only the mangled slug from the rifle.) More important, he combined a *Jeopardy!* contestant's knowledge range with an extraordinary memory that Dunaski believed would be equal to the data-intensive task at hand. Duff, moreover, had an earnest boyishness that encouraged people to trust him. If Mead could have passed for an elementary teacher, Duff might have been a high school baseball coach. Together, Dunaski, Mead, and Duff formed a congenial trio. Though Dunaski had not a day's more seniority than Duff, he was, in Duff's words, "our de facto leader and the lead investigator. He was a great interviewer—that's what he did." Mead, whose partners dubbed her the "Angel of Death" after two different individuals happened to die not long after speaking with her, was the easy-to-talk-to "unDunaski" (Duff's term), especially effective dealing with other women, of whom there were many on their list of potential sources. Duff's strength was prizing information out of old files, obscure archives, and scattered databases, the way a miner gouges precious metal out of rock.

"I wanted Scotty because I knew he would lose sleep at night about this, like we did, and that he would go to the wall with us because that's what was going to make it happen," Dunaski said later. "We had to have people who were totally dedicated and weren't just worried about what they were going to get paid for overtime."

The trio did not devote every hour of every day to the Sackett case, but large parts of most days were allotted to it, beginning in mid-2003. Given the obsessive nature of good detectives, even when they weren't actively working on the case, the case was working on them. "It was always on our mind," Dunaski said later. Other St. Paul detectives, including Thomas Quinlan, Robert Merrill, and Timothy McCarty, as well as FBI special agent Matthew Parker, helped out with surveillance, "trash pulls," and other tasks as needed. By the time the case could properly be called closed more than seven years later, hundreds of city, county, state, and federal law enforcement officers from dozens of jurisdictions in Minnesota, Nebraska, Colorado, Illinois, and elsewhere would touch at least a piece of it.

The original investigators were more than happy to lend a hand. All told, Dunaski's team was able to confer with about a half-dozen of them.

"Every one of them was the lead investigator, when you talked to them," Dunaski said later with a laugh. Ernest Williams presumably had the best overview of the case as it originally unfolded, but he had died in 1998. As they did with other deceased investigators, Dunaski's crew sought out Williams's widow and children, asking about any notes and other documents the detective might have stashed in a closet after retiring. "We all take our notes home with us," Dunaski explained. "Someday they might come in handy. Ernie did, too, but his family said they destroyed them after he died." Carolen Bailey and Earl Miels *were* able to put their hands on important material, and while Ted Collins could not produce a court reporter's transcript (because it never existed), his wife brought out a nearly complete set of newspaper clippings she had saved from the Trimble trial.

Tom Opheim was eighty years old when Dunaski's crew contacted him, but he was sharp and quick. He told them Trimble had confessed to him—had told him everything—during her first evening in jail. "I went in and told Captain Williams, 'She just told me the whole story,'" Opheim told Mead. "A few minutes later she said, 'I'm not saying anything. I want a lawyer.' You've got to have my report in there somewhere." But Mead did not have Opheim's report. There was a report recounting their conversation the day *after* Trimble's arrest, when she retold the story of the mysterious written instructions and the ploy to bust Gerald Starling, but nothing that would qualify, then or later, as the "whole story."

"Opheim swore up and down, 'There's got to be that report in there—she confessed to me,'" Mead said later. "Opheim wasn't the type of guy who was going to say it unless he thought it was a fact. I think she might have admitted to *some* things, and with the passing of time he misremembered it. She no doubt did say, 'I made the phone call.' But the question was: did she know what the phone call was for? Maybe that's what Opheim remembered and brought to the captain. Who knows?"

Opheim died a short time after meeting with the task force detectives, fatally injured while riding his motorcycle in Florida.

Criminal investigations—especially large ones such as Sackett—are messy, chaotic, maddening affairs that almost never come together like the tidy jigsaw puzzles cops assemble on TV. Sometimes dragging on for years, they are marked by tedium and frustration, bum steers and dead ends. Potential witnesses die, leave town, and change their names. Sources lie, misremember, make things up, or inadvertently get their facts wrong. Paperwork is mislabeled, filed in the wrong drawer, or destroyed. Evidence disappears or was not there in the first place. Different jurisdictions have different agendas. Priorities and protocols diverge, egos clash, phone calls and e-mails are not returned in a timely fashion or not returned at all. Multiply such difficulties by a large number if you're talking about a case that is more than three decades old.

Duff, the task force's new guy, spent "literally weeks, maybe months" poring over the historical files, those in the boxes and those in the department's microfiche room. Sometimes he and Mead went in on the weekend so they wouldn't get in the way of the records staff's normal weekday activity.

"We'd develop a list of names and then go back and pull up the old police reports the individuals may have been mentioned in and put people together," Duff explained. When the police stopped a car on Selby Avenue, for example, their report would usually indicate who was in the car besides the driver. Duff would jot down those associations, as dated as they were, and when calling on one of the names mentioned in the report the detectives would have the other names in their pocket. "'I don't remember anything,' some guy would tell us," Duff said, "and we would say, 'Well, you used to hang out with So-and-So.' And if the guy said, 'No, I didn't know him,' we'd say, 'Well, back in 1969 you guys were together during a DUI stop. Your friend was driving and didn't have a license.' And the guy would say, 'Oh, yeah, I forgot about that.' It was tedious, digging up that information, but sometimes it paid off."

Some sources, of course, were more promising than others. In those instances, the detectives might take the individual out for coffee or lunch. "Often we'd just sit and talk about nothing," Duff recalled. Over time and additional contacts the source might develop some trust and confidence in their hosts and begin remembering interesting people and events from back in the day that he or she had forgotten or neglected to mention.

Many of the persons the team members spoke to had personal histories they didn't care to share with the police, unaware of or forgetting about the statute of limitations in Minnesota for most crimes except murder. "Look," an investigator would tell a stone-walling source whose police record the investigator had reviewed only minutes before his visit, "we're trying to solve a homicide. We don't care about those burglaries when you were a kid." That assurance, coupled with a reminder of the limitations statute, would often—though not always—be enough to loosen the person's tongue. Interestingly, albeit irrelevant to the Sackett investigation, by the time they had finished their probe the detectives figured they had effectively solved two dozen thirty-year-old bank robberies, scores of burglaries and gun thefts, and numerous arsons-for-hire—"stuff," as Duff would describe it, "that just came up in those conversations."

Shortly after joining the team, Duff received the go-ahead from Dunaski to check out a handful of individuals beyond the circle of presumed suspects, "so we could say we touched base with everybody and to see if any of the earlier stories had changed," Duff said. These included persons who might have had reason to hold a grudge against Jim Sackett, setting aside, for the sake of thoroughness, the virtual impossibility of the assassin knowing that Sackett would be the officer responding to the phony call. Duff tracked down and talked to the burglar that Sackett had shot and wounded in March 1970. The man—whom Duff found lucid but in questionable health in a state hospital—was quickly crossed off the list of dubious possibilities. A couple of other persons, whose names had been collected by the original investigators, had supposedly talked about Sackett roughing up or otherwise harassing African Americans on the street, but the allegations were vague and seemed to have been second- or third-person hearsay even at the time.

Duff also made contact with one of the brothers of Keith Barnes, who had been killed by a plainclothes officer in February 1970. But the man had nothing to say. "I could respect that," Duff said later. "The guy didn't want to talk to a white cop about another white cop killing his brother." Such attempts had to be made nonetheless, Duff said, "because you had to figure that down the road the defense attorneys would be looking at these people, too."

Most of the task force interviews took place on the Hill or with persons who lived there in 1970. Word of the reopened investigation had spread quickly, reinforced by Nelson's cable television spot and other public statements. Neighborhood reaction was predictably mixed, though mainly ranging from a resigned "Here we go again" to a weary "Why can't they let sleeping dogs lie?" The code of silence that thirty years earlier kept many residents from talking to police may not have been as strong and pervasive, but, much to the frustration of the latter-day investigators, it still was in force. Now, however, it wasn't young people in pool halls telling other young people to keep quiet. Mature men and women, grandparents in many instances, were talking in supermarkets and coffee shops, cautioning each other about discussing certain events of the past. When they did speak to investigators, they often brought up old grievances.

"Some of the people we talked to had been teenagers who got pushed around during the Stem Hall riots and were still on us about that," Dunaski said. "Then there were people who remembered Barnes and Massie. You could see it in people's eyes. They might look at us and think, '*They're* not like that, but some cops back then were.' Some of the people we talked to told us about being kids, watching on TV and seeing Angela Davis getting arrested and Martin Luther King getting shot. You could understand why black people were angry."

The bitter memories went back a long way and often revealed parallel realities—one white and one black. When St. Paul civic leaders, police, and their families gathered to honor their fallen officers in May, Sergeant Allan Lee, killed in the 1949 shootout with Oliver Crutcher, was among the names for whom the memorial bell tolled. For many of the hundreds of neighborhood residents who had watched the six-hour drama that long-ago September day, however, Lee was not the only victim. In the minds of many of those citizens—and their children and grandchildren, who grew up hearing the story—Crutcher had been executed by the police, an example of "street justice" that black people believed was all too common in their neighborhood. Some blacks still said, for that matter, that Paul Paulos "didn't have to kill" Wayne Massie when Massie and Byrd Douglas emerged from the stereo shop in 1970, never mind the official version of events that night that had Paulos returning Massie's fire. In both cases (and many others), the black reaction of skepticism, doubt, and distrust of official accounts of deadly confrontations would resonate the length of the long Sackett narrative.

Would an African American investigator have made a difference, in 1970 or later?

There were no blacks in St. Paul's homicide unit in either 1970 or 2003, but there were sworn black officers in the department and black investigators in nearby jurisdictions whom the task force could have utilized. Finney was, of course, an African American and from the neighborhood to boot—as was the late James Griffin, who, long after the Lee-Crutcher case, became St. Paul's first black sergeant, captain, and deputy chief. John Harrington, who succeeded Finney in 2004, was also black. Black officers, including Griffin and Finney, who worked in the neighborhood experienced, in any event, a mixed reaction from many of the people they policed, perceived by some of their neighbors as sellouts and lackeys of the white establishment. The feeling among both whites and blacks, police and civilians, seemed to be that during the Sackett investigation the ethnicity of the investigator didn't matter much. If you subscribed to the code of silence, you didn't talk to cops regardless of the color of their skin.

Nearly as detrimental to the investigation as the racial divide was the passage of time. Gone were potentially important witnesses, evidence, documents, and the memories of countless persons who once may have had material information about the events immediately before and after Sackett's murder. "We'd tell potential witnesses, 'Just think about it—we know it's been a long time.'" Mead said. "Then we'd call them in a month or so and sometimes they'd say, 'You know, I remember something else.' We'd read them what they told us the last time, and they'd sometimes add to that or make corrections. With some people we did that four or five times. I mean, it *was* more than thirty years ago."

"The most unfortunate fact in this case," Dunaski groused, "is that it should have been reviewed many years ago."

Whether the man was honoring the code of silence or merely acknowledging a failing memory, the reaction of a middle-aged Summit-University resident was typical of the responses the task force was hearing in 2003. The man had been identified as a childhood friend of both Reed and Clark, but, when told by Dunaski why he and his partner were standing at his door, he was visibly conflicted. The man took a deep breath, stared at his feet, then exhaled. "I can't help you," he said at last. "I don't know anything."

Like Kelly Day, Eddie Garrett was high on the list of long-ago associates of Ronald Reed and Larry Clark that the task force detectives were eager to contact. Garrett, after all, had told the police to "watch the rooftops" a week before Sackett's murder and had been interviewed at the scene within an hour of the shooting. If Garrett had been vetted later by one of Williams's investigators, there was no record of it in the surviving files. He was not called to testify during the Trimble trial (though he was available), nor was there any indication that he had ever been a serious suspect in the Sackett case. But in 1970 he was clearly one of the Hill's angry young men.

Unlike Day, Garrett was still alive in the spring of 2003 and apparently innocent of any illicit activity that might provide the police with leverage in their quest for helpful testimony. He was not difficult to find, because for the past several years his had been a euphonious voice on KBEM-FM jazz radio, broadcasting from studios in north Minneapolis. He was, as Dunaski and his partners would quickly discover, an easy person to like. It would, however, take Garrett more than a year to get comfortable with them.

Garrett was a large man with a commanding presence. Now in his middle fifties, he was a father and grandfather with many family members, friends, and jazz-radio fans in the Twin Cities. Born in Iowa, he grew up in St. Paul. He graduated from Monroe High School in 1966 and then, like a lot of young men without better prospects, enlisted in the Army. He spent a year in Vietnam—an infantry marksman with an "expert" rating—before returning home in late 1968. He got to know Reed, Clark, Day, and others who had organized themselves in a small group called the United Black Front, hung out at the

Inner City Youth League and other sites around the neighborhood, and espoused the revolutionary, anti-imperialist philosophy of the Black Panthers and Mao Tse-tung. Quick-witted and self-confident, Reed was the group's leader, and Garrett was, at least for a time, its "minister of information." At their meetings, which rarely included more than a handful of participants, they would discuss everything from armed resistance to the police to the kind of community programs for kids and the elderly that Black Panther chapters had established in other cities. Later, Garrett studied radio broadcasting at a local trade school, then held jobs at several different stations in the area, apparently helping make ends meet when necessary by driving a bus or a limousine.

The first time Dunaski and Mead contacted him, Garrett correctly supposed they wanted to talk about his "rooftops" comment. According to the detectives' report, he told them he had made the remark out of anger after his car was stopped by patrolmen Jerylo and Lee and a pistol he kept in the car's glove box was confiscated. The "rooftops" language, he acknowledged, was standard Panther rhetoric. The night of Sackett's murder, Jerylo and Lee briefly detained him again. While he sat in the back seat of their squad car, Reed and Day stood on the sidewalk and glared at him—under the circumstances, he said, a frightening experience. At that moment, he said, "he had a gut feeling that [Reed and Day] did it," if for no other reason than that they had been advocating attacks on police at their meetings.

The way Dunaski remembered that May 2003 conversation, Garrett did a "little song and dance" for them, conceding a relationship with Reed, Clark, Day, and others but not telling them much more than they already knew. Still, wittingly or not, Garrett said enough about what the investigators understood to have gone on and who was doing what back in the day to believe he had indeed been part of Reed's circle and could be a credible source. "This guy knows more than he's telling us," Dunaski said to Mead after that initial meeting.

Obviously, the fact that Garrett had been an expert marksman in the service made the investigators wonder if *he* might have killed Sackett. Neither Dunaski nor Mead—dead shots themselves—believed the Sackett shooting had required a great amount of skill. They had heard from other sources that Reed and his pals took target practice at various sites, including in the ICYL's basement, but, for all they knew, Sackett's assassin had been dumb lucky (Dunaski's opinion), striking his target "center mass." Nevertheless, Garrett *had* had military training and combat experience. "Sure, we were thinking Eddie could have done it," Dunaski said later. "This could have been the guy they talked into pulling the trigger. There was that crew, and for a while Eddie was part of it."

It's not clear when the investigators put the question to Garrett directly, but it probably wasn't long into their relationship. Dunaski was not the sort who beat around the bush.

"*You* didn't do it—didja, Eddie?" he asked him.

"No, I didn't," Garrett replied.

"You *sure* you didn't do it?"

Garrett said he was sure, and, pending further revelations, Dunaski was inclined to believe him.

The detectives would maintain contact for as long as necessary, knowing it would take time to establish a bond. Like most of their sources, Garrett was plainly wary of the police. He didn't like cops when he was twenty, and he didn't like them much more when he was fifty-five. In addition, he had become a known quantity, if not exactly a celebrity, in the Twin Cities' black community. Why would he want to risk his standing by talking to detectives? Dunaski and Mead decided they would play it easy, staying in touch but not applying any pressure. They would spring for lunch and, on one occasion, buy gas for Garrett's car. They would be there when he had something to tell them.

Jeanette Sackett was skeptical when she first heard from Tom Dunaski—whom she knew of only from seeing his name in the paper—telling her the task force had reopened Jim's case. She and her now grown children had heard little after the initial burst of optimism that followed Tom Hauser's discovery of Connie Trimble in Colorado a decade earlier. She and Chief Finney didn't get along, Glen Kothe was keeping his distance, and Nelson and Bohlig were no longer working the case. She and her children wondered if there would ever be an end to the story.

Not long after taking the case, Dunaski and Mead invited Jeanette to meet them at a Bakers Square restaurant near her home. As it happened, Jim's siblings, David and Corrine, were available that afternoon, so there were three Sacketts who sat down for lunch and talked about their common history. It turned out that, in classic St. Paul fashion, Dunaski was related by marriage to Jim Sackett's niece.

Dunaski, as was his practice, did most of the talking. He told the family about the cold cases that he and Mead had closed and said they were now going full throttle on the Sackett case. He said they were going to work it as hard as they could and they were going to get results. Jeanette rolled her eyes. She thought, *Yeah, I've heard that before.* "But he kept talking, and I kept listening, thinking, *It would be so nice to get this done.*" The presumption, apparently among everyone at the table, was that Reed and Clark were the killers; the task at hand would be proving as much. At any rate, by the time the investigators picked up the tab and Dunaski stopped talking, Jeanette was beginning to believe that could happen.

Afterward, David Sackett told her, "They'll never do anything with that case. It's too old."

But Jeanette shook her head. "You know," she said, "I think they will. I like them. I think they're for real. Something tells me they're going to find those answers."

4

B y the beginning of 2004, the task force investigation had developed a momentum that justified Jeanette Sackett's confidence. Despite confronting many more dead ends than open doors, Dunaski, Mead, and Duff were slowly making friends and developing sources who would direct them to additional sources, some of whom would likewise become friends and direct them to others.

Their task was to build a roster of credible witnesses who could put Reed and Clark at the center of a conspiracy to kill a police officer. If additional conspirators could be implicated, well and good, but, based on what the detectives were learning, that seemed unlikely. Kelly Day may have been one of the conspirators, but Day was now beyond prosecution. Eddie Garrett's complicity was not out of the question, yet based on what the team's sources were telling them and their own intuition, he was not a likely suspect. Both logic and experience told the detectives that the more people who were directly involved, the greater the chances that someone would have either accidentally or on purpose gone public with probative information during the previous three and a half decades. There was a conspiracy, they believed, but it had been a small one.

The task force was reminded, among other things, that the line between revolution as it was preached in 1970 and the street crimes perpetrated by "revolutionaries" and their associates was often thin or nonexistent. Focusing on a loose group that hung around the Selby Avenue pool halls and the Inner City Youth League, for instance, the detectives found all manner of "interesting" people. "You got a crew of revolutionaries, you got a crew of wannabes, and you got a crew of stickup men, burglars, pimps, and gangsters who kind of floated in and out and used [the sites] as cover," Dunaski explained. "There was a lot of that back then—where they'd go out and pillage, then come back and hang out and shoot a little stick." Then there were the neighborhood business owners who often lived in tonier parts of town and occasionally hired young men to light a fire or set off an explosive—arson and insurance scams in the guise of social upheaval.

Dunaski, with thirty-plus years on the job, knew many of the now middle-aged men and women whose names emerged from the files and interviews. "Some of them, like the pimps and prostitutes, I might have had some involvement with when I was working vice," he said later. "Some guys I put away on drug charges years ago. Jane would read the names, and I'd say, 'Yeah, I know that one.' And, 'Yeah, I know that one, too.'" A few of the individuals were still in prison, where Dunaski had put them ten or fifteen years earlier. They would all, of course, be called on and talked to and, more often than not, revisited again and again. The investigation had become, in Dunaski's words, "gumshoe police work."

During the course of 2004, the detectives and their colleagues in other jurisdictions in Minnesota and around the country sought literally hundreds of people in connection with the Sackett murder, contacted several dozen, and enjoyed productive conversations with maybe half of those.

The persons they actually spoke with included aforementioned inmates in county, state, and federal prisons; individuals who had shared a jail cell with one of the suspects; staffers at correctional institutions where the suspects had been incarcerated; former high school teachers, counselors, and classmates; long-ago landlords and roommates; retired police officers and federal agents whom the detectives had overlooked or missed earlier in the probe; officials of the long-defunct Inner City Youth League and other community organizations; African American activists past and present; historians, commentators, and journalists; and a former FBI behavioral scientist who headed the International Cold Case Investigative Association.

The richest information came from the scattered cohort of no-longer-young men and women who hung out with Reed and Clark in 1970. Thanks to early reports and the grapevine that still connected many Summit-University families, few people seemed surprised to hear from the investigators. One woman told them she had dreamed they were coming. The majority of these persons, Dunaski wrote in March 2004 with uncharacteristic delicacy, were "less than cooperative . . . living in a time warp and [still] loyal to the revolutionary ideals of the time." Dunaski reckoned that such individuals "either share some responsibility [for Sackett's murder], have direct knowledge about the plot . . . , or fear for their own safety." The one-time acquaintances who did talk, however—either openly or as an identity-protected confidential source—often contributed specific information about the suspects, the murder (and other, less serious crimes), or both, and reinforced or corroborated information and impressions acquired from other sources.

Much of the commentary, however, was confused, contradictory, unsubstantiated by other data, or patently wrong. Several sources prefaced their replies to the investigators' questions with the same unimpeachable excuse: "It's been a long time." One source said he thought Sackett's murder might have had something to do with prostitution. Another insisted Reed had been driven to kill a cop by the fatal police shooting of a close friend following a suburban restaurant holdup—though in fact the friend's death occurred in 1976, six years after Sackett's murder. While nearly everybody from the period mentioned the Black Panthers, there was little agreement as to whether the Panthers were active in the Twin Cities at the time, whether Reed and Clark were "certified" Panthers, whether the Panthers really advocated the murder of police officers, et cetera. A consensus said that Reed and others wanted to attract the attention of the Panthers' national leadership in order to be sanctioned for a St. Paul chapter.

As to the more crucial issue of the shooting itself, sources disagreed as to who fired the shot. Because no one claimed to have witnessed the assassination, the best that any one of them could do was repeat what Reed, Clark, or somebody else allegedly told him or her. Even then, the statement was rarely *that* specific, but rather came wrapped in circumspect language, referring to the murder as "taking

care of business" and "something that had to be done." In the eyes
of the law, it would not matter who literally pulled the trigger—both
(or all) participants were equally liable. But the prevailing opinion
among both sources and investigators held that Reed was the literal
shooter.

In any event, the bulk of the substantive information from their
sources provided the task force with the building blocks of a case
against the primary suspects. According to those sources, Reed and
others talked frequently about killing a "pig." Reed was the leader of
a group of young men, including Clark, who had easy access to guns
and explosives and were known to be involved in criminal activities, from armed robberies and drug dealing to arson and an alleged
airplane hijack plot. Most important, minutes prior to the Sackett
murder, Reed had been present when his girlfriend made the call
that lured the officer to his death; minutes after the murder, Reed
was identified among the spectators who gathered at the site. Apparently, in the first few days after the shooting, several persons
bragged about being the shooter; only Reed and Clark, however,
continued to talk about it months later. The task force did not yet
have enough information to ask a grand jury for indictments, but
they believed that day was on the horizon.

The information the detectives were gathering was also adding
flesh and blood to the profiles of the two suspects at the center of
the case.

Among the group of self-styled militants, Reed was, according
to acquaintances, the undisputed leader—a firebrand with a vision
and agenda. Clark, who was six months Reed's junior, was the dutiful
sidekick.

Reed was the third son of a respected Summit-University family,
hard-working, wage-earning people who had come north from Mississippi after World War II. One of his brothers, Duane, would become, in 2004, president of the Minneapolis chapter of the NAACP
after retiring as an executive at Cargill, Inc., the Twin Cities–based
agribusiness giant. Ronnie was smart, assertive, and always part of
the neighborhood mix, where he was widely known as "Little Reed."
One summer, his mother took him across the river to be a "cast
member" in the popular *Romper Room* TV series locally produced
at the Channel Eleven headquarters in the Calhoun Beach Hotel.
From fourth to eighth grade, he was enrolled at St. Peter Claver, a

respected Catholic academy located on Oxford Street near his home. He later played Midget League baseball with future Hall of Fame star Dave Winfield at the Oxford playground, was a member of Central High's Twin Cities champion football team, and was elected Central's annual Icicle Day King. Photos in the school's 1968 yearbook show a slight young man with close-cropped hair variously in a suit, a prom tuxedo, a football helmet, and a winter-pageant crown.

At some point during his middle teens, Reed, increasingly at odds with his parents, had fallen in with a loose assemblage of juvenile lawbreakers who hung out at the neighborhood's parks and pool halls. ("I had a lot of energy . . . a lot of connections," he said much later.) A couple of burglary charges, which he denied, resulted in a few months in reform school. Still, Reed's personal popularity and solid family ties made him an unlikely suspect in the eyes of many friends and neighbors.

"When they said who did it, I thought: I know his mama, I know his grandma, I know his brother, I know *him*," said a woman who lived near the Reeds. "We all grew up together. They went to Pilgrim Baptist Church. I don't remember when I first heard that Ronnie was supposed to have done it, but it just didn't seem conceivable. Not at all."

It also seemed clear that even all these years later Reed was still held in warm regard by some former classmates and acquaintances. "How *is* Ronnie anyway?" another woman from the neighborhood inquired earnestly when Jane Mead brought up his name.

Clark's early profile was less distinct than Reed's, his family not as well known. He was reportedly born in Louisiana, the oldest of four siblings whose family came to St. Paul by way of Illinois. The family lived, at least for a while, on Dayton Avenue. Clark's own Central High career was best remembered, acquaintances seemed to agree, by his membership in its Afro-American Club and his suspension for hawking Black Panther newspapers on school grounds during his senior year. Since their high school days together, Clark had been part of Reed's politically oriented circle.

During their conversations with the Sackett investigators, acquaintances described the post–high school Reed as intelligent and articulate. He was a serious chess player and read voraciously—by that time political texts by Marx and Mao and black nationalist writings by Malcolm X, Eldridge Cleaver, and others. At some point in 1969 or 1970 he began sporting an Afro hairstyle and wearing military-type clothing that reflected, friends said, a "militant attitude" on racial issues. Berets, leather jackets, fatigue pants, and polished combat boots had in fact become popular among many young African Americans in the provocative commando fashion of the Panthers, and Reed and several friends adopted the look. The fatal 1976 shooting of his friend Freddrick ("Freddie") Price by Roseville police following an apparent holdup could not, as believed by other friends, have radicalized Reed, but something or someone did at least six years earlier. One acquaintance said Reed had been a member of the far-left Students for a Democratic Society while attending the university. (Reed later vehemently denied that, along with many other details of his "official" biography, which, he complained, made him out to be much more the angry young militant than in fact he had ever been.) Others said he was among a handful of local men who traveled to Des Moines, Omaha, and/or Oakland, depending on the source, to meet with Panthers and other black radicals. Reed was reportedly comfortable with guns, having hunted small game with adults since he was a kid, and was an excellent shot with a rifle. Some sources said he was into drugs at the time; others insisted that, per official Panther strictures, he kept himself clean.

When Reed was mentioned, so was Clark, though inevitably in a supporting role. Few acquaintances could recall Clark speaking to the group, let alone any specific messages. His antipathy toward the police was probably every bit as fervid as Reed's, but he was not the one who acquaintances remembered standing up and articulating his anger in front of the others.

Reed's and Clark's lives since 1970 had been dominated by their years in the Nebraska prison system, following their 1971 convictions in connection with the Omaha bank job. Again, Reed's history was longer and more interesting than Clark's—in October 1976 he had not returned to the Nebraska prison while on a work-release program and spent a year on the run, reportedly in California. Despite the unauthorized absence, he had been paroled in 1981; less than two years later, however, his parole was revoked for alleged drug use. He was granted a parole a second time in 1984 and finally discharged from parole in 1986. In 2003 he was known to be living quietly in Chicago, where he installed sprinkler systems in commercial buildings and belonged to a union. He was said to be close to his family in the Twin Cities and to his daughter, Cherra, who had grown up and become a parent herself. He owned a dog or two, barbecued chicken for the annual block party in his South Side neighborhood, and regularly attended church. (A neighbor later described him to a reporter as a "saved man.") His record since his release from prison included only a 1999 arrest for soliciting a prostitute.

Little was heard from or about Clark following his parole in 1979, other than that he had become a practicing Muslim and was using the name Sharif (or Shariff). He was occasionally spotted in the Twin Cities and in Omaha, where he was known to have family and friends. One of the investigators' St. Paul sources said he would sometimes see Clark riding a city bus. Neil Nelson believes he saw him stocking shelves in a Midway neighborhood grocery store, but Clark did not have a trade and was often out of work. In January 2004 he was questioned (but not arrested) by St. Paul police following the apparent theft of an acquaintance's ATM card. "Clark is believed to be staying at Dorothy Day [a downtown St. Paul shelter] and is homeless at this time," the incident report stated. Informants said he was hostile to white people in general and to the police in particular.

In June 2004, Dunaski contacted Reed in Chicago. Dunaski explained why he was calling—as though Reed couldn't guess—and Reed, according to Dunaski's report, agreed to meet when he returned to the Twin Cities to see his family and attend a Central High reunion later in the month. He also said, Dunaski reported, he wanted to take a polygraph test while he was in St. Paul, apparently to clear his name. Dunaski told him he would pass on his request to Jeff Paulsen, the Assistant U.S. Attorney.

But Dunaski later said he never heard from Reed, though he learned that Reed had in fact attended his high school reunion at Phalen Park. Paulsen, meanwhile, had approved the polygraph exam and told Dunaski to inform Reed. By the time the investigator got hold of Reed, however, Reed said he was on his way to the Wisconsin Dells, after which he would be returning to Chicago. Dunaski told Reed in that case investigators would likely call on him in Chicago. Reed, who didn't seem to like the idea of the police visiting his place of employment, insisted he had tried to contact the detective while he was in St. Paul, but Dunaski said he had not received any such messages.

Much later, Reed told a reporter that *he* had initiated the contact with Dunaski, suggesting the lie-detector test, but that Dunaski had ignored his request. At any rate, there was never a meeting of the two men, and Reed never took the test.

The task force had achieved, however, a major breakthrough a few weeks earlier, which Dunaski may or may not have mentioned to Reed when they spoke on the phone in June (it is not in Dunaski's report) but which Reed probably knew about in any event.

On the Thursday before Memorial Day 2004, someone in the homicide office contacted Dunaski at task force headquarters and told him Connie Trimble had called; she said she wanted to speak to one of the Sackett investigators. Obviously, news of the reopened probe had reached Colorado, since no one in St. Paul law enforcement had talked to her since her short series of uninformative phone conversations with Nelson and Bohlig nine years earlier. When Dunaski called back, she told him that she'd heard the police were revisiting the case and that she would be willing to talk to them, though she was not up to traveling to Minnesota to do so. Dunaski said the detectives would come to her. After hanging up, Dunaski called Mead and Duff and told them to cancel their holiday plans. They were driving to Colorado.

The next day, the three detectives loaded the now several boxes of Sackett files into a van and headed west, reviewing yet one more time the familiar case history as they drove. When they reached Denver after a sixteen-hour journey, they checked into a Comfort Inn and, in Dunaski's words, "hashed things out" in preparation for meeting for the first time one of the three central characters in their all-consuming drama.

Trimble was now living in Aurora, a large, inner-ring suburb on the eastern edge of the city, where she shared an apartment with her husband, Manuel Smith, and her daughter Cherra's son, Eddie Coleman III. When the detectives arrived at about ten o'clock on Saturday morning, she greeted them at the door.

"Come in," she said. "I've been expecting you."

The smallish apartment was untidy, according to the detectives, and Trimble, at fifty-two, looked haggard. Her visitors recalled the plump, middle-aged woman they had observed in Tom Hauser's 1994 video and found the woman they were finally meeting in the flesh thin and drawn by comparison. She was wearing a wig, Mead noticed, and it wasn't on quite straight. Trimble introduced them to her husband, who apparently had health problems of his own, and her grandson, who appeared to be in his late teens. While both men were friendly, neither was interested in being part of the conversation. Smith went back to working on his car outside, and young Coleman came and went. After some small talk, the detectives offered to rent Trimble a room at their hotel, where they could have a leisurely dinner and talk without distractions. Trimble said that might be okay, but she needed some time to get herself and the apartment together. The detectives agreed to come back in a few hours.

When they returned about one-thirty that afternoon, the apartment was still a "mess," as Mead remembered it, but Trimble had dressed up a little. She was having trouble getting organized, she told them, and to the detectives she seemed edgy and uneasy in a way she hadn't been that morning. Dunaski figured she was having second thoughts about speaking to them, perhaps having "talked to some people" while they had been away. The detectives again suggested that the four of them go back to their hotel, but Trimble did not want to budge.

"Can't we just do it now?" she said abruptly.

"We sat right down," Mead recalled. "You could've heard a fricking pin drop."

"Go ahead," said Dunaski, as Mead grabbed paper and a pen.

The subsequent police report quoted Trimble saying, "Ronnie was the one who asked me to make the call. I didn't know any of Ronnie's things that he did. I want to [be] clear [about] this. I didn't know. Right after the phone call we went over to Larry's house. I think we went to get weed or something." A few moments later, according to the report, she said, "Ronnie said he didn't [shoot the police officer], but he was with me at the phone booth. Right after that we went to Larry's house. Larry lived right up the block from the house where the policeman was shot."

As she had told investigators and the Rochester jury years earlier, Trimble went on to say—according to the task force report— that she thought she was calling the police to set up a pot-party bust at 859 Hague, that she hadn't learned of the murder until she heard about it on the news the next day, and that she was too afraid to say anything to anyone afterward. When she later talked to Reed about going to the police, he warned against it, hinting at retaliation by the killers. When she asked him if he was involved in the murder, she said he told her, "What you don't know you can't tell." She said that was his response whenever she asked him about suspected criminal activity.

As she talked, Trimble's visitors sat on the edge of their chairs. Her account of the couple's movements immediately after making the bogus call was especially interesting.

"So you were in the car, by the phone booth, with Ronnie?" Dunaski said.

"Right."

"And after the phone call you went down the street, then parked in the alley behind Clark's house."

"And Larry," she said, "is standing at the back steps in a raincoat."

She said that she and Ronnie (and six-month-old Cherra, whom they had with them the entire time) went inside the house, where she believed Larry's girlfriend, Diane Hutchinson, was asleep with her children, and while she was in the bathroom for a few minutes Reed and Clark were either in the kitchen or had gone outside—she wasn't sure which, since she couldn't see them from the bathroom. At any rate, they stayed at the Hague address for five or six minutes, as best she could recall, before Reed drove her and Cherra back to their apartment on Fuller. Reed then went out again, she said, though she didn't know where he was going.

The detectives exchanged glances. This information was not in the files, in any of Trimble's previous statements to investigators, or in her 1972 trial testimony as recorded by participants and reporters. For the first time, a witness had placed Reed and Clark together at the scene—within a few yards of the spot where the fatal shot was believed to have been fired—moments before the shooting. Though Trimble said she hadn't seen any guns, it was easy for the cops to imagine what Clark might have concealed beneath the raincoat.

"We were floored," Dunaski said later.

Trimble didn't think she was breaking new ground. "I already told them this," she said. "When I was on the stand? Didn't I testify to all this?" The detectives knew, of course, that she had spent thirty days in jail for refusing to tell the court who was with her when she made the call that night and that she had not publicly implicated Reed until Hauser called on her in 1994.

Then, amazingly, she said the memory of pulling up behind Clark's house had just come to her. "I woke up in the middle of the night, and I remembered Larry standing by the back door," she told the detectives. "I had forgotten all about that—Larry standing on the back steps with a raincoat on."

As the detectives gingerly probed for additional revelations, Trimble insisted she had not seen a gun that night and hadn't heard a gunshot either, even after the detectives told her that neighbors reported hearing a loud noise at about the time she and Reed were visiting Clark. She said there had been a lot of thunder that night, which could have masked the sound of a gunshot. In fact, as the investigators were well aware, the thunderstorm that swept across St. Paul on May 22 occurred approximately three hours after the shooting.

Their conversation lasted about an hour and a half. According to the police report, Trimble insisted again that despite her fears and suspicions, she didn't really think Reed knew that an officer was going to be murdered that night, nor was she aware, until she found a box of cash in the basement, of the bank robberies Reed had apparently been involved in before his arrest in late 1970. (Based on the comments of other sources, the task force believed Reed, Clark, Day, and others may have held up the Grand Avenue bank two or three different times.) She said Reed seemed to have changed and become "more rebellious" after a trip to Black Panther headquarters in California sometime prior to the murder and that family members had worried about his association with a St. Paul man named John Griffin, who was known to be heavily into drugs and criminal activity to support his habit. At one point, she told the detectives, she thought Kelly Day was Sackett's killer, though she didn't explain why. Interestingly but not particularly relevant, she said she had happened to be shopping at Dayton's department store on the Saturday afternoon in August 1970 when Gary Hogan, whom she knew through Reed and thought was "crazy," nearly killed a woman with a bomb planted in a first-floor restroom.

Dunaski said that she echoed the regret she had expressed to earlier investigators. "It was like," he said, quoting her, "'If I had known what was going to happen that night, I never would have made that phone call.' Or, 'If I would've known what was going to happen, I never would've gone with Ronnie.'" Whether her regret was the same as remorse he couldn't know.

Late in the day, Dunaski and Duff went out to buy a bottle of zinfandel and some chicken for dinner (Trimble had declined another invitation to go out and eat) while Mead remained at the apartment and helped her clean up the kitchen. Trimble talked about her health problems and frequent doctor appointments. She seemed to relax when speaking with another woman, and she went on to tell Mead about her marriage, which didn't appear to be in very good shape at the time, and her constant struggle to make ends meet.

At no point, Mead would insist, did Trimble talk about expecting financial support from the police. The money, or its absence, became an issue later and played a prominent role in the family's accounts of the investigators' Memorial Day weekend visit, but Mead and her colleagues always said that money wasn't part of the conversation at that time.

Trimble, for that matter, did not seem curious about who else the detectives had been talking to about her, Reed, and Clark.

That night the investigators returned to their hotel and reviewed what Trimble had told them. On a laptop computer Mead typed her notes into a rough draft that they would review with Trimble the following day—"to make sure we got everything right," in Mead's words.

When they returned to her apartment the next morning, however, Trimble was apprehensive. She looked as though she hadn't gotten much sleep.

"She was more emotional than she'd been the day before," Mead recalled. "Like she was thinking, *Did I really do this?* Maybe she drank that entire bottle of zinfandel after we left, I don't know."

"She was concerned," Dunaski said. "She was asking herself, 'Am I in trouble again? Am I going to be indicted?' We told her, 'No— there was no double jeopardy.' We even offered to get Jeff Paulsen on the phone so he could tell her that she wasn't going to be charged with anything again."

"Her daughter was living with Ronnie at the time, and I think that really bothered her," said Mead. "I think she was worrying that she had driven another wedge between her daughter and her."

Duff said, "Maybe she'd talked to Cherra, and Cherra said, 'Why'd you tell them *that?*'"

By the time they had gone over Mead's draft and chatted some more, Trimble had calmed down. The detectives said good-bye to her believing that they had secured at least one piece of critical information and established a tenuous rapport with an essential witness. They left Aurora with hugs, good wishes, and mutual promises to stay in touch, which they did through the rest of the summer.

5

In June 2004, St. Paul's police department inaugurated a new chief. John Harrington succeeded William Finney, who was retiring after a dozen years in the top job.

Harrington was a burly, physically intimidating, yet cerebral career cop who had grown up on Chicago's South Side listening to his father, a Cook County deputy sheriff, and his dad's cop friends exchange "war stories" on the family's back porch. Much to his father's displeasure, John had hung out for a while during his teenage years with a "younger chapter" of the Black Panthers. He had also listened intently as his father and his father's friends discussed the fatal shootings of local Panther leaders Fred Hampton and Mark Clark during a blazing pre-dawn police raid on a Chicago apartment in December 1969. The account young John heard was dramatically at odds with the official version broadcast by the media. Contrary to those accounts—and as eventually confirmed by state and federal investigators—all but one of the nearly one hundred bullets that tore up the Panther apartment had been fired by the raiders, not by the occupants, which surely made the deaths of Hampton and Clark sound like cold-blooded murder. Harrington, nonetheless, wanted to be a cop, and, after pleasing his mother by earning a bachelor's degree at Dartmouth College in New Hampshire, found his way to the St. Paul department, which was then seeking minority-member recruits, and became a sworn officer in 1977.

Coming from Chicago, Harrington was amused by the differences between the two cities, especially as those differences pertained to race. He recalled with a laugh being driven down Selby Avenue by St. Paul relations and seeing what they referred to as the "ghetto" where "the black folks lived." He said he looked at "all those substantial houses, with grass in the front yards—all the cars had their wheels, nobody had burglar bars on their windows—and I kept waiting to get to the *ghetto*. We got down to the Cathedral [at the eastern end of Selby], and I'm thinking, *Hey, this is nicer than any place I've been living.*" Even many of St. Paul's so-called "militants" struck him, by Chicago standards, as "intellectual, academic, and pretty tame" for the era, "not exactly the type to throw a Molotov cocktail at a squad car."

The racial divide was quantitatively less dangerous than it was in his hometown—and was somewhat improved over what it had been in St. Paul seven or eight years earlier. St. Paul's police department, following the settlement of a federal anti-discrimination lawsuit, now included about thirty persons of color among its four hundred–plus sworn officers. The Sackett assassination, however, was still fresh in the minds of the city's senior officers, whatever the pigmentation of their skin. While patrolling the neighborhood, an older partner would point out the relevant sites: "This is the house where Sackett got killed." "That's where we think they ditched the rifle." Occasionally, Harrington rode with Glen Kothe, who would mention Sackett's murder but didn't offer any details. Making an arrest in a bar at Selby and Dale, Harrington said, "we'd been taught, 'Go in, grab your prisoner, then drive as fast as you can out of the neighborhood.' The explanation for that? 'Sackett.'"

Now, in the summer of 2004, Harrington was briefed on the reopened Sackett case by Tom Dunaski. Harrington, like many in the department, viewed the pugnacious investigator as a force of nature who was impossible to put off, let alone ignore. Dunaski brought the new chief up to speed on the investigation and urged a "full-court press" to wrap up the case.

"Connie's health is bad," Dunaski told him. "Some of our witnesses' health is bad. They're old and they want to get this off their chest."

Harrington, who had by now been part of the community for almost thirty years, believed Reed and Clark were legitimate suspects.

"It wasn't just the police department's position," he said later. "Folks who were credible to me—they were cops, they were black, they had grown up in the neighborhood—this is what *they* said was the truth." Then there were the task force's reports recounting the dozens of interviews with Reed's and Clark's associates, among them, most recently, Connie Trimble. "You could see things were moving," Harrington recalled. "You felt that the case was building to a point where it was really going to happen."

The chief had the support, moreover, of the mayor, Randy Kelly, and the city council, which, at the time, included Sackett's power shift sergeant, Dan Bostrom, and Deborah Gilbreath Montgomery, the Summit-University kid who had grown up to be a nationally prominent civil rights activist and the department's first female patrol officer and senior commander "who happened to be black."

"We'll find a way to get you what you need," Harrington assured Dunaski at the end of their first meeting.

Somewhat to the investigators' surprise, the hundred-thousand-dollar "Spotlight on Crime" reward, though publicized in the local media, had not yielded any significant information. Neither had Jeanette Sackett's recent appearance in the paper and on TV asking the public's help to bring "closure" for her family. Money from Dunaski's task force budget was provided in small amounts to a few informants, but that was by no means unique to the Sackett investigation and, according to the investigators, was never a factor that would make or break the case. Almost everyone on the police and prosecution side would come to credit some combination of the investigators' relentlessness and the eventual willingness of aging and conscience-driven witnesses to tell what they knew for their ultimate success.

The relentlessness was clearly part of Dunaski's DNA and no doubt a component of Jane Mead's and Scott Duff's makeup as well. And while all three insisted that they would expend the same effort on any case—as the long, arduous Coppage and Gillum investigations seemed to verify—they also conceded that the victim at the heart of their current investigation made the case personal in a way that most cases would never be. The fact that the shooter seemed to be aiming at Sackett's badge—whether he was or not, the symbolism of the bullet striking so close to the shield was potent—and the stories they picked up about young men firing at silhouettes of police officers in the ICYL basement, though never proved, couldn't help but stoke the investigators' emotions.

"I mean, who were these guys that they thought they could shoot at the uniform that I wear?" Dunaski, in high dudgeon, wanted to know. That Sackett was responding to a pregnant woman needing help only added to the deep well of indignation. "We'd all worked the stretcher cars and emergency trucks and broken our necks getting to an O.B. call," Dunaski said. "That made this case even more special."

That summer one potential witness stayed close without the investigators having to make pests of themselves. Following the detectives' visit in late May, Connie Trimble called Mead often, usually relating her personal problems and sometimes asking for help. At one point, Mead asked the prosecutors what they could do. "How are we going to keep in contact with this woman, for God's sake?" she demanded. "She doesn't have *anything*." Mead ended up sending Trimble small amounts of cash, intended to be spent on necessities such as groceries and the telephone, though the detectives suspected she was drinking and using drugs. "We wanted to help her out, keep her going," Mead said. The financial assistance was also a way to help insure the witness stayed where they could find her. The detectives knew, of course, how important Trimble was to their case, but Mead also felt a personal affinity with the troubled woman. Regardless of what she had been a part of, Mead thought, Connie had been through hard times in her life, and Mead couldn't help but feel both compassion and a certain fondness for her.

During the summer and through the rest of the year, the task force kept working its sources, with mixed results. There were still the hard-core cop-haters who made no bones about their unwillingness to help; how much they could actually reveal was never certain, but their contempt for persons who did was plain. "I know the whole thing," one man told Duff, "but I ain't a snitch like some people." Others lectured the detectives on the local civil rights movement and its heroes. A few of the no-longer-young men they tracked down readily conceded they had been "too busy pimping" or "sticking needles" in their arms to get involved with "politics." A few admitted taking potshots at squad cars back in the day but swore they had nothing to do with killing Sackett.

The detectives couldn't locate Gerald Starling, whose marijuana party, Trimble continued to insist, was the reason she made the fatal call and who happened to share a Ramsey County jail cell with Reed after Reed's arrest in November 1970. Diane Hutchinson, who had, according to Trimble, been asleep in the house she shared with Larry Clark the night of Sackett's murder, said she knew nothing. She insisted she didn't even recall testifying at Trimble's trial in 1972. "I can't remember back ten years, let alone that far back," she told Dunaski and Mead.

More talkative, though not especially helpful, was Kofi Yusef Owusu, formerly known as Gary Hogan, who was convicted of the 1970 department store bombing. Owusu, paroled after serving only three years of his twenty-year term (presumably because of his age and good behavior while incarcerated), had long since lived in Washington, DC, where he worked for the Peace Corps, the National Black Caucus of State Legislators, and other organizations. The St. Paul investigators viewed Hogan/Owusu as one of the militant young blacks back in the day but not among the youthful crowd at the scene on the night Sackett was murdered. Now Owusu told the FBI agent and District of Columbia detective who called on him at the task force's request that he corresponded with Trimble when she was in jail and was still friends with Reed. He referred to Reed's job and residence in Chicago and said his friend had "gone citizen."

A couple of years earlier, Owusu went on, Reed had visited him in Washington. While in town, he said, Reed had toured the National Law Enforcement Officers Memorial, where he located James Sackett's name among the thousands of fallen policemen and women; Owusu said he had done the same thing during an earlier visit to the site. Why they visited the memorial was apparently not discussed. The FBI report said only that, according to Owusu, the two men "briefly discussed finding the officer's name on the wall as a mere curiosity." As for Sackett's murder, Owusu said he had heard the commotion from the bedroom window of his grandmother's house but didn't know what had happened until the next day.*

Closer to home, the detectives talked to a man named Donald Walker, who recalled attending meetings at which Reed and Clark, claiming to be Panthers, quoted from Mao's Red Book and inveighed

---

*Owusu died unexpectedly, of undisclosed causes, in Washington, DC, in 2010.

against capitalism and the police. More important, Walker told Dunaski and Rob Merrill that at least twice during that period Reed and Clark had asked him to stow a rifle, wrapped in a "sheet type" cloth, in the trunk of his car. Walker was away, in the Army, when Sackett was killed.

Besides Trimble and Eddie Garrett, whom the detectives were assiduously cultivating in 2004, no one, however, would prove more important to the case than an inmate at the federal penitentiary in Oxford, Wisconsin. Not that John Griffin would be readily amenable to helping the cops, especially in light of the fact that one of the detectives had helped put him in prison on a drug charge.

Mead was reading a list of possible witnesses she had assembled from police records and other sources when she came to Griffin's name. "Well, hell," Dunaski said. "I pinched that guy for dope back in about eighty-nine. He should still be in the pen."

Griffin had been part of the group of young men who congregated in the Hill's hangouts in the late sixties and early seventies and had reputedly been close to Reed for a while. Though some sources identified him as an actual Panther who had been "sanctioned" by the national organization while on a trip to California, others said he was more accurately described as a burglar and stickup man with a serious drug habit. He had been in and out of prison for most of his adult life, and, when Dunaski and Mead first went to see him at Oxford, he was about halfway through a thirty-year sentence. Arrested in a heroin bust, he had turned down a plea bargain of ten years, was convicted at trial, and received 360 months in federal prison. Griffin was a bitter man with a fearsome appearance. Stabbed with a ballpoint pen during a prison fight, he was blind in one eye and saw poorly out of the other.

Sitting down with Griffin was difficult for everybody—"like sandpapering a bobcat's ass in a phone booth," as Dunaski memorably described the first meeting. "He about went nuts."

But the investigators would visit Griffin at Oxford several times. On one occasion, they brought along Bill Finney, who had known the prisoner when they were kids. Another time, the investigators brought Griffin a new pair of eyeglasses. Jeff Paulsen, the federal prosecutor, called on Griffin as well, to discuss the possibility of a sentence reduction in exchange for his testimony in the Sackett case. "We started seeing the human side of him, and he started seeing the human side of us," Dunaski said later. "That's what it takes, and that's why it takes so long to develop that relationship where they start trusting you and open up."

Griffin did not, however, open up without some incentive. While he did tell Dunaski and Mead he had valuable information about Sackett's murder, he wanted to speak to a lawyer before deciding if he would tell them what he knew, and he wanted to speak further with the prosecutor about the chances of reducing his prison time.

The investigators were also during this period reexamining the physical aspects of the case. That meant revisiting the crime scene and pressing their search for the murder weapon.

Scott Duff was the task force's logistics and firearms expert, and one day in August 2004 he recalculated the ranges from several plausible sites to the spot where Sackett was struck. Such estimates had been made during the original investigation, of course, but this time Duff used an electronic range-finder and Tom Dunaski served as the "target" standing at the front stoop of 859 Hague. The readings, taken at points between several of the houses on the south side of the street kitty-corner from the target, ranged from fifty yards at the corner to 102 yards near Larry Clark's former residence—all of which would have been within a realistic striking distance of a shooter with a scope and a few practice sessions behind him.

The neighborhood itself had not changed much so far as the investigators could determine. The two blocks of single-family homes, duplexes, and small apartment buildings did not look greatly different from how they appeared in the crime-scene photos taken moments after the shooting, or, for that matter, when Glen Kothe stopped there with Duff two years later. The street lighting had been improved, and several of the majestic elms, ravaged by disease, had been replaced by smaller trees. But the lawns were green, the elms' successors were in full summer splendor, and the street itself seemed an improbable spot for the assassination of a police officer. The nondescript frame house on the northeast corner of Hague and Victoria had been freshened up. Newer awnings shaded the windows on the west side, and a built-up set of stairs led to the back door where Kothe had hollered to his partner to watch out for a dog.

In addition, Duff made four separate test drives from the southwest corner of Selby and Victoria—where Trimble's phone booth once stood—to the backyard of 882 Hague, where Clark had been living and where Trimble said Reed had driven after making the call. Duff covered the .15-mile distance in between twenty-seven and thirty-one seconds. On yet another occasion, Duff followed the route that Sackett and Kothe had taken on May 22, 1970. Without using red lights or siren, Duff made the roughly two-mile trip from the Capitol to 859 Hague in six minutes.

One day, Duff drove up to Kothe's home north of the Twin Cities. The two men once more reviewed Kothe's experience on the night of the shooting. Afterward, at Duff's request, they went outside and Kothe lay down in the position in which he recalled Sackett had fallen. Duff took Polaroid snapshots of Kothe on the ground for the files.

About the same time, the investigators received word from an informant regarding the location of the assassin's rifle. The weapon was rumored to have suffered several different fates—cut into pieces and thrown in the trash, tossed from either the Lake Street Bridge or the High Bridge into the Mississippi, or buried at some undisclosed site in the city. At any rate, for many years the gun was believed to be gone for good. The informant's tip not only suggested the rifle still existed but made a find seem distinctly possible. The word was that the rifle, having been moved among several hiding places, had been secreted in its current spot since 1986.

For the investigators, the rifle would be a tangible piece of evidence in a case with precious few such pieces. It was possible, though not highly probable, that the weapon would bear the killer's fingerprints all these years later and that those prints would be legible and distinct from those of the other individuals who might have handled the gun over time. DNA evidence, unrecoverable in 1970, was another possibility. The actual rifle, moreover, would increase the chances of the investigators connecting the recovered slug with the weapon that fired it and perhaps, if a serial number had not been erased, its provenance. (The odds were good that it had been stolen.) A short time earlier, the BCA had reexamined the jacket from the fatal bullet, and the results allowed the investigators to narrow the likely types of rifle used in the murder to two: a .30–30 and a .30–06 bolt-action hunting rifle. Finally, juries tend to be impressed when a prosecutor holds aloft the "actual murder weapon," which if nothing else provides a tangible connection between the victim and his accused killer.

Armed with detailed directions from their informant and a search warrant signed by a Ramsey County judge, the detectives descended into the basement of a house on Concordia Avenue, once the residence of one of Reed's associates. They removed per their instructions a length of air duct—Dunaski, the former "tinner," knew a little something about ductwork. But in the camouflaged stash space they found nothing.

They were surprised and disappointed. The informant was reliable, the address was plausible, and the instructions were spot on— "everything was as described," the detectives noted in a subsequent report. So, assuming the rifle had in fact been there, what had become of it, and where was it now?

Perhaps whoever had updated the ductwork discovered the gun and innocently removed it. With that possibility in mind, Duff tracked down the contractor in a Minneapolis suburb. Amazingly, when the detective identified himself on the phone, the man asked, "Are you calling about the gun in the ductwork?" Excited again, Duff and Dunaski hurried over to St. Louis Park in the west metro. But when they arrived, they learned that the gun the contractor had discovered was a .45-caliber pistol, not a bolt-action rifle, and that the ductwork he had installed was at a different St. Paul address.

So how many St. Paul basements, the frustrated detectives had to wonder, had firearms tucked away among the flues and pipes?

Jeff Paulsen was looking for a way to prosecute the Sackett case in federal court. Paulsen and Dunaski had successfully collaborated on federal prosecutions of the earlier high-profile cold cases and wanted to proceed similarly with Sackett. The problem was finding an applicable federal statute. In most situations, the murder of a municipal police officer, like the murder of an ordinary civilian, was prosecuted under state law—so what, in Sackett's case, might allow a federal prosecution, with its generally more stringent rules and tougher penalties, including, in some instances, a sentence of death?

"We looked at everything," Paulsen said later, referring not only to his office but to the FBI and the Justice Department in Washington. "That included civil rights violations and even treason, believe it or not. It was writ large that the ultimate goal of the Black Panther Party was the violent overthrow of the government, and Sackett's assassination could be viewed as a step toward that. But, obviously, [treason] was pretty tenuous." Other possibilities, such as murder in aid of racketeering activity, did not become federal law until years after the Sackett murder and could not be applied retroactively. Still others, including the murder of a state employee because of his or her race, had not become a federal offense until later. Paulsen eventually decided that to proceed behind such questionable charges would pose too great a risk to their case. Better at this stage in the investigation to offer his temporary services, with the U.S. Attorney's blessing, to Ramsey County as a special assistant county attorney, urge the county to convene a grand jury, and help try the case under state law.

It would be an unusual step. Paulsen could think of a couple of instances in which a state prosecutor had functioned as a special assistant federal attorney but not of a single case where it proceeded the other way around. But his boss at the time, U.S. Attorney for the District of Minnesota Thomas Heffelfinger, gave him the green light, and he joined forces with Ramsey County prosecutor Susan Hudson, with the federal government paying his salary for the duration.

Ramsey County Attorney Susan Gaertner and prosecutors Hudson and Paulsen agreed that the time had come to ask the grand jury to hear evidence in the Sackett case. The list of cooperative sources had reached a more or less critical mass, but many of the individuals were considered shaky—vulnerable to pressure from family and community members and capable of memory failure, second thoughts, or flight. (Anybody who had studied the Sackett history would be aware of the Kelly Day no-show during Connie Trimble's trial.) A grand jury would compel by subpoena skittish witnesses to testify under oath and document their sworn testimony for later use at trial. And it would be the grand jury's job to return the indictments directing the arrest and trial of the suspects, if the grand jurors believed the evidence justified such action.

Beginning on August 25, 2004, the Ramsey County grand jury met three times to hear testimony concerning the murder of Patrolman Sackett. The witnesses called and examined by Paulsen, Hudson, and the unidentified jurors included Glen Kothe and Scott Duff, who re-created the event and provided logistical detail, and several men who had known and associated with Reed and Clark at and around the time of the murder. There was a woman, too—Constance Louise Trimble, who had returned to St. Paul from Denver to testify. Though the task force detectives had talked to her many times on the phone since they visited in late May, none had seen her until that morning. Given her condition when they left Colorado, the cops were crossing their fingers that the woman who appeared would, as she might say herself, "have it together." She did. As a matter of fact, when she walked into the Ramsey County Courthouse with grandson Eddie Coleman, the investigators couldn't have been more pleased.

"Oh, my gosh!" Mead said later. "She looked great. She had makeup on, and she was beautiful."

Her state of mind seemed to have brightened, too. "She was very positive about things," Dunaski noted.

To Mead, the improvement in Trimble's appearance and outlook reflected her belief, in the detective's words, "that this was important—that *she* was important. I think she felt she was doing the right thing."

In her lengthy testimony Trimble confirmed what she had related to the investigators in May: that Reed had told her what to say when she made the phone call, though she didn't know, and didn't think Reed knew, the real objective of the call; that immediately after making the call Reed drove her and their baby the block and a half to Clark's house, where Clark was waiting outside the back door wearing a raincoat; that while she was inside, in Clark's bathroom, Reed and Clark may have been in the kitchen or outside—she didn't see them for a few minutes; and that after the brief visit, Reed drove her and the baby home, where she went to bed and he left for parts unknown; that the following day, when she first learned of Sackett's murder, Reed said their lives would be in jeopardy if she said anything about their activities the previous night. She said he told her, "You could be killed. The baby could be killed. I could be killed."

She was older now and "closer to God," Trimble told the grand jury. She had come close to telling what she knew many times and wished she had done so years earlier. "I was never afraid of Ron Reed," she said at one point. "I was afraid of what I didn't know and who was behind Ron Reed"—though she didn't shed any light as to who that might have been.

Other witnesses testified about the times, the Inner City Youth League, the effort to establish a Black Panther chapter in St. Paul, "police oppression," "black empowerment," the meetings, guns, and furious rhetoric. Also described was the heady mix of global revolution and local street crime that attracted many young people. "We went over to the West Bank and robbed some hippies for a bunch of weed," one witness recalled of a not-atypical adventure. Sometimes the recollections were mistaken. Once again the deadly 1976 shooting of Reed's friend Freddie Price was conflated with Sackett's murder. Occasionally the testimony reflected the rueful self-understanding that sometimes comes with advancing age. Everybody was aware of the Panther movement at the time, one man said, and "we all wanted to identify with it. . . . That's the way we thought back then—you know, revolution. 'We need to do something for the community. We need to do something drastic.'" Ronnie, Larry, and a few others were "into it—you know, the tam, the black jacket, the buttons, the look, the imagery." But this witness said he himself was never a "real card-carrying Panther," adding, "I would have liked people to think that I was. But I wasn't."

Witnesses said that prior to Sackett's murder there was a great deal of anger and violent talk about letting "the pigs know we are tired of this shit"—which included the fatal police shootings of Barnes and Massie in February. "We got to do something back," said one witness. "You know, we got guns!" After the officer's murder, there was "celebration" and "bragging." Nobody who testified said he or she witnessed Reed or Clark (or anyone else) shoot Sackett, but many of their acquaintances seemed to believe one or the other had done it. "Why not?" said one man. "That is what they preached." Another witness was more specific: a couple of weeks after the murder, Clark said, "Yeah, we took care of business. We did what had to be done." And a short while after that, the witness said, Clark told him that "Ronnie did it" and had used Connie to make the phone call "because they were sure she wouldn't tell."

John Griffin, having established a level of trust with Dunaski and Paulsen, had agreed to tell the grand jury what he knew, despite the fact, he said, that the government "[hadn't] really offered anything in return." What the government had done, Paulsen explained, was agree to make a motion to Griffin's sentencing judge requesting a reduction of Griffin's term, provided he offered "substantial assistance" in the Sackett case; any decision regarding his sentence would be up to the judge. But Griffin said he was also motivated by letters sent to him in prison by Jeanette Sackett. (At the investigators' suggestion, Jeanette had written to Griffin as well as to Trimble, asking for cooperation.)

Griffin described himself to the grand jury as an authentic Black Panther who hung around with Reed, Clark, Day, and the others and occasionally resorted to robbery to help fund Panther-style community activities, such as free breakfasts for neighborhood kids and lunches for the elderly. He said Reed, who was "knowledgeable" about black history, Communism, and other "political things," had emerged as the group's leader, believing that "we should get on the map . . . and that we needed to, you know, spread our wings and make a statement." Reed was especially focused on the police, who, Griffin said, were "coming into the black community" and beating people up. "And then the conversation came around to killing a cop," he said.

Griffin himself was in prison from the summer of 1969 until the late winter of 1971. But when he got out and returned to St. Paul, he said, Day showed him the rifle that Day said had been used to kill Sackett. He repeated a long, convoluted story that he said Day told him about how Reed shot the officer, Clark shoved the murder weapon in some bushes, and Day eventually ended up with the gun—the .30–06 bolt-action rifle that Day was showing to Griffin. Later, during Trimble's trial, he said, Reed contacted him from the Nebraska prison where Reed had been sentenced for the attempted bank robbery and asked him to keep Day from testifying against Trimble. Reed told him, he said, that if Trimble was convicted, she could "hurt him really bad." (Reed also told him, Griffin said later in his testimony, that he never told Trimble the truth about the shooting, which would seem to raise the question of why Reed thought Trimble could "hurt" him.) Griffin said he and another, unnamed person did in fact hold Day at gunpoint to prevent him from going down to Rochester to testify. Day did, however, appear in court the day after he was called by the prosecution, apparently none the worse for wear, though he was now unwilling to take the stand. For that, Griffin said, Reed had been grateful. So grateful, Griffin said, that years later, when both men were out of prison and back in St. Paul, Reed thanked him for his help—and then, incredibly, described for him Sackett's murder.

"When I pulled back the bolt and locked the bullet in and put the bead on that dude, I felt more powerful than I've ever felt in my life," he quoted Reed as saying. "Then, when I pulled the trigger and I knew it hit him, I really felt fucked up."

A few moments later, Griffin told the spellbound grand jurors, "All of us had the propensity for violence. That's what we did. But Ronnie was taking it to another level."

The Ramsey County grand jury indicted Ronald Reed and Larry Clark on Wednesday, January 12, 2005, and a Ramsey County district court judge promptly issued felony murder warrants for their arrest.

Two days later, at about a quarter to four in the afternoon, near the intersection of Penn Avenue North and Twelfth Street, a pair of Minneapolis squad cars, acting on the Ramsey County warrant, stopped a brown Ford pickup truck with South Dakota license plates and took its sole occupant into custody. Moments later, Tom Dunaski, Jane Mead, Scott Duff, Rob Merrill, and other members of the task force, tipped that Larry Clark—who was said to attend Friday prayer services at a North Side mosque—was in the area, arrived at the scene. Dunaski and Duff put the unresisting Clark in the back seat of an unmarked car and advised him of his rights. Clark refused to acknowledge the rights that were read to him or to make a statement. It was a cold, wet, midwinter afternoon, and, according to the subsequent police report, the prisoner's only comment was a request to turn up the heat in the car.

Reed was arrested a few hours later, at his home on Chicago's South Side. Apprehended without a struggle by members of Chicago's cold-case squad acting on the Minnesota warrant, he was advised of his rights and driven to the Cook County jail. If Reed said anything of note that evening, the Chicago cops didn't record it.

Despite the arrests, the St. Paul investigators weren't popping champagne, nor were the prosecutors in either the federal or the Ramsey County courthouse. After a two-and-a-half-year paper chase, after tracking down and interviewing dozens of sources, after three sessions of a grand jury and the indictment of two suspects, they still had no confessions, no eyewitnesses, and no murder weapon. Many of their witnesses—assuming those witnesses would be there for them when the case went to court—were not the kind of citizens a jury would eagerly embrace. Then there was the fact that thirty-five years had passed since the crime. Could even the most credible individual be trusted to remember critical information from that far back in the past?

The cops and the prosecutors agreed: difficult as the case was to investigate, it would be at least as difficult to win a conviction at trial.

"We never knew how it was going to turn out," Jane Mead said much later. "Frankly, we thought that if we got them indicted, we won. We never thought the case would be a slam dunk in the courts."

Jeff Paulsen told the detectives, "The good news is, they're indicted. The bad news is—they're indicted."

The arrests were front-page stories in the Twin Cities papers, never mind the fact that many readers and perhaps some of the reporters had not been alive when James Sackett was murdered. Though neither the investigators nor the suspects were quoted, plenty of other interested parties were. One of his Chicago neighbors told the *Star Tribune*'s Joy Powell that Reed was a quiet man who minded his own business. His daughter, Cherra, who was living with Reed at the time, told Powell that her father's "mantra" was "Be responsible." "We just knew him as our dad," she said. Powell said Clark's stepfather, Phillip Porter, told her that the family was shocked by the arrests, though he hadn't spoken to Clark in several years.

Several Twin Citians weighed in on the distant times disinterred by the arrests, offering their perspectives on the Black Panthers and other exotic life forms of the era.

"People had decided they weren't going to take it anymore," Bill Finney told *Star Tribune* columnist Nick Coleman. "We were all revolutionaries back then, but we didn't all take the same path."

Longtime members of the Summit-University community may—or may not—have captured the current ethos of the neighborhood following the arrests.

"There were rumors circulating about this for thirty-five years," Nick Khaliq, St. Paul's NAACP president, told Coleman. "So for this to come to a head now makes people wonder whether [the police] have their facts right, or if the clock is ticking and they have to hurry up and rush to judgment. You think things are getting better, and then you wonder if we are going backwards. There are a lot of mixed feelings."

Educator and neighborhood activist Kathleen ("Katie") McWatt surely summed up the situation as succinctly as humanly possible that day. She told Coleman that she was "amazed" when she heard about the arrests, then added, "Those times seem so far in the past. But here we are."

Rookie patrolman James Sackett on Christmas Eve 1968, his
first night on the job. (Courtesy Jeanette Sackett Monteon)

859 Hague Avenue shortly after Sackett's murder. Expecting to help deliver a baby, officers Sackett and Kothe had arrived at the site in the camouflaged traffic car at the curb. (St. Paul Police Department)

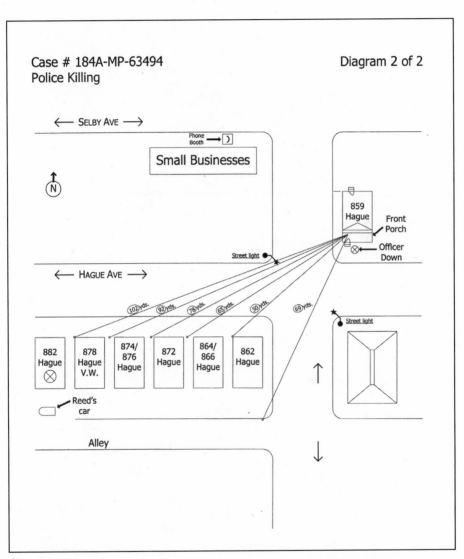

An investigator's diagram of the crime scene, including the comparative
distances between Sackett's position and the shooter's possible locations.
(St. Paul Police Department)

The view looking north toward Selby Avenue along Victoria Street from the front yard of 859 Hague. Connie Trimble placed her call from a phone booth around the corner of the store at the far left. The building directly across Selby housed the Inner City Youth League. (St. Paul Police Department)

Looking toward 859 Hague from the southwest quadrant of Hague and Victoria. Investigators believed Sackett's killer fired from approximately this position. (St. Paul Police Department)

Jeanette Sackett at her husband's burial with six-year-old Jim Jr., four-year-old Jennifer, and the patrolman's father, Melvin Sackett. (Craig Borck, *St. Paul Pioneer Press*)

Sackett's partners and supervisors carry his casket to its Fort Snelling grave site. Glen Kothe, wearing glasses, is in front at right. (Craig Borck, *St. Paul Pioneer Press*)

Class photos from Central High School's 1968 yearbook: senior Ronald Reed, left; Larry Clark, a junior; and sophomore Constance Trimble.

Reed was Central High's 1968 Icicle Day king.

Ronald Reed's mug shots following his arrest in November 1970. (St. Paul Police Department)

Larry Clark and Connie Trimble in fall 1970 police photos. (St. Paul Police Department)

John Harrington, center, succeeds William Finney, left, at a police department ceremony in 2004. Finney, the department's first African American chief, was in charge when the Sackett cold case probe was initiated; Harrington, St. Paul's second black chief, presided at its closure. (Joe Oden, *St. Paul Pioneer Press*)

The St. Paul task force was honored in 2007 for its work on the Sackett case by the International Homicide Investigators Association. From left: Sergeant Jane Mead, Assistant U.S. Attorney Jeffrey Paulsen, Sergeant Thomas Dunaski, Assistant Ramsey County Attorney Susan Hudson, Sergeant Scott Duff, and IHIA executive Bill Hagmaier. (Courtesy Thomas Dunaski)

Part Three

The Burden of Proof

"This case is about the events of May 1970, but it is also about so much more than that. It is about the passage of time. It is about memories that fade or that are replaced by new ones."

"The passage of time is both an enemy and an ally."

1

As if the city needed a reminder of the crime that it would soon be reliving in court, another St. Paul police officer was murdered in the spring of 2005.

Early on the morning of May 6, Sergeant Gerald Vick, a forty-one-year-old, highly decorated, sixteen-year department veteran, a husband and a father of two, was shot and mortally wounded in an alley off East Seventh Street. The murder seemed to make even less sense than most. Vick and his partner, Sergeant Joseph Strong, had been working undercover on a prostitution-related assignment when they left Erick's Bar, on East Seventh at North Forest, about 2 AM. Outside, they spotted a man urinating against a wall. The officers exchanged words with the man and the man's friend, after which the cops each climbed into an unmarked car and prepared to leave the neighborhood. The argument continued, however. Vick and Strong got out of their cars, and Vick followed one of the men into the alley, where the man turned and fired three shots at point-blank range. Strong returned the fire, but Vick was down and the two men escaped unhurt. After a brief, intensive manhunt, Harry Evans, a thirty-two-year-old Chicago native, and twenty-seven-year-old Antonio Kelly, also originally from Illinois, were separately found hiding a few blocks from the shooting site, the suspected murder weapon nearby. Within a few hours of their arrest, Kelly had fingered Evans as Vick's killer.

Five days later, the city once again came to a somber standstill for a policeman's funeral. The image of a thousand uniformed cops with black bands across their shields, massed in formation and saluting a flag-draped coffin as bagpipes skirled on an otherwise unmemorable weekday afternoon, took nearly every adult reading about it in the paper or watching reports on TV back to August 1994, when on successive days they witnessed similar rites for Ron Ryan Jr. and Tim Jones. Older citizens, primed by the recent, highly publicized arrests of Ronald Reed and Larry Clark, would remember even further back—to a previous cop-killing on a dark May night, thirty-five years earlier.

But Jerry Vick's murder was not an assassination. It was likely, in fact, that his killer did not know Vick was a police officer when he shot him. Whether the killing could be considered "racially motivated" was debatable, though Vick was white and Evans black. To all appearances, the murder was the ugly end-point of a random confrontation exacerbated by alcohol, testosterone, and bad judgment. That the victim was a much-honored cop and the alleged shooter an ex-con with a long record of arrests and a conviction for attempted murder in Illinois seemed to be grotesquely coincidental.

Nonetheless, if dissimilar in most aspects from the Sackett case that was just beginning to grind its way toward a courtroom resolution, the Vick murder reanimated the gut-churning emotions that surge up around a cop-killing and reminded the Sackett investigators both how much was at stake and how much had yet to be done.

In May 2005 the Sackett team was preparing to go to a trial in late summer or early fall. That month, they began turning over to the defense counsel investigative information as required by the rules of discovery. After fighting extradition for nearly two months, Reed had been returned to Minnesota from Illinois and had been held since March by Ramsey County authorities in lieu of two million dollars bail. Clark's bail, originally set at the same amount, had been reduced by half, district court judge Gregg Johnson agreeing that Clark, supposedly because of an ailing mother in the Twin Cities and a connection to a local mosque, did not pose a significant—or *as* significant a—flight risk. Both men were assigned public defenders. The pair would be tried in a state court under state law, and the prosecutors intended to try them together.

The task force believed they had a strong case. Not a sure thing—no one who ever conducted business in front of a jury believed in sure things—but a solid, persuasive argument capable of both winning over a dozen impartial citizens and standing up against the barrage of appeals that would inevitably follow the trial. Even without confessions, eyewitnesses, or significant physical evidence, they believed they could place both Reed and Clark at the scene of the crime at the time the crime was committed and accord them convincing motivation for committing it: to retaliate for heavy-handed police behavior in the neighborhood and to attract the attention of the Black Panther leadership in California. Several witnesses, including Connie Trimble, presumably would testify to that effect.

The local rumor mill, both on and off the Hill, had pointed out or at least speculated about the witnesses since Dunaski and his colleagues began making the rounds of the neighborhood more than two years earlier. Everybody seemed to know that Trimble had spoken to the detectives in Colorado and to the grand jury in St. Paul. Then, in late July 2005, Trimble, John Griffin, and a handful of other prospective prosecution witnesses were identified in a pretrial hearing before Judge Johnson, making those names part of the public record. Griffin's grand jury statement quoting Reed describe his feelings before and after firing the shot that killed Sackett, even sanitized for a newspaper audience, made electrifying reading in the *Pioneer Press.*

Predictably, the defendants' attorneys questioned both the integrity and the reliability of the state's likely witnesses, pouncing on admissions that prosecutors had offered some of the witnesses financial assistance and others the possibility of reduced prison time. (A good deal less credible under the circumstances was the defense's assertion that the state had purposefully delayed filing charges for three and a half decades—presumably for either a strategic or tactical advantage that wasn't readily apparent to anyone except perhaps defense counsel themselves.) Just as predictably, some of the outed witnesses complained that they were being ostracized—privately by old acquaintances in familiar neighborhood haunts and publicly in the columns of local media commentator Ron Edwards. It escaped no one's notice that Reed's brother Duane was president of the Minneapolis NAACP and that Duane Reed's St. Paul counterpart, the widely respected Nick Khaliq, was publicly skeptical of the state's case. Small wonder that task force members were beginning to notice some of their sources asking themselves (and the detectives), in one man's words, "Can this possibly be worth all the shit I'm having to take?"

A police department memo stated the challenge succinctly: "The longer the delays, the more difficult it is to keep witnesses on track and shore up their confidence."

The defense, meanwhile, was asking for thousands of pages of documents, ranging from FBI files detailing the bureau's surveillance activities circa 1970 to copies of Jeanette Sackett's letters to Trimble and Griffin. Connie Iversen and Thomas Handley, Clark's court-appointed attorneys, also asked the judge to compel federal agents past and present to testify about their activities vis-à-vis black militants a generation earlier. In early September, with the trial scheduled to begin in a month, the defense asked for still more historical paperwork, including the criminal records of several of the prospective witnesses and federal reports regarding not only black nationalist organizations but sundry antiwar and radical counterculture groups as well. Judge Johnson, who might have begun suffering nightmares not only about delays but of an eventual trial of unlimited scope and endless dispute, finally said enough. "This is not going to turn into a trial about terrorism in the 1970s," he told the lawyers. "This is not going to be a trial about the Black Panthers, the Weathermen, or the Symbionese Liberation Army."

In mid-September, defense counsel laid out the defendants' alibis, or at least their whereabouts at the time of the murder. Reed, said his attorney, public defender John Pecchia, was at home at 996 Fuller Avenue, a mile from the crime scene. According to Iversen and Handley, Clark was also at home, at 882 Hague (where Trimble said she had seen him). A "third-party perpetrator," unnamed by the defense, was blamed for the officer's murder.

At about the same time, the defense also asked the state court of appeals to overrule Johnson's refusal to throw out the case or try the defendants separately. By this point, no one was expecting a trial to begin in October. And on October 3, Johnson rescheduled the start date to November 7, to give the defense more time to prepare its case.

* * *

There *was* an upside to the delays from the task force's point of view. The investigators had more time to track down additional information and to cultivate potential witnesses who were still guarding their secrets. They hoped the arrests of Reed and Clark would encourage previously reluctant sources to come forward now that their testimony might make a difference.

True enough, some of the team's efforts that summer came to naught. In June, for instance, investigators secured a search warrant for the two-story brick building on the northwest corner of Selby and Victoria that decades earlier housed the Inner City Youth League. Sources dating back to Paul Paulos's surveillance days prior to Sackett's murder had insisted that the ICYL maintained a firing range in the basement—with bales of hay stacked against the walls and targets in the shape of police officers—despite the steadfast denials of the organization's leadership and the absence of tangible proof that such a thing existed. If the investigators could recover bullet fragments from among thirty-five years of dust and detritus, and if those fragments corresponded to the fragments of the bullet that killed Sackett—well, that would be a breakthrough. Without such a connection, what relevance the presence of a target range might have been to the guilt or innocence of Reed and Clark, other than adding credibility to certain prosecution witnesses, was a separate question.

In any event, a front-page story in the *Pioneer Press* on July 9 suggested something important had been found—according to the headline, A NEW LEAD IN OFFICER'S 1970 SLAYING. The accompanying story described investigators leaving the building (which had long since been given over to unrelated commercial activities) with three bags of "possible lead fragments mixed in with concrete." There were no subsequent stories about what might have been salvaged from the basement, however, and later in the year the investigators would note in a terse report to their bosses, "No bullet fragmentation or trace evidence [had been] located" during the search, nor anything else "of evidentiary value."

The investigators had better luck with a couple of sources—one of whom they had been patiently calling on for much of the past year and one who seemed to appear out of nowhere.

The latter was a middle-aged man dragging a lengthy police record. His name was Arthur Harper, and he was part of Reed's loose cluster of acquaintances in 1970. Harper told the investigators about something they hadn't heard from anyone else up to that point—the existence of what Harper called a "revolutionary house." Situated at 844 Dayton Avenue in 1970, the house had been torn down long ago. At the time, it was actually a rental duplex, the first floor of which functioned, Harper told Dunaski and Mead, as a sort of clubhouse for Reed and his friends, who would gather for conversation, political instruction, and games of chess. The apartment was full of Black Power posters and guns, Harper said; Reed and some of the others wore "all that Black Panther shit," discussed Mao's Red Book, and spoke frequently about killing a cop, though never in specific terms. The apartment had been rented in the spring of 1970 by Kelly Day and was located two blocks north of Hague Avenue. More interesting yet, Harper said, half an hour before Sackett was murdered, he and his pal Arling Reese saw Reed and Clark leave the house and walk in the direction of Hague. Reed, he said, was carrying a bolt-action rifle. (Reese subsequently told investigators he didn't remember being at the Dayton Avenue house with Harper or anything else about the night Sackett was killed.)

Harper went on to say that while he didn't witness the shooting itself, he heard the shot and shortly afterward watched from near the corner of Selby and Victoria as squad cars swarmed into the neighborhood. He said he saw Reed—but not Clark—standing around after the shooting; he said he had not seen Connie Trimble with the men at all that night, though it was later generally accepted that Reed had talked her into making the call that drew the officer to his death. Harper denied the rumor (brought up by the detectives) that he and Reese had served as "lookouts" during the shooting.

Describing himself back in the day as more of a "snatch and grab"–type thief than a revolutionary, Harper was not eager to talk to the police, either as a youth at the time of the murder or as a middle-aged man in 2005. He had never flown high on the local radar, at least so far as the investigators were concerned, and it no doubt took a good deal of their persuasive powers to get him to open up. "We didn't know anything about Arthur Harper, but his name was brought up by a couple of other people," Dunaski explained later. "So we go talk to Art, and Art is one of the ones that saw [Reed and Clark] when they left that place with the gun. He just took a liking to us, and we got more and more out of him."

The other important source to respond to the detectives' entreaties at about that time was Eddie Garrett. Dunaski, Mead, and Duff had been in touch with the local deejay for months, getting to know him and building trust, and finally the detectives' patience was rewarded. After talking to members of his family, Garrett decided to tell what he knew about the Sackett murder, or at least about the events leading up to it. He now told them about a conversation he'd had with Reed a few days before Sackett's murder. The two men, Garrett said, had been sitting in his baby-blue Cadillac on Selby Avenue when Reed asked him if he wanted to participate in—Garrett's words quoting Reed—"taking down the first pig." Garrett said he assumed his combat experience had prompted the invitation. In any event, he said, he told Reed he wasn't interested and from that point on did his best to stay away from his friend.

The value of the two sources' recollections was obvious. In Harper the task force had a witness who could, like Trimble, place Reed and Clark in the immediate vicinity of the murder within minutes of the shooting. Harper could put a bolt-action rifle in Reed's hands as well. Garrett gave the prosecution Reed's stated intent to kill a police officer a few days before the murder. Granted, Harper's checkered past—like Trimble's, Griffin's, and that of several of the other prospective witnesses—would be an issue in court, as would Garrett's anti-cop fervor, not to mention the combat vet's skill with a rifle and proximity to the scene on the night of the crime. But the task force would worry about that when the witnesses took the stand—assuming the case ever reached trial.

On Sunday, November 6, the *Pioneer Press* published a long front-page feature intended to be a preview of the trial scheduled to begin in Judge Johnson's Ramsey County courtroom the next day. TRIAL TO RECALL BITTER ERA, the headline read. The story, by staff writer Shannon Prather, contained many of the familiar details of what had become by this time a sort of local mythology, as well as the comments of familiar citizens who formed a veritable Greek chorus in the background—Bill Finney, Nick Khaliq, and Ron Edwards among them. Edwards, another one of the ICYL's founders, railed against the state's allegations in the *Minnesota Spokesman-Recorder,* a weekly newspaper serving a primarily African American audience, and his energetic blog. Quoted by Prather, he declared Reed and Clark victims of a "botched" vendetta mounted by a group of "obsessed" police officers less interested in solving the case than in "retribution and revenge." Of the two defendants, Edwards said, "They were both strong. They were black. They were intellectually competent. They were well respected by their peers." To which he added, "To be young, black, and gifted generated animosity and jealousy." Edwards did not say "animosity and jealousy" among whom, nor did he or anyone else included in the story offer the names of other possible suspects or, for that matter, an alternative explanation for the murder.

Neither Reed nor Clark was quoted by Prather. In a brief interview in the *Spokesman-Recorder* about the same time, however, Reed declared both his innocence of the murder and his ignorance of the killer's identity. He also wondered aloud why in thirty-five years none of the investigators had asked to speak directly to him—an assertion that, of course, ran counter to the stated experience of investigators such as Carolen Bailey and Russ Bovee. Reed also said he had offered to take a lie-detector test but the authorities weren't interested. Tom Dunaski, who would have provided a contrary version of Reed's lie-detector account, apparently wasn't asked to comment.

The November 6 story's coda was provided by yet another familiar voice, Jeanette Sackett's. "I am just anticipating the start of the trial to let our justice system do whatever it needs to do so our family can have closure," she said.

But instead of commencing the next day, the trial was once again postponed while defense attorneys continued to review the complicated history of the "bitter era."

Actually, there were several bones of contention delaying the trial start. The admissibility of evidence, such as the guns and the copies of the handwritten notes confiscated when Reed was arrested in November 1970, the admissibility of the earlier arrests themselves (Reed's in June as well as November 1970, Clark's in October 1970), and the admissibility of the defendants' convictions in connection with the Omaha bank case were among the issues debated before Judge Johnson in preliminary hearings that dragged on into the late fall of 2005. There were defense motions to quash the indictments and to sever the trials, and a challenge to the "ten-year rule" limiting the admissibility of a witness's prior convictions. And there were the seemingly interminable arguments about discovery, during which defense counsel accused the prosecutors of withholding relevant information.

"How long are we going to go on with this where everyone is complaining that they haven't received this and they haven't received that?" the judge demanded of the lawyers at one point. "We will never get this case tried. . . . I don't really want to spend a lot of time talking about what took place in Omaha, Nebraska, twenty, thirty years ago. I mean, I understand that may have some relevance and we are going to take that up at a Rasmussen [evidentiary] hearing, but I'm getting kind of frustrated with thirty years of discovery disputes."

Johnson was another hometown boy and an almost exact contemporary of the defendants in this case. Born in 1950, he grew up on the city's East Side, which had produced considerably more cops than judges, and graduated from Johnson High School, Jim Sackett's alma mater. Johnson studied economics at the University of Minnesota—he was an undergraduate there when Sackett was murdered—and for a few years worked as a stockbroker and on the staff of the Metropolitan Council, the Twin Cities' regional planning agency. He eventually followed a longtime interest in the law ("I noticed that lawyers were persons people listened to," he once explained) and earned a juris doctorate from St. Paul's Hamline University. He started his own practice and then worked for almost nine years as a public defender before being appointed to the district court bench by Republican governor Arne Carlson in 1992. Two years later, he was elected to the post, then reelected in 2000. (In Minnesota, district judges are usually appointed but then must stand for election and reelection every six years.) He had presided over antitrust cases and class-action suits as well as a couple of extensively publicized homicide cases. Since 2004, Johnson had been the Second Judicial District's chief judge, elected to the position by his district court colleagues, so it was appropriate that he appoint himself to preside over the trial of a pair of alleged cop-killers, which was about as high profile a criminal case as a judge was likely to get in St. Paul.

Johnson's neatly trimmed salt-and-pepper mustache and goatee made him appear only slightly less boyish than he might have otherwise, though he would hardly match most stereotypes of a senior judge. He was an avid recreational tennis player, cross-country skier, and runner who kept himself fit during the winter by jogging up seventeen floors of the courthouse during his lunch break. He was married and the father of four daughters. His wife, Susan Haigh, was a former Deputy Ramsey County Attorney and currently president of the Twin Cities chapter of Habitat for Humanity. Temperamentally, Johnson was known to be easygoing, evenhanded, and cautious, respectful of the lawyers in front of him yet not a pushover, as well as a well-organized manager of complicated trials. Asked about his judicial philosophy, the judge once replied, "I'm neither liberal nor conservative. I'm middle-of-the-road, as in my politics." Despite his several years as a public defender, county prosecutor Susan Hudson, who had tried other cases in front of him, considered Johnson fair and unbiased.

As the holidays came and went and January 2006 marked a full year that Reed and Clark had languished behind bars on the murder charges, Johnson and the battling attorneys approached the point where there was not much left to do but try the case. Johnson set February 6 as the new start date.

While defense counsel continued to press the judge for separate trials, the prosecutors continued to press the task force investigators for additional material to bolster their case. The state's several dozen exhibits would include photos of a uniformed James Sackett in front of the family Christmas tree and the murdered officer in the county morgue; audio recordings of Trimble's O.B. call and Kothe's cry for assistance; the bullet jacket removed from Sackett's body and the bullet fragments taken from the doorframe at 859 Hague; photos of the crime scene and maps of the immediate area, with measurements from several possible firing sites along the south side of Hague to the front stoop at 859. The state paid federal forensic experts a reported twenty thousand dollars to construct a scale-model mockup of the Hague and Victoria intersection that would presumably enhance the jurors' understanding of the crime scene. (The mockup was an expensive clinker, according to several participants: overpriced, incomplete, and inaccurate—adding a steeple, for instance, to the steeple-less Shiloh Baptist Church on the corner.)

At the same time, Dunaski's crew was keeping close watch over the jumpy witnesses—"babysitting them," as he described the frequent contacts and surveillance—lest anyone be scared off before he or she could testify. There were also health issues to be concerned about. The *Pioneer Press* had reported during the summer that Connie Trimble was dying of cancer, which did not now seem to be true, but she was too important a part of the prosecution's case for her guardians not to fret about her. In addition, several of the retired cops—who would be called on to provide the jury with law enforcement's perspective on the events of 1970—were in their seventies or older and couldn't be expected to stand by forever.

Trimble's situation involved more than her physical health. She was known to be in contact with members of Reed's family, if not directly with Reed himself. Late in 2005, citing family emergencies in Colorado, she turned down a request from prosecutors to come to St. Paul to be deposed prior to trial. And, perhaps worried that the prosecutor would renege on his promise of immunity, she hired her own attorney. Then, in early January, Reed's lawyers told the court that they may call on her to back up *his* alibi. Publicly, the prosecutors expressed confidence in their witness, but privately they worried.

On January 27, with another district court judge, Kathleen Gearin, presiding, a Ramsey County jury ruled Harry Evans guilty of murdering Gerald Vick the previous May. In that case, Evans's companion, Antonio Kelly, had provided critical testimony for the prosecution. Insisting on his innocence, Evans was nonetheless sentenced to life in prison without the possibility of parole; Kelly, who wasn't charged, walked free. The case, of course, raised at least two obvious questions among those watching the Sackett drama lurch toward trial: why was it taking so long to get there, and had the state applied pressure to one or the other of the Sackett defendants with the objective of achieving a similar outcome? The first question could only be rhetorical, absent a concise and satisfying answer. As for the second, the answer was a qualified yes. The task force had talked about making a deal with Clark, by which he would testify against Reed, believed to be the case's alpha conspirator, in exchange for a prison term significantly lighter than life without parole—but Clark, true to form, refused to listen to such a proposition.

Evans would appeal his conviction, but Sergeant Vick's ineffably sad case—all the sadder for its senselessness—was essentially closed. Only one cop-killing remained to be adjudicated in St. Paul.

* * *

February 2006 began with the two sides arguing, still in pretrial hearings, about, among other issues, the enigmatic, multifaceted role played by Kelly Day. Reed's old neighborhood playmate had been dead for more than three years, yet his shadow continued to drift across the proceedings. Was he, defense counsel wondered aloud, the actual shooter? Without offering any evidence supporting the notion, Tom Handley suggested that Day "may well" have pulled the trigger. The prosecutors, conceding between themselves that there was always that possibility, were willing to rely on Trimble's testimony on the subject. She was on the record saying, after all, that Reed had told her to make the phone call and that Clark was the only other person she saw at Clark's house. Her comment to detectives that she initially thought Day might have done the deed was deemed either a red herring or a frivolous notion and not taken seriously. Judge Johnson ruled that the defense could ask witnesses if Day had been a police informant; beyond that, he said, "we'll have to wait and see."

On another matter, Johnson ruled that the Black Panther Party could be mentioned by name during the trial, though he would not allow extended discussion of the group and its nationwide activities. The defense had argued against the very name's admissibility, insisting the term was both irrelevant (because the Panthers were not active in St. Paul at the time of the murder) and inflammatory (because jurors would likely be aware of the group's violent image). The prosecution argued that the defendants' desire to impress the Panthers' national leadership was at least part of their motivation to kill a police officer. Though often walking a fine line, the judge seemed determined to make sure that whatever else might come up, *State of Minnesota v. Reed and Clark* would focus on the murder of James Sackett, not on its parlous times and peripheral players.

Then on Friday afternoon, February 3, with the start of the long-awaited trial scheduled for the following Monday, Johnson ordered that the two defendants be tried separately. The court had ruled against severance the previous summer, but Clark's lawyers had re-opened the issue on Wednesday. The two sides discussed the matter, and the prosecution agreed to sever, with the proviso that Reed be tried first. The judge said Reed's trial would begin on the following Monday, Clark's on April 10.

Later, Paulsen said that agreeing to sever was one of the prosecution's most difficult decisions. A single, joint trial, he explained, is usually easier on both the victims and the witnesses. Conversely, it's usually more difficult for one defendant to shift the blame when the other defendant is seated a few feet away in the courtroom. The rules had been changed during the 1980s to allow joint trials in Minnesota, and Johnson had until that point okayed a joined proceeding. "But thinking about it," Paulsen continued, "we realized that using a 1980s law for a 1970 crime could be construed as ex post facto or retroactive application of the law, and we didn't want to risk a reversal on appeal. So we took the conservative approach and agreed to try the case as we would have tried it in 1970—in separate trials."

Trying Reed first was the key to the decision. "I'll be the first to say our case was stronger against Reed than it was against Clark," Paulsen said. "The downside to that was that Trimble would be the star witness, and she was probably going to shade things in Reed's favor. Still, that was pretty much the way we were thinking: *Let's get the main guy first.* And Reed was always, in our view, the main guy."

2

ourtroom 840, on the eighth floor of the Ramsey County
Courthouse in downtown St. Paul, was not Judge Johnson's
first choice for the trial of Ronald Reed. Despite the fact that
840 had been part of an extensive 1990s renovation of the twenty-
one-story, seventy-four-year-old Zigzag Moderne masterpiece, one
of the city's architectural glories, the judge preferred to do business
in the more familiar and convenient confines of his own courtroom
four floors above, where the Sackett case's pretrial hearings had
been held.

But Reed's trial was, by all indications, going to draw a large
crowd, and 840, with a gallery capacity of about two hundred, was
the largest of the building's twenty-five courtrooms. Court officials,
moreover, believed they could provide more effective security in 840
than they could upstairs, and there was reason to believe security
would be a concern. Johnson would not reveal whether the county
had received specific threats, but he quietly authorized certain pre-
cautions, such as special parking spaces for the attorneys for the duration of the proceedings. The visible police presence was increased
throughout the building, reflecting what several visitors and courthouse regulars described as a pervasive tension.

The courtroom itself—paneled in Cuban mahogany over a red
Italian marble base, with its rosewood bench, jury box, and gallery

seating, and original Art Deco light fixtures, bronze railings, wall clock, and window grates—had been the site of earlier trials of major community interest. Scarcely a week before the Reed trial began, Evans was found guilty of Vick's murder there. But Reed's trial (and Clark's to follow) would revolve around a homicide case unlike any other in the city's history. It would revisit a brutal moment in the distant past and stir up agonizing memories. While attempting to determine whether one man (and then a second) was responsible for murdering another man in cold blood, it would call up a dire and complicated context that was both ancient history and all too current. It would rely on aging men and women recounting events and conversations from their youth. Individually and in the aggregate, it would pit black against white or, more precisely, black against *blue,* which then as now was mostly white—and which then as now was America's most combustible, destructive dynamic. A large number in the gallery would believe that justice in the nearly thirty-six-year-old assassination of Patrolman Sackett was long overdue. Another large number would believe that justice in a "white court" such as this was impossible for an African American.

And sure enough, when the standing-room-only crowd filed into Courtroom 840 on the morning of February 6, 2006, they split the difference—the family, friends, and supporters of James Sackett, mostly white, gathered on the right side of the gallery's center aisle facing the bench, while the family, friends, and supporters of Ronald Reed, almost all of them black, took seats on the left. Other interested parties—the task force detectives, retired law enforcement officers, courthouse staffers, Central High alumni and other citizens who remembered the Sackett murder "like it was yesterday," and no small number of plainclothes sheriff's deputies—filled the rest of the large gallery. (Uniformed deputies were stationed around the courtroom as well.) There was no obvious hostility between the two sides. There was no interaction at all, which some observers thought was depressing in its own right.

Like regulars in church, the Reeds and the Sacketts sat in the same place on the pew-like benches for every session. The defendant's mother, Lillian Reed, as proper and impeccably attired as though she were in fact at Sunday worship, sat with son Duane and other relatives. Across the aisle sat Jeanette Sackett, still girlish and likewise carefully dressed for the occasion, bearing an expression that seemed at once sad, defiant, and proud. Sitting beside her was her husband, Simon Monteon, and at least two of her four children: forty-two-year-old Jim Jr., taking time off from his job as a registered nurse, and Julie, now thirty-eight, a college computer technician who took meticulous notes during the proceedings. (Son Jerel came when he could. Daughter Jennifer chose not to attend.) The families were advised to avoid contact with the "other side" and were ushered in and out slightly ahead of or behind the other. During breaks, the two groups would gather at opposite ends of the ornate hallway outside Courtroom 840 or in separate rooms provided by the court.

Jim Sackett Jr. didn't think he and his family would ever be sitting there. "Each year that passed I thought the chance of going to trial was less and less," he said afterward. "People seemed to be less interested. People were getting old and memories were fading. We waited and waited. Mom was skeptical at the beginning of the most recent investigation. I was, too. Another false start, we thought. But then came the grand jury and the arrests, and then, finally, we were in court."

One of the curiosities of the Ramsey County courtrooms is the fact that the prosecutors and defense counsel sit on opposite sides of the same table, facing each other across four feet of polished walnut. The prosecutors sit on the right side of the table, with the judge and the witness stand to their right, the gallery to their left, and the jury seated in two rows of commodious swivel chairs a few feet behind them. The defendant and his counsel sit on the left side of the table; the judge and the witness stand are on their left, the gallery on the right, and the jurors face them behind the prosecutors. During the examination of witnesses, unless the judge grants them permission to approach the bench or the witness stand, the lawyers must stay close to the table. Counsel usually remain seated in their own comfortable swivel chairs while questioning the witnesses, lending the proceedings a certain relaxed appearance even when the proceedings are decidedly not.

Reed's lead attorney, John Pecchia, was familiar with the drill. He was a methodical, low-key public defender with almost thirty years of legal experience. The second chair was occupied by Marcus Almon, a young African American who had clerked for Kathleen

Gearin. He also had been appointed by the court to this case and was definitely working in the brightest light of his three-year career. Because of the differences in experience, Pecchia (pronounced PEE-cha) would perform the lion's share of the courtroom duties during the trial ahead.

On the other side of the table, Jeff Paulsen and Susan Hudson each brought more than twenty years of courtroom history to the trial. This was the first case, however, that they had worked together and for Paulsen a rare instance in which he shared a prosecution with anyone. Because this was a state case and because Paulsen, a federal prosecutor headquartered in Minneapolis, was on temporary duty with Ramsey County, Hudson could have claimed home-field advantage. But, in actual practice, she would say later, "we were co-equals."

Despite obvious differences in temperament, style, and courtroom strengths—this was yet another odd pairing in a narrative full of them—they seemed to have little difficulty dividing responsibilities. "It was not a matter of first and second chair," Paulsen said. Hudson would handle the jury selection and what Paulsen called the "*CSI*-type testimony"—the medical examiner, ballistics experts, et cetera. He would examine most of the neighborhood acquaintances, police officers, and other non-technical witnesses. The wisecracking Hudson referred to her colleague as a "control freak who always had to get in the last word" but said their disputes tended to be "tactical, not strategic, differences." Both believed there was much at stake. Both felt the additional pressure of prosecuting an accused cop-killer in a case that had the city's rapt attention. Both believed this might be the most challenging case of their careers.

It remained to be seen, though, who among the officers of the court would face the greatest challenge from Ronald Reed. Before Johnson had a chance to bring in prospective jurors for the voir dire on Monday, Reed's lawyers asked the judge to recuse himself. In the defense motion Almon said, "The judge is biased against the defendant." Reed's counsel also moved once more to dismiss the murder and conspiracy charges against him. (A separate motion, filed in U.S. District Court, sought federal intervention to stop the trial, arguing, among other points, that several of the state's witnesses had been bribed to lie to the grand jury. The motion was denied.) Johnson refused to disqualify himself and began the jury-selection process, which was expected to consume the better part of the opening week.

On Tuesday Reed decided he was not interested in going any further under the current arrangement. He told Johnson he wanted to fire Pecchia and Almon, declaring them incompetent. Then, after several interruptions of the voir dire, he told the judge he no longer wanted to be part of the courtroom proceedings. Johnson replied that the trial would continue whether Reed was in the courtroom or not. He said that Pecchia and Almon were adequately prepared and competent and that, at any rate, the defendant did not have an "unbridled right" to choose his public defenders.

Reed's motion, which his brother Duane (who was not a lawyer but was in almost daily contact) had written at his request, was sealed by the judge after Reed attempted to read it out loud. The motion stated that Pecchia had met with him six times at the most* during the previous several months and had "not partnered with me in preparing my defense." As a result, "I am in the dark as to the strategy to be used in my case." Despite offers of family and friends to make "resources and individuals within the community available to John," the lawyer had "not pursued such opportunities." Almon, Reed continued, was cocounsel "in name only," and "Marcus can not adequately advise me or assist me in preparing my defense because there is no substantive communication" between the two attorneys. By contrast, Reed praised Larry Clark's lawyers, whom he had observed during the lengthy pretrial run-up, for their "attentiveness to detail and perseverance." "Counsel for Mr. Clark," he said, "is clearly prepared to take on the prosecution in proceeding to trial."

Meanwhile, there were certainly several persons on the premises who flashed back to Judge Julius Hoffman's federal courtroom during the chaotic Chicago conspiracy trial of late 1969 and early 1970, when a profanely contemptuous Bobby Seale, the only African American among the antic caucus of "anarchists" accused of riot and other crimes during the 1968 Democratic Convention, was handcuffed and gagged on Hoffman's orders. Reed himself would have known about the episode; perhaps Seale was his inspiration. Ronnie Reed, however, was not Bobby Seale, and Judge Johnson, who remembered the Chicago debacle and prayed he wouldn't have to

---

*Paulsen later noted for the record that, according to the county jail visitors log, Pecchia and defense team investigator Pat Robinson had seen Reed on twenty-two occasions and that Almon had visited ten times.

deal with a similar situation, maintained a cooler head than Judge Hoffman. At Johnson's direction, Reed was peaceably escorted to a small, secured anteroom, where, thanks to quick work by courthouse technicians, he could monitor the ongoing jury selection via closed-circuit TV. The next day he was back at the counsel table, seated between Pecchia and Almon. Pecchia promptly told the judge that the media's coverage of Reed's first two days in court had made a fair trial in Ramsey County impossible and asked for a change of venue, which Johnson just as promptly denied. Resigned or merely catching his breath, the defendant sat quietly while jury selection went on.

Sympathetic observers said Reed had been acting out his frustration with the system. Cynics believed he was continuing a year-long strategy of distraction and delay, hoping key prosecution witnesses would disappear or die before having the opportunity to testify. Some suggested that Reed had tried to provoke Johnson into an ill-considered response such as Hoffman's, with an eye toward a later appeal. Reed, for his part, said he was asking for new counsel only to make sure he received a fair trial.

The Sacketts, seated up front and to the right of the center aisle, had a roughly three-quarters view of the defendant's face during the proceedings. Jeanette Sackett said later, "We could see him, and he could see us." The trial was the first time family members had seen Reed in person. As children, hearing only the name and making the mental connection with the murder of their father, they had imagined a monster. As adults, they pictured a young terrorist with a rifle. Now, in the crowded courtroom, they saw, in Jim Jr.'s words, "just a little old man with salt-and-pepper hair." There wasn't much eye contact between them, Jim would recall, but "he knew we were there."

Because it was a first-degree murder trial, more than the usual number of citizens were polled for the jury. The prosecution, as usual, was looking for "law-and-order types," said Hudson afterward. "Obviously, we didn't want jurors who'd had unpleasant contacts with the police. We wanted people who remembered the era. Not necessarily the crime, but the era." The defense was seeking people of color and a certain age, though the pools of prospective jurors are drawn randomly from county voter-registration rolls, and, as it happened, there weren't many African Americans in their fifties and sixties in the pool. What there were, curiously, were several convicted felons whose civil rights had been restored and were thus eligible for jury duty. "Jeff was appalled," Hudson recalled. "He said, 'We don't have convicted felons in federal jury cases.' I said, 'Welcome to the real world!'"

It took the two sides six days to select the all-white, seven-man, five-woman jury, plus three alternates (one of them an African American woman), but that included the time required to deal with Reed's interruptions. All things considered, six days didn't seem very long.

At nine-thirty-five on Tuesday morning, February 21, Jeff Paulsen rose from the counsel table and began the prosecution's opening statement. Using the oversized mockup of the neighborhood as a visual aid, he walked the jury through the familiar landscape and events—familiar to most of the spectators in the gallery if not to every member of the jury—culminating with the gunshot that killed James Sackett. "He was twenty-seven years old, Officer Sackett was, when he was murdered," Paulsen said. "He left behind a wife and four young children. The youngest child was only three weeks old. In fact, this was Officer Sackett's first night back on the job after the birth of his child."

Then Paulsen articulated the core of the state's case.

"One of the men who planned and carried out this cold-blooded assassination thirty-six years ago is in the courtroom today. And it is the defendant, Ronald Reed. You see, it was his girlfriend at the time, Constance Trimble, who made the call to the police about a woman in labor. He, Mr. Reed, tricked her into doing it. He didn't tell her it was a setup for an ambush to kill a policeman. He just told her to make the call. Mr. Reed was with her at this phone booth a block and a half away when she made the call. He told her what to say. He knew what was going to happen because Mr. Reed planned the entire event and he helped carry it out."

The specific charges against Reed and Larry Clark, Paulsen pointed out, were aiding and abetting and conspiracy to commit murder. The conspiracy charge alleged that Reed directed Trimble to make the phone call that drew the victim into the ambush. He said the evidence would show that Reed was the shooter, Sackett's literal killer—but, whether he was or not, he was guilty of aiding and abetting the murder as well as of conspiracy. "People who help carry out a crime are just as criminally liable as those who commit the crime."

As for motive, Paulsen continued, the evidence would show that Sackett was "killed not for who he was, but for *what* he was. He was a police officer, and Ronald Reed hated police officers. And he wanted to make a statement by killing a police officer." Paulsen described Reed as a "member of an organization" that was "basically . . . affiliated with the Black Panther Party." While there was no Panther chapter in St. Paul at the time, he said Reed could be described as a Panther "organizer."

At that point, John Pecchia raised the first of what would be several objections. Paulsen accordingly refined his description: "These were people who were interested in the Black Panther philosophy, interested in that movement, and were seeking to get a Black Panther type of organization established here in Minnesota."

Paulsen continued to lay out the state's case, implanting in the jury's consciousness the names Eddie Garrett, Connie Trimble, and John Griffin. He conceded that "some of these witnesses you are not going to like" and that the state had provided about $3,700 in "financial assistance" to help Trimble through tough times during the past year and had agreed to help Griffin seek a reduction in his federal prison sentence. Though a hundred-thousand-dollar reward had been offered for information in the case, he added, no one had received, nor had anyone been promised, "a penny of any reward." "The key witnesses in this case all gave their statements before they even knew about the existence of any reward," he said.

Pecchia, rising to counter with the defense's opening, quickly set about questioning the motivation and credibility of the state's witnesses:

"John Griffin is looking for a ticket out [of prison]. John Griffin wants to get back on the street. . . .

"Eddie Garrett . . . is a military veteran, trained in firearms, and a shooter. . . . [O]n May 22, 1970, within an hour or so after Officer Sackett was murdered, Eddie Garrett was in the back seat of a police car. . . .

"Constance Trimble . . . has told more than one different story. . . ." He would later tell the jurors that Trimble had problems with drugs and alcohol.

The state's witnesses, Pecchia said, had received or been promised "inducements" for their testimony, either money or the "chance to get out of jail." It was those inducements, he said, that brought the state's witnesses forward at this time. "Where were they in 1972? Where were they—pick any year along the way? Where were these witnesses who knew what this was about? Why didn't they come forward? Why only now?"

Pecchia also raised questions about the state's competence and credibility. Where was the transcript from Trimble's trial? Where were the guns and the alleged hijack notes—the prosecution had only photocopies of the original documents on its list of exhibits— seized during Reed's November 1970 arrest? "Gone. And whose possession [were they] in? The state's." The state, Pecchia concluded, would not be able to meet the burden of proof in this case.

The prosecution's first five witnesses were Jeanette Sackett Monteon, Glen Kothe, Jerry Dexter, Harold Alfultis, and Joe Corcoran. Each answered counsel's questions as anyone familiar with the case would have expected: Sackett Monteon with a somber recitation of her husband's brief police career, their truncated family life, and the events of May 21 and 22, 1970; Kothe describing the call from dispatch sending Squad 327 to 859 Hague, their arrival at that address, the barking dog, the flash and explosion, and his partner's body on the sidewalk in front of the house—Kothe's testimony augmented by scratchy recordings of both the dispatch and his distress call moments later; Dexter, Alfultis, and Corcoran about their respective experiences at the crime scene after the shooting.

Alfultis, in charge of the department's crime lab at the time, said a preliminary examination of the site and recovered slug fragments suggested the shot came from somewhere south of Hague and west of Victoria and was probably fired from a bolt-action rifle. With the exception of a dusty black cap, a shoe-print cast, and the phone booth at the corner of Selby and Victoria (its telephone and bat-wing door were removed after the shooting and taken to the crime lab), there was nothing else by way of evidence retrieved at or near the scene. The cap, shoe print, and phone-booth surfaces all proved to be worthless. There were no usable fingerprints, nor was there yet the DNA technology that might have been employed if there had been meaningful evidence left behind.

Alfultis's frustration was still apparent when asked about the evidence search in the moments following the shooting.*

Q: What, if anything, did you find?

A: Nothing. Nothing of evidentiary value.

Corcoran had assisted Alfultis on May 22. Almost thirty-five years later, long retired to the north woods but back in St. Paul for Reed's trial, he had driven from his downtown hotel to 859 Hague the night before he was scheduled to testify. His experience as a sex-crimes cop investigating pedophiles and their protectors had long ago put him off the Catholic Church, but he still believed in the power of prayer. That night, in front of the house where Sackett had been murdered, he sat alone in his car and beseeched God for justice. Then, addressing the dead officer, he whispered, "Jim, I'm sorry we couldn't solve this case sooner. But we're going to get them now."

The next day Corcoran's testimony left a vivid image hanging in the hushed courtroom air.

Q: What do you remember about the weather while you were at the crime scene?

A: Well, we spent quite a bit of time there and then just as we were getting ready to leave the skies opened up and it began to rain real heavy. And I never forgot that night because I could watch Officer Sackett's blood run down the sidewalk into the street.

Before they were finished four days later, the prosecutors called a total of twenty-three witnesses, including the Ramsey County medical examiner, a ballistics expert, and another ten law enforcement officers past and present. Thomas Owens re-created his and Tony Bennett's false medical-assistance call to another, nearby Hague Avenue address on May 20, 1970. James Jerylo described his and Laverne Lee's May 15 encounter with Eddie Garrett and Garrett's admonition to "watch the rooftops." Minneapolis officer Dennis Bernstrom and retired Minneapolis cops Douglas Danielson, John Locke, Phillip Bishman, and William Chaplin recounted Reed's November 1970 arrest. Retired Ramsey County jailer Gregory LaRock said he overheard Reed tell Gerald Starling after Reed's 1970 arrest that he had instructed Trimble "to not say anything to the pigs" if she were picked

---

*Unlike Trimble's 1972 trial, the trials of Reed and Clark were documented in complete transcripts, which are quoted here and on the following pages.

up. Former St. Paul investigator Russ Bovee also told of overhearing Reed's conversations when he was in the county lockup, mainly to the effect that Reed was confident that, in Bovee's words, "his people would not talk to the police about anything." Scott Duff talked about sniper rifles and a rifle's "killing range" ("you can actually kill out to a thousand yards"), driving times between the Capitol and the crime scene, and other forensic matters. Jane Mead described the detectives' Memorial Day weekend visit to Trimble's apartment in Colorado.

But five individuals from the old days on the Hill would provide the heavy artillery of the state's attack.

Donald Walker, who described himself as a fifty-five-year-old artist currently working as an employment counselor, talked about participating in Black Panther meetings ("That's what we called them") with Reed, Clark, Trimble, and others. The meetings, usually led by Reed and Clark, were the site of "hate talk about the government, the police, and the white establishment."

Walker could not, at Paulsen's invitation, recollect anything specifically hateful that was said at the meetings, nor could he recall when exactly during the summer of 1969 Reed and Clark placed a "wrapped-up" single-shot, bolt-action rifle in the trunk of his white Chevrolet and he drove them and the rifle to a house "mid-block just west of 859 Hague" (Paulsen's words). He did say he transported the rifle on a second occasion after a meeting, this time with only Clark in the car. At some point, he said, Clark "felt I was going to get stopped by the police. So he got out of the car and took the rifle," his destination unknown.

When Paulsen asked if his testimony had been motivated by news of a reward in the paper, Walker said no.

Q: Why did you come forward?

A: A lot of reasons. It was the right thing to do. The community was now looking for the people responsible for [Sackett's] murder and it just—it is human nature. A human being got killed and if you know something about it, you should come forward.

Paulsen then led Joseph Edward Garrett through the familiar terrain: the organization headed by Reed, which met at the ICYL and nearby Dayton Presbyterian Church, also the location of its Panther-inspired breakfast program for kids, his own role as "information minister," and Reed's relationship with Connie Trimble. As for the group, Garrett said, "we mostly talked about protecting and providing for the community. . . . We would talk about patrolling, keeping an eye out, and protecting ourselves, our children, and our property.

Q: From whom?

A: From the oppressor, from the police, from whoever would bring us harm.

Q: Were the police considered the allies of your community, or the enemy?

A: The enemy.

Q: And there was talk at these meetings about, you said, protecting the black community from the police?

A: From the oppressor and whatever means—*by* whatever means necessary. . . .

Q: He [Reed] said, "By whatever means necessary"?

A: Correct.

Q: Would that include violence against police?

A: Yes.

After discussing the glut of guns in the neighborhood at the time, Paulsen and Garrett returned to the talk of violence.

Q: At the meetings . . . was there ever a specific plan articulated by anyone to kill a particular policeman?

A: In the meetings there was never a mention of a specific plan. It was just generally stated that we should protect ourselves, we should protect our community.

Q: Did there ever come a time when you had a conversation with Mr. Reed about a specific plan?

A: Yes.

Q: When was that?

Garrett said the conversation took place a "few weeks" prior to Sackett's murder. Reed had approached Garrett, who was "chilling, so to speak" in his blue Cadillac parked in front of the Celebrity nightclub on Selby Avenue. Garrett said Reed climbed in and, after some general discussion, asked, "Do you want to be involved in getting our first pig?"

Q: What did he mean by that?

A: He meant did I want to be involved in killing a police officer.

Garrett said Reed's statement, while it didn't surprise him given the group's rhetoric, left him shaken. He said that while he bore similar feelings toward the police, after his tour of duty in Vietnam—"experiencing human death firsthand"—a cop-killing "wasn't something I wanted to be involved in." He said he never discussed the matter with Reed again and "avoided contact" with his friend. He also said that by his "watch the rooftops" comment to Jerylo and Lee a few days after his conversation with Reed, he "may have subconsciously been warning them."

Q: Warning them about what?

A: About . . . if you are going to start using your sticks, Mace, and guns if necessary, to watch yourself.

A week later, at the scene of the Sackett shooting, Garrett said, Reed and Day saw him sitting in the back seat of Jerylo's squad car.

Q: Did that affect your willingness to tell the police what you knew about the offense?

A: No doubt.

Q: And you were afraid you were going to be killed?

A: Well, yes, to answer your question. I was afraid for my life, yeah. . . .

Q: So you kept your mouth shut that night.

A: I did.

In his cross, Pecchia asked Garrett about his familiarity with rifles and brought up an episode that Garrett had mentioned to task force detectives early in their discussions. Garrett and another man were "patrolling" the neighborhood with rifles one night, and when they spotted a uniformed security guard sitting in his car outside Marshall Junior High School, they briefly debated whether they should shoot the man. They decided against it and left the guard apparently unaware that he had nearly been in somebody's gunsight.

Garrett's imposing presence and mellifluous voice made his testimony compelling even beyond the riveting content. At fifty-seven, he seemed to be at peace with himself and his past and at least outwardly unruffled by defense counsel's insinuations that *he* might have been Sackett's killer. On his way out of the courtroom following his testimony, someone on the Reed side of the aisle said something to him sotto voce. He stopped, leaned down, and, according to spectators sitting nearby, asked, "You got something to say to me?" The other man apparently did not, because Garrett said, "I didn't think so," and walked on.

* * *

At two o'clock on the same day, February 22, Connie Trimble took the stand. Some observers referred to her as the state's star witness, though the state's lawyers applied the term ironically. The truth is, despite the investigators' trips to Colorado, the multiple heart-to-heart conversations dating back to the Nelson-Bohlig initiative more than a decade earlier, her grand jury testimony in the summer of 2004, and the task force's "babysitting" of the woman since then—the prosecutors didn't know for certain what she was going to say in court.

On the night before her scheduled testimony in *State v. Reed*, the prosecution knew only one thing for sure: she went bowling with the Reeds.

Dunaski's crew was aware that she had been talking to Reed over the previous several weeks. Prisoners' phone calls are monitored and recorded (the prisoners know they are being eavesdropped; there are signs on the jail walls), and the task force had listened to the former Central High sweethearts chat about the forthcoming trial. They were careful what they said, but it seemed clear to the cops listening in that Trimble was doing her best to assure Reed that she wasn't going to hurt him in court. She had been close to the Reed family for a long time. Lillian Reed had taken care of Cherra while Connie had been in jail awaiting trial. More recently, Connie reportedly spoke on the phone to Lillian as often as once a week. So it could not be surprising that she would connect with family members when she returned to the Twin Cities. There was nothing illegal about a reunion. Trimble was a witness, not the defendant. She could come and go as she pleased, so long as she showed up in court as directed. So, for the two evenings prior to her scheduled testimony, her minders—members of the police department's Special Investigations Unit—dutifully followed her out of her downtown hotel to dinner and bowling with the Reeds, then back to the hotel, her temporary home in St. Paul.

The state, of course, had her grand jury testimony to compare and contrast. If the testimonies diverged, Reed's jury would decide which version to believe.

Trimble Smith (as she was called for the court record) did not exhibit the confident glow that she had worn for her grand jury appearance a year and a half earlier. She looked sick and weary and worn down. On the stand, she described herself, when Paulsen asked if she was currently employed, as "disabled." At the prosecutor's invitation, she then spoke for several minutes about her medical history, which was woeful and extensive, the result of on-the-job accidents and illnesses exacerbated by alcohol and cocaine. She said her marriage had been "pretty difficult" and she had spent time in a shelter for battered women.

Paulsen directed Trimble Smith back to 1969 and 1970, when she lived with Reed and hung out at the Inner City Youth League. She readily admitted making the phone call to police on the night of May 22 and repeated her account of setting up Starling. She eventually conceded that Reed had asked her to make the call and sat in the car with their baby while she called from the phone booth.

Paulsen played the recording of her call. The jury listened attentively to the young woman's unexcited request for help and Officer Kinderman's businesslike response.

—*Yes. I was wondering if you could send a squad car down to 859 Hague.*

—*What's the trouble?*

—*Uh, my sister's getting ready to have a baby, and we have no transportation.*

—*Okay, just a moment. Eight-six-nine?*

—*Eight-fifty-nine.*

—*Eight-five-nine.*

—*Hague. . . .*

The prosecutor then resumed his questions.

Q: Do you remember making that call to the police?

A: Yes, I do.

She insisted, though, that she believed what Reed had told her—that "Gerald would be busted for dealing drugs" when the police arrived at the house.

Trimble Smith next described driving with Reed and the baby from the phone booth to Clark's house at 882 Hague, a little more than a block away.

Q: Larry was at the back door?

A: Yes.

Q: As if he was expecting you?

A: Yes.

She said that she and Reed took the baby inside, where Larry's girlfriend, Diane Hutchinson, was asleep with her kids. They were in the house "not more than five, seven minutes," she said. "I was sitting in the dining area holding the baby and waiting for Ron to say, 'Come on, let's go,' and go home." After which "we left and went home." They returned to their Fuller Avenue apartment in a storm, she said—"it was thundering and lightning and raining real bad." She said she first heard about the shooting of the police officer the next day, while watching the news on TV. She described her confusion and fear and the anonymous note warning her not to go to the police. Even after she was arrested and charged with murder, she said she believed—"not knowing what was going on and who was behind it"—that both she and Reed "were still in danger." She said she believed Reed had not known an officer was going to be killed and had been "set up like me."

At Paulsen's request, Trimble Smith recalled the visits to Colorado of newsman Tom Hauser and the two teams of St. Paul detectives ten years apart. Paulsen then directed her attention to her grand jury testimony in 2004. "And there are a couple of differences from what you are testifying to today, aren't there?" Paulsen said. She agreed that there were, but, considering the passing of thirty-five years, not to mention the "different medications" she'd been taking and even the interference of her subconscious ("I dream a lot"), the difficulty she experienced remembering details was understandable. "It is a long time, and it is very confusing," she said, for once not having to fear contradiction.

Paulsen took her back yet again over the couple's actions beginning at the phone booth and proceeding to the house at 882 Hague.

Q: And do you remember going inside or going up to the door and seeing Larry Clark waiting for you?

A: Yes.

Q: And all of those things are clear in your mind?

A: Somewhat.

Q: And do you remember being at that house for five to seven minutes?

A: Yes.

Q: And is it your testimony today that Mr. Reed and Mr. Clark did not leave the house during those five to seven minutes?

A: No, they did not.

Q: Because this is one of the things that you said differently in the grand jury. Do you remember?

A: Well, no, I don't think I did. I think they got that wrong. Because I have always said they did not leave the house and we were there only a short period of time.

Q: Do you remember saying in the grand jury that when you first went into Mr. Clark's house . . . you had to use the restroom?

A: Yeah. The restroom, it was by the—you know, I don't even remember that. That was just brought to my attention today. I don't even remember that. I really don't. . . .

Paulsen referred to the grand jury transcript that he had shown her before court that morning. She replied that "anybody could have wrote anything in there."

Q: And I showed you the transcript where you said four different times that you used the restroom at Larry Clark's house?

A: Yes, you showed me. But I didn't write the transcript. . . .

Q: In the grand jury, you were asked whether it was possible that Ronnie Reed or Larry Clark left the house during that five to seven minutes. And do you remember what your answer was?

A: I may have been confused about that, because I know today—

Q: Well, do you remember what your answer was?

A: No, I don't.

Q: You said, "Yes, it's possible."

A: Oh, well, I was mixed up on that one, because I know they didn't leave the house because we were not there that long for them to leave the house.

Paulsen was not surprised by the testimony. Trimble Smith would not be the first witness to revise her grand jury narrative when the case reached trial. It was one thing to testify in a grand jury's cloistered, almost conversational setting—quite another in open court, with the entire community watching and listening. There was also, for Trimble Smith, the pressing bonds of kith and kin, which had to be impossible to ignore as she looked out from the witness stand and saw the defendant, family members, and old friends staring back at her.

At that juncture, Paulsen pointed out for the jury's sake Trimble Smith's continuing relationship with the Reeds—which she was quite willing to affirm.

"They are still family to me," she said. Ronald Reed "will always be a part of my life. I had a child by him, an only child."

Q: Do you still care for him?

A: Yes, I do. I care for everybody.

Q: Even though the thing that he asked you to do that night, to make that phone call, led to all these problems for you in your life?

A: Well, I don't really feel that he was responsible. I really don't. I think he was just an innocent agent, like I was on this matter.

After almost an hour of direct examination and a short recess, Pecchia began a brief cross. He walked Trimble Smith back through her testimony about the Dunaski team's visit to Colorado. She had said the detectives had found her lying on the couch—"sick, going through withdrawals"—and had given her a hundred dollars, supposedly to be used for pain medication. Instead, while they were gone for a few hours, she used the money to buy crack cocaine. She'd said she used the crack and consumed part of a bottle of wine before they returned to the apartment.

Q: And so you would say you were pretty much under the influence at the time you were talking to them that first time that they met with you?

A: Yes, I was.

She also mentioned that she had taken morphine for pain prior to testifying before the grand jury.

Q: And did that affect your ability to understand and answer the questions?

A: Pretty much, I guess. Yeah, because I don't remember saying a lot of things that I said. . . .

In his even briefer redirect examination, Paulsen reminded Trimble Smith of a statement she had given an investigator employed by the defense, covering much of the same ground as her grand jury testimony.

Q: And then there was a question that came up about whether Ronald Reed knew that a policeman was going to be killed. And do you remember your answer?

A: No, I do not.

Q: I will read it to you. "I don't know if he knew what was going to happen." Is that a true statement you made when you said that?

A: Yes, I remember that now.

Q: So you don't know whether Ronald Reed knew that a policeman was going to be killed as a result of that phone call?

A: Wait a minute. I'm not understanding you clearly.

Paulsen pressed the point, but the witness insisted she didn't remember saying that, even after Paulsen showed her the line in the transcript of the defense investigator's interview.

"Nothing further," Paulsen said.

Afterward, it was difficult to determine whose side had been better served by Trimble Smith's messy testimony. Her earlier statements, especially those made under oath before the grand jury, were surely more credible than her contradictory trial iterations, and her memory lapses, while plausible given her chemical history and the passage of time, often seemed pathetically transparent. Her most genuine statement may have been the acknowledgment of her continuing relationship with the Reeds.

At least one observer on the prosecution side of the aisle was sympathetic. "I think for the first time Connie felt she was an important part of their family," Jane Mead said later. "That's just my opinion, but I've thought about it a lot—about the way she back-pedaled on the stand. It was maddening. The evidence was there. The truth was there. But that was still her family, and Ronnie Reed still meant a lot to her. She'd probably loved him all that time."

Anthony Foster, in his middle fifties, told the court he had done cabinet-assembly work until he was laid off after being subpoenaed in this case. He, too, recalled the racial tension of the late 1960s and early 1970s and the meetings in the neighborhood that discussed the need to establish a Black Panther chapter in St. Paul. "There weren't a whole lot of black people in St. Paul," he said. "And we did have our share of problems. And they"—Reed, Clark, Kelly Day, and others—"felt that the only way that they could get national recognition was to do something very drastic."

Foster brought up the shooting of Wayne Massie by the police in February 1970. "Wayne was my cousin," Foster testified, and Massie's death, he said, was one of several incidents that Reed and others were referring to when they said, "They are killing us, so we have to kill them." Foster referred to the abundance of guns—"all different types"—that were available to the group as well as target practice in the ICYL basement and at a farm "somewhere up north."

Then Paulsen led Foster through an "encounter" he'd had with Reed a few days after Sackett's murder. Foster said they were at his apartment. He was drinking wine with Reed, Arthur Harper, and Arling Reese; all but Reed were also smoking marijuana. Paulsen asked if Reed was acting unusual that day. Foster said Reed wasn't wearing "his Army fatigues and everything. . . . Usually he did." When Foster mentioned the Sackett shooting, Reed said nothing.

Q: Did that surprise you, that Mr. Reed didn't say anything about the murder?

A: Well, you know, seeing as it was such a big thing, yes. But I just let it go.

Foster also acknowledged that after his name appeared in the paper on a list of possible witnesses, he had been given "about $1,300" by the state to relocate and an additional amount for the first month's rent at the new location.

John Pecchia, on cross-examination, asked Foster if he had taken notes at the time or if he was relying on his memory of "what someone said or may have said thirty-five years ago." Foster acknowledged he was relying on his memory.

Q: And it would be fair to say that sometimes your memory may not be perfect—correct?

A: Yeah.

Pecchia also brought up some of the other characters on the scene at the time, including the ex-Army marksman Eddie Garrett.

Q: And you knew [Garrett] always carried a gun, right?

A: A lot of the time.

Q: And you saw him with rifles?

A: Yes.

On redirect, Paulsen said, "Mr. Pecchia asked you why you didn't go to the police back in 1970 or 1972." Foster replied, "Well, they never came and questioned me. . . . And there was a code of silence. We don't talk. That's just the code. And it is something that is very hard to break. It is hard to break today. Because we don't talk."

Q: Do you feel you might suffer repercussions from being in this courtroom today?

A: I may.

Q: Why did you agree to talk to the police when they sought you out in 2004, 2005?

A: Well, a lot of things have changed. A lot of things have changed in my life. So, you know, they asked me the questions and . . . I could only tell them the truth, what I know of.

The final recollections from the old neighborhood were provided by the federal prisoner John Henry Griffin, currently in the middle of a thirty-year sentence for possession of and conspiracy to sell heroin. Following Paulsen's lead, Griffin explained his extensive criminal history, his hope to have his sentence reduced after testifying for the prosecution in this trial, and the fact that the government had paid him approximately $1,200 for a new pair of glasses, phone calls, and other, "miscellaneous things." "The state hasn't offered to do anything specific other than let [my] sentencing judge know that I did cooperate in this case," he told the court. He said he understood the procedure as explained by the prosecutors and that, even though a motion would be filed with the federal judge who had sentenced him, there were neither promises nor a guarantee of a reduced sentence.

Griffin described his introduction to the Black Panthers while visiting the Bay Area to cut a drug deal in 1969. He said the Panthers were "looking for members and . . . nationalizing" at the time. And while the organization expressed interest in St. Paul ("the place that snows all the time," he said he had to tell the Californians, who seemed unsure of the city's location), he wasn't authorized to set up a local chapter or "make somebody else a Panther." The "little group" led by Ronald Reed in St. Paul followed the Panther philosophy and articulated the Panther program, he said, but they were never, strictly speaking, Black Panthers.

When asked about the group's activities, Griffin mentioned the breakfast program for kids and a "senior citizens program that we were thinking about doing." Unfortunately, he said, the group didn't have the funds to meet the need. "So we did other things for money."

Q: So criminal activity?

A: Criminal activity, yeah.

Griffin described the group's desire to become a Panther chapter and how it was generally agreed that something sensational would be necessary to impress the national leadership. Cops had been attacked in other parts of the country, and Reed seemed interested in that approach, Griffin said.

Q: What was Ronald Reed's attitude toward the police during this time period?

A: Well, we all had a negative attitude toward the police at that particular time. His attitude was like all of ours. You know, we called them "pigs"—[for] police in the ghetto. We felt that they were coming in and, you know—well, they were coming in and beating people up and all of that at the time.

Despite his own animosity toward the police, Griffin said, he believed that killing a cop "would create a lot of problems" for the St. Paul organization. He said he didn't think it would ever happen.

Griffin was in prison following a robbery conviction when Sackett was murdered and didn't return to St. Paul until early 1971, by which time Reed and Clark were awaiting trial for the Omaha bank job. He next saw Reed sometime in the 1980s (he couldn't be more specific), when they sat in a West St. Paul supermarket parking lot and talked about old times. Griffin was following, almost verbatim, his testimony before the grand jury in 2004. Again, the recounting of his conversation with Reed was startling. Connie Trimble didn't know what had gone down, he said, but she still could have caused problems for Reed ("she could have put him there"—at the crime scene), so Reed thanked Griffin for helping prevent Kelly Day from testifying for the state at her trial. During that conversation, Griffin continued, Reed suddenly described the shooting itself, telling him "that when he put a bead on that officer, on that cop . . . he felt powerful, he felt strong. . . . [B]ut when he seen the bullet hitting him . . . he never felt more fucked up in his life."

Paulsen, who of course had heard the story before, was struck by how quiet the courtroom had become. "Griffin was the only witness who came right out and said Reed shot Sackett," the prosecutor said later.

Pecchia tried to counter by pounding on Griffin's desire to reduce his sentence. Griffin responded directly about his wife and his five children, none of whom he saw very often, and his offer to Tom Dunaski two years earlier to provide "information that would solve the Sackett case" (Pecchia's words) in exchange for a shortened term. Counsel also reiterated Griffin's behind-the-scenes role on behalf of the defense (actually, on behalf of Reed) during the Trimble trial and his lifelong "problem" with heroin. But nothing then or the next day, when Pecchia concluded his cross-examination, seemed strong enough to diminish the force of the convict's testimony.

*   *   *

On Friday morning Jeff Paulsen told the court that the state rested. Several individuals who had been included on the prosecution's witness list—long-ago acquaintances of Ronald Reed for the most part, with clouded histories of their own—were no doubt relieved to not have been called. The state's lawyers believed they had made their case, and with additional testimony they risked muddying the already not-exactly-crystalline waters. At any rate, it would be difficult to improve on the revelations of Garrett and Griffin.

More surprising was John Pecchia's announcement, following the weekend recess, that the defense also rested. The defense had not called a single witness.

Counsel's decision followed a certain logic. If Pecchia had called witnesses to testify on Reed's behalf, the state could have challenged the character evidence by introducing other crimes in which Reed had been involved, most notably the Omaha bank robbery attempt, which had been off-limits. Discussing the point out of the jury's earshot, Paulsen said that, if given an opening, the prosecution would bring up the Nebraska crime to show the defendant's willingness to use a gun to harm a police officer (the moonlighting security guard). The prosecutors had in fact spent the weekend preparing cross-examinations of the several potential witnesses listed by the defense. They were as surprised as the rest of the courtroom when, on Monday, the defense announced that it would call no one.

Once again, though, the defendant was determined to speak for himself. Prior to resting, Pecchia had asked him if he wished to take the stand. Reed said he didn't. "Under extreme duress, I am inclined to waive my right to testify in my behalf," he explained to the court.

Judge Johnson, as might be expected, responded quickly to the "extreme duress" assertion. "I want to make it clear that this is a decision that you are making of your own accord," he told Reed.

Reed said, "Yes, sir. . . . Under extreme duress, I am inclined to waive my right to testify in my own behalf."

Pecchia asked to speak, but Reed was on his feet, calling for the judge's attention. After a short, off-the-record conversation at the bench, Johnson gave Reed permission to address the court.

"Your honor," Reed said, "it is my understanding that it is the position of the court that if I were to proceed with my defense . . . and if I attested or any of my witnesses would attest to my good character, that this court would allow the prosecution to then impeach my testimony by introducing into evidence a twenty-five- or thirty-five-year-old conviction. . . . So the court, I feel, is placing an albatross around my neck."

"Okay," said Johnson.

"And that is the only reason that I am inclined to forego my rights to testify in my own behalf and to present a defense," Reed concluded.

The following morning, both sides offered their closing arguments. Susan Hudson played the recording of Trimble's phone call, reprised the subsequent events of May 22, 1970, and reviewed the evidence against Reed. "The state does not have to prove that Reed himself actually fired the shot which killed Officer Sackett, although you could so find because there is evidence from which you can conclude that he did . . . ," she told the jury. "What you do have to find, however, is that this defendant knowingly aided and abetted someone in the shooting of Officer Sackett." The second count of the indictment required the jurors to find the defendant guilty of conspiring with at least one other person to commit murder.

Pecchia attacked the quality of the investigation that followed Sackett's murder, the lack of a precise determination of the fatal bullet's origin, the paucity of tangible evidence, and even the accuracy of the scale-model reproduction of the neighborhood that sat at the foot of the jury box. He again challenged the motivation and credibility of the state's witnesses and the reliability of grand jury testimony without the presence of a judge or the cross-examination of witnesses. He reminded the jurors that Connie Trimble had been acquitted in the same case.

The jury was given Reed's fate at noon on February 28.

At 4 PM the next day they returned their verdict: Ronald Lindsey Reed was guilty of aiding and abetting murder in the first degree and guilty of conspiracy to commit murder in the first degree.

The defendant remained seated and silent, his hands clasped in front of him, while the judge read the verdicts. In the gallery, family members and supporters on both sides of the aisle stirred, cried, and offered each other congratulations or consolation, though the response was generally restrained. Several of the old cops who were there for the finale squeezed each other's hands. St. Paul's mayor, Chris Coleman, who was eight years old when Sackett was murdered, stood next to councilmember Dan Bostrom, who had been Sackett's supervisor. Chief John Harrington, a formidable physical presence in his dark blue uniform, stood alongside the Sacketts.

Before Johnson handed down the sentence, Jeanette Sackett Monteon, her second son, Jerel, and daughter Julie offered brief statements. Jerel, who was the three-week-old infant his father had reluctantly left behind when he went off to work that night, told Reed, "Hopefully, you and your family will now have a chance to experience the loss that I have had for the past thirty-five years." In a letter read by Susan Hudson, Julie enumerated the several personal milestones—her high school graduation, her wedding day, the birth of her children, and others—for which her father had been absent. Jeanette, after briefly describing the family's loss, said, "Today, I feel content. I have waited for this day. And I hope that with Ron Reed being incarcerated, he will know the pain and the suffering that I have gone through and will go through the rest of my life."

A moment later, Reed rose and addressed the court. "Your honor, and to Mrs. Sackett and her family and to the Minnesota community at large," he said, "if my unjust conviction brings consolation and closure to Officer Sackett's legacy and to his beloved family, then I accept the consequences gladly and without malice toward anyone.

"Also, your honor, I beg the court's indulgence if it has perceived that I have disrespected it in any way. That was not my intention."

Johnson, who seemed surprised by the apparent apology if not by the weirdly self-exonerating statement of acceptance, told Reed he hadn't felt disrespected. He then sentenced him to life in prison. Under the rules of 1970, by which the case was tried, that meant Reed would serve at least seventeen and a half years before becoming eligible for parole.

Johnson then offered his customary benediction before Reed was led out of the courtroom. "Good luck to you, sir," he said.

"Thank you," Reed replied.

A juror told the *Pioneer Press* that shortly after beginning their deliberations seven members of the panel had voted for Reed's conviction and five were undecided. The group debated the case the rest of Tuesday afternoon, then took another vote first thing Wednesday morning. That vote was ten for conviction and two undecided. The jury eventually passed word to the judge that they wanted to listen again to the recording of Trimble's phone call. They did, and then cast a unanimous vote: guilty on both counts.

"The remaining two people thought that call from Connie was rehearsed," the juror, who asked to remain anonymous, explained to reporter Bill Gardner. "She rehearsed it. She was aware of what she needed to tell the police."

Still, according to the paper, the decision had been difficult and emotional. Everyone was sad. A few of the jurors cried. They had reached the verdicts by noon on March 1 but wanted some "quiet time to reflect." So the twelve of them shared pizza in the jury room before telling the court what they had decided.

3

Who was Larry Clark?

After more than thirty-five years of on-and-off public conversation, three separate police investigations, three grand jury hearings, dozens of media references, and a high-intensity trial in which his name was frequently invoked, Clark's identity as well as his role in the assassination of Patrolman Sackett remained murky enough for his own counsel to raise the question in a context where it might have been evident: *State of Minnesota v. Larry Larue Clark.*

Moments into his opening statement, public defender Tom Handley answered his own question by telling the jury who Larry Clark *wasn't.* "He is not a yes man," Handley said. "He is not a scapegoat. He is not a hateful person. He is not a follower. He wasn't then, he isn't now." More to the point, Handley added a few moments later, though Clark "knew Ron Reed" and "considered him a friend," Clark was "not his fall guy or understudy . . . or co-conspirator in this case." Jeff Paulsen, opening the state's case, had already linked Clark with Reed in a conspiracy to kill a police officer, telling the jury that "each one in a conspiracy is the alter ego of the other." Clark, Paulsen said, was Reed's "right-hand man, the person he was closest to," and that "anything Ronnie Reed said or wanted, Mr. Clark would back it up by words and actions."

The fact that both sides spent more time talking about Reed than about Clark spoke volumes about both the nearly thirty-six-year-old case and this year's successive trials. In the thousands of pages of reports and transcripts dating back to 1970, when Clark's name was mentioned it was almost always as half of a Reed-Clark tandem, and usually the latter half at that. Even in the recollections of old neighborhood acquaintances, Clark rarely had an extended speaking part but was rather a voice in the anti-"pig" choir. Speaking to a journalist after the trials, former police chief Bill Finney, who knew them all growing up in the neighborhood, recalled the "loud-mouthed radicals" who hung around the Inner City Youth League and Dayton Avenue Presbyterian Church. Reed, he said, was the leader. "Clark—he was just kind of in there with them."

The task force investigators who spent almost four years trying to learn more about Clark could, in the end, add little to the state's profile. "Clark was just Reed's gofer," Tom Dunaski said with a shrug. "What happened that night was the high point, his one claim to fame. After that, he helped rob that bank in Nebraska and went to prison. Then what? He came back, and he'd steal a lawn mower and buy a little crack. We had people who were into him, but he never talked about the Sackett case. He never talked much about anything. He'd mentioned robbing another bank once in a while, but that never happened. He was just a petty thief."

At trial, Clark's lawyers would seek to shorten that bleak biography even further by removing the reference to Sackett. It was not a crime, after all, to be a cipher. Clark may have been Reed's friend, they would argue, but it wasn't Clark who told Trimble to make that phone call; nor had anyone placed Clark at the scene in the hour or so after Sackett's murder. In his antipathy toward the police and the white establishment, he was one of countless young men and women who talked the talk in those days. Unfortunately for his defense, Clark didn't have to be anything more prominent than a mostly silent partner. Aiding and abetting, after all, meant merely *helping* with the commission of the murder, and to be part of a criminal conspiracy you had only to agree to and in some way assist with the plan.

The state did not have to prove that Clark pulled the trigger. It would be enough to prove that he had knowingly and purposely been there—as he had often been there—at Ronnie Reed's side.

*   *   *

Clark's trial had gotten under way in Courtroom 840, the Honorable Judge Gregg Johnson again presiding, on April 10, 2006, five and a half weeks after Reed's conviction in the same elegant venue. The gallery was not as crowded as it had been for Reed's trial, and the often nearly palpable tension of the first trial had been dialed down a few clicks as well.

Once more, members of the Sackett family and their supporters sat on the right side of the aisle facing the bench, while Clark's kin, friends, and partisans sat on the left. The unaligned spectators were present as well, but there were fewer of them at this trial. Seated between his public defenders on the left side of the common counsel table was another grandfather with salt-and-pepper hair and a thickening midsection wearing an inexpensive suit and tie provided for the occasion by the state—though no one expected this defendant to be as vociferous as his predecessor. Indeed, because it was Larry Clark in that chair, no one expected the defendant to say anything at all.

But if anyone anticipated a swift and efficient march to a verdict, he or she had badly miscalculated.

Handley and cocounsel Connie Iversen, a pair of hardworking, experienced defenders, were going to pick up where they left off during the past year's seemingly endless parade of pretrial hearings, beginning, at trial, with a challenge of the jury pool. Counsel pointed out that only one of the sixty-five prospective jurors available for the Clark trial was an African American, which seemed blatantly insufficient considering that an African American was on trial, even in a county where fewer than 6 percent of possible jurors were black. But after hearing testimony from the official in charge of Ramsey County's jury operations, Johnson denied the defense motion to dismiss the pool, citing the randomness of its makeup and pointing out that a jury's fairness and impartiality were more important than its ethnicity. Handley and Iversen had served notice, though, that they were ready to fight. It was a scrappy assertiveness that Reed, grousing about *his* court-appointed counsel, had said he envied but also an in-your-face approach that had rubbed the prosecutors the wrong way from the beginning. "I thought they accused us of operating in bad faith at times," Paulsen said later. "That made the case more acrimonious than it had to be."

What's more, as it became readily apparent during Handley's opening, the defense was going to drag the bad old days of the late 1960s and early 1970s into the trial proceedings, never mind the judge's admonition to hew to matters of the crime itself. In Handley's words, "This case is about the events of May 1970, but it is also about so much more than that. It is about the passage of time. It is about memories that fade or that are replaced by new ones." And before he sat down he had evoked memories of the Vietnam War, the invasion of Cambodia, the Kent State shootings, Martin Luther King's assassination, Richard Nixon, J. Edgar Hoover, and the Black Panthers. (At one point, Hudson objected; at another, Paulsen, arguing irrelevance. In both instances, the objections were sustained.) "Closer to home," Handley continued, the Stem Hall riots, the police shootings of Keith Barnes and Wayne Massie, and the Morrill Hall takeover at the University of Minnesota "mirrored" the problems and protests of the larger world. There may not have been a great deal to say about the defendant, counsel seemed to be suggesting, but there was no end of the points to make about the times.

The prosecution began its case with the historical accounts of Jeanette Sackett Monteon, Glen Kothe, Jerry Dexter, and Harold Alfultis. All but three of the state's twenty-three witnesses had testified against Reed. This time, however, Handley and Iversen gave most of them a rigorous cross, bringing up, for instance, Kothe's grand jury testimony in which he claimed to have seen Connie Trimble in the crowd at the crime scene following the murder and questioning the retired officers about everything from the absence of footprints in the alley behind Clark's house to the investigators' bullet-trajectory calculations. Long-ago neighborhood youths Donald Walker and Anthony Foster were grilled by the defense on various points of their previous trial testimony, counsel not always rehashing especially relevant details but continually raising the issues of past time and the limits of memory.

"Okay," said Iversen, for example, examining Walker, "when you testified under oath in February . . . about transporting the rifle, you laid out a specific route that you took."

Walker acknowledged that he had.

Q: Today, when asked which route you took, you said either Selby or Dayton.

A: Yes.

Q: Which route did you take?

A: I can't remember. I mean I can't get specific. All I know is I went in that direction—west. I could have used Dayton. I could have used Selby. But I went in that direction.

"In February," Iversen continued, "when you testified at Mr. Reed's trial, instead of having them bring the rifle across the street to your car, this time you said you went and got your car and brought it into the parking lot of the church. Is that what you testified to?"

"Yes, but again, you are talking thirty-some years ago," Walker replied. "You get the general idea. I either went across the street or they came across the street. But the general idea is that the car—the gun was placed in my trunk, period."

Q: But you don't remember specifically.

A: I don't remember driving over to the parking lot specifically. I don't.

Trimble Smith took the stand on the state's behalf on the afternoon of April 19. Whatever her questionable star quality, she was in fact the only witness who could place Clark with Reed at the site where the prosecution said the fatal shot was fired. Even so, her helpfulness again extended only so far. Well into her direct examination, Paulsen asked if the events of May 22, 1970, as she described them during Reed's trial, were still clear in her mind. "Yeah, they are clear," she replied.

Q: When you and Mr. Reed went to Larry Clark's house that night after making the phone call and stayed five to seven minutes, do you know whether either Mr. Reed or Mr. Clark left the house during that five to seven minutes?

A: No, they did not.

Q: And you say that based on what?

A: I know it to be a fact. They did not leave that house.

Q: Because you previously testified about that matter in the grand jury. Do you recall that?

A: I recall.

Q: And do you recall saying something different in the grand jury?

A: It is only what I was showed on paper. I don't recall saying that. . . .

Q: And you had told the grand jury that during that five to seven minutes in Larry Clark's house, you needed to use the restroom.

A: I don't remember saying that at all.

Q: You also told them that it was possible that Reed and/or Clark could have left the house.

A: I do not recall saying that, and I don't believe I did say that. I really don't.

Q: But if it is in the transcript, would you agree that you said it?

A: Nope. Because anybody can write anything. . . .

Even on the Reed-Clark relationship Trimble Smith's assistance was dubious. The two men were friends, she replied to Paulsen's query.

Q: How good of friends?

A: Pretty good friends. I was friends with Larry. We both were.

Q: Mr. Reed and Mr. Clark spent a lot of time together?

A: I wouldn't say that. Ron was going to school and working a lot, so I wouldn't say they spent a lot of time together. But then I wasn't with him all the time so I really couldn't say that.

During her cross, Iversen likewise had to deal with Trimble Smith's apparent amnesia. Clark's lawyer nonetheless pressed the issue of the witness's conversations with Hauser, the TV reporter, in 1994 and with detectives Bohlig and Nelson a few weeks later.

Q: They asked you if you had made the call?

A: Yes, they did.

Q: And you admitted that you had?

A: Yes, I did.

Q: And they asked you if Ron Reed was with you. Did you tell them that that was accurate?

A: I don't remember.

Q: But, again, you didn't tell them anything about going to Larry Clark's house, did you?

A: I don't—no. I don't remember. I don't really remember. . . .

Reviewing the May 2004 visit of Dunaski, Mead, and Duff, Iversen asked if she remembered telling them she had initially suspected that Kelly Day shot the officer and that she was going to tell them Day told her to make the call. Trimble Smith said she didn't remember saying that.

Q: Do you remember . . . telling them that it was only a few days prior to their visit that you recalled having seen Larry Clark standing at the back door of the Hague address wearing a raincoat when you and Reed came to the address on the night of the shooting?

A: I don't remember that right now. . . .

Q: When you told them in 2004 that you went to Larry Clark's house after you made the call, that's the first time that you said that you and Ron Reed went to Larry Clark's house on Hague Avenue after making the call. Isn't that correct?

A: I don't remember. . . . I was questioned so many different times. I cannot remember every detail about every questioning. So I really don't remember.

Trimble Smith would not budge from her account of the brief visit ("maybe six or seven minutes") to Clark's house (to get some marijuana) and that she never saw or heard police cars in the neighborhood that night and never heard a gunshot. Iversen did not ask her about using the bathroom while she was at Clark's, or the possibility that one or both of the men stepped outside while they were out of her sight.

Trimble Smith did discuss, responding to Iversen's questions, the cash the task force had given her during the past couple of years. That, of course, went to the defense's larger point that the state's witnesses were not only unreliable, they had been corrupted by bribes. Still, it is not difficult to discern both frustration and perhaps a certain malice in counsel's concluding back-and-forth with Trimble Smith, which began with mention of the government's promise of immunity in this case.

Q: There is an exception to that immunity that's been granted to you. Is that correct?

A: I don't understand what you mean—"exception."

Q: The only exception to being prosecuted is if you commit perjury. Isn't that correct?

A: Yes, I understand that.

Q: What is perjury?

A: It means lying under oath.

Q: Is that the reason why you keep telling us you don't remember what your previous testimony has been?

A: No. I tell you I don't remember because I don't remember.

Iversen had nothing further.

The state would not call John Griffin in Clark's trial because his testimony focused only on Reed. Eddie Garrett, however, took the stand in the second trial on April 21. His testimony, too, followed the earlier narrative, with a few additional details. He said, for instance, that he had provided the police with "disinformation" the night of Sackett's murder when he told Jerylo and Lee about seeing "new faces" in town. He also mentioned, for the first time, Kelly Day's comment after Day spotted him in the squad car at the shooting site. "Kelly Day told me I better keep my fucking mouth closed," Garrett told Paulsen. "Excuse my mouth, but that's exactly what he said." Garrett said he was still concerned for the safety of himself, his children, and his grandchildren.

On cross-examination Handley established Garrett's familiarity with a diverse group of local characters at the time. Handley also elicited from Garrett an admission that he had told investigators "it was possible" (Handley's phrase) that one of several rifles he had stolen from a Veterans of Foreign Wars or American Legion post earlier in 1970 was used to kill Sackett. Under Handley's questioning, Garrett also confirmed he had recanted and then reaffirmed his statement about Reed's invitation to "bring down the first pig."

As with most of the testimony, there was little mention of Larry Clark, whom Garrett said he had last seen (until this trial) at a party in Minneapolis in 2003 or 2004. Garrett said Clark didn't recognize or remember him.

Arthur Harper, who had not testified in Reed's trial, was one of the state's witnesses against Clark. He was fifty-six years old and awaiting sentencing on third-degree burglary charges. In a mumbling voice that the defense repeatedly asked him to raise, Harper described the so-called "revolutionary house" on Dayton Avenue where Kelly Day lived and where he, Reed, Clark, and others were frequent visitors. There was a great deal of talk at the house—with Reed doing most of the talking, Harper said—about the police "oppressors." Reed would say the police "were killing our brothers," Harper recalled.

Q: What did Mr. Reed want to do in response to that?
A: Give them a lesson. Revenge.
Q: Namely?
A: Kill one of them. Teach them a lesson.
Q: Did you hear Mr. Reed say that?
A: From time to time. . . .
Q: And would Mr. Clark be present when Mr. Reed was advocating teaching the police a lesson by killing one?

A: Yes.

Q: What was Mr. Clark's response to that?

A: He would agree.

Harper said Reed and Clark were the "best of friends. . . . They run together. When you seen one, you seen the other one. They were always together."

Harper told the court what he had told Dunaski and his colleagues earlier—that late on the night of May 21, 1970, he and Arling Reese encountered Reed and Clark coming out of the Dayton Avenue duplex. "Ronnie," he said, "was carrying a rifle, headed south, with Mr. Clark coming out the back door." Fifteen to twenty minutes later, he heard a shot and shortly after that "noticed police cars heading south on Victoria." He said a few moments later he, Day, and Reed stood on a corner near the Inner City Youth League building and watched the police activity at Victoria and Hague. He said Reed was not carrying the rifle he had seen earlier. He said Reed "had a smile on his face." He said he did not see either Trimble or Clark.

During Iversen's cross-examination ("Use your outside voice," she told him), Harper conceded that he first talked to task force investigators about the Sackett case after he had been arrested on suspicion of burglary. He said he had not hung out at the ICYL or attended meetings "where the Black Panther Party platform or program was discussed" (Iversen's words). He said he and Reese often stayed on the upper floor of the house on Dayton.

Then Iversen said: "You are aware that this Arling Reese person you are talking about was arrested in April of 1970 for an aggravated robbery in Moorhead, Minnesota?" And wasn't it true, Iversen pressed him, that Reese was AWOL from the Marine Corps at the time and was in custody in Moorhead until he was returned to the Marines in August 1970?

"I'm not sure," Harper responded. "It just seems to me he was with me that night in May."*

A few moments later Iversen asked him about seeing Reed and Clark with the rifle.

Q: You didn't see Mr. Clark with a rifle, did you?

A: No.

---

*Reese later testified that he had been in jail in Moorhead on May 22, 1970.

Under further questioning, Harper denied that a deal had been struck with the state—a reduced sentence for a pair of recent third-degree burglary convictions in exchange for his testimony. "I'm not expecting nothing, period," he said. Harper also admitted, responding to Iversen's question, that he had during just the previous week confessed to, in Iversen's words, a "serious felony offense." He hadn't received any consideration from prosecutors concerning *that* crime either, he said.

What the jury didn't hear was that the "serious felony offense" was, incredibly, murder. While talking to investigators about his upcoming testimony, Harper had confessed, without prompting, to an unsolved 1969 homicide quite possibly forgotten by everyone except the victim's family, a few friends, and Harper himself. According to Iversen, as quoted by the *Pioneer Press,* the victim was a twenty-one-year-old Macalester College dropout named James Berg. Harper told the detectives that Berg was shot while struggling for Harper's gun while Harper and two other men tried to rob him during a drug deal. The *Pioneer Press* quoted Harper telling the astonished investigators, "I don't know why I'm saying this. I guess it's because you guys have been there for me."

"We were talking to Harper about the [Sackett] case," Tom Dunaski said later. "We told him that before he testified he had to tell us about anything else he might be involved in that might jeopardize the case against Clark. So out of the blue he tells us about this other thing." Dunaski laughed. In his long career he had seen and heard a lot, but this was a first even for him. "We went back to Paulsen and said, 'Arthur's in the game [with his Clark testimony]. Also, we solved another murder.'"

Prior to Harper's testimony, Johnson had ruled that the Berg murder was not relevant to the Sackett case and he wouldn't allow the confession heard in its specifics in court.*

Late in the afternoon of Wednesday, April 26, after calling its twenty-third witness, the state rested its case.

---

*After considering the circumstances and surviving evidence in the case, Ramsey County authorities decided not to prosecute Harper for the 1969 homicide. He served slightly less than two years on the burglary charges.

Connie Iversen rose and, with the jury out of the courtroom, asked the court to acquit Larry Clark on both counts of murder. "There has been an abundance of evidence presented regarding Mr. Reed," she said. "However, the evidence against Mr. Clark does not show his participation and in any way that he aided or abetted or helped the commission of that offense." As for the conspiracy count, she continued, the evidence showed that Clark was not present during Reed's "bring down the first pig" conversation with Garrett, nor was there evidence showing that Clark had anything to do with Trimble's phone call. "There is nothing in the evidence to show that a conspiracy existed between Mr. Reed and Mr. Clark between the dates of May 15 and November 13 of 1970."

Paulsen, responding, said there was "ample motive evidence in the testimony of several witnesses." Furthermore, two witnesses placed Clark "at or near the scene of the crime at the time of the crime," and a witness reported seeing Clark and Reed in possession of a bolt-action rifle moments prior to Sackett's murder.

Johnson said, "The court believes this is an issue for the jury to decide," and he denied the request for a summary acquittal.

The defense began its case by calling Neil Nelson, the former homicide investigator. Nelson, who now commanded a task force investigating Internet crimes against children, would be one of ten street cops and detectives that Clark's lawyers called over the next five days. It was, to say the least, an interesting mix, comprising, among others, Dunaski, Mead, and Duff, retired sergeant Paul Paulos, long-ago homicide detectives Earl Miels and Carolen Bailey, John Labossiere, who was among the first officers to reach the murder site, and James Mann, one of the handful of African American officers in St. Paul thirty-six years earlier. The witness mix became an even more curious mélange when the defense added erstwhile Hague Avenue resident Myrna Patrick, an independent forensic consultant named Matthew Noedel, African American historian Mahmoud El-Kati, former Urban League director Katie McWatt, and three leaders of the much-discussed, long-defunct Inner City Youth League: Robert Hickman, William Wilson, and William Collins.

The defense witnesses conjured up a variegated panorama of Summit-University's underside circa 1970. Now-familiar names were elicited from both the old cops and the former residents, among them Gary Hogan, John Griffin, Kelly Day, and Harold Mordh.

There was testimony about shootings, stolen weapons, dynamite caches, electronic surveillance, and confidential informants. Questioned by Iversen, Paulos, who at eighty-four appeared both able and willing to take back the streets of the meanest neighborhood, described his confrontation with the teenaged robbers coming out of the University Avenue stereo shop in February 1970. The details were all the more chilling for the crisp precision with which Paulos recounted them.

Q: Who was holding the gun?

A: Massie.

Q: And he opened fire on you?

A: Yes.

Q: How many times did he shoot at you?

A: Three times.

Q: Did you return fire?

A: Yes.

Q: With what?

A: A twelve-gauge shotgun with double-aught buck.

Q: Did you strike Wayne Massie?

A: Yes.

Q: Did he die?

A: Yes.

Q: How about Byrd Douglas?

A: I shot him in the legs.

Q: But he didn't die.

A: No.

Bailey recalled in careful detail the voice-print evidence against Connie Trimble, the bizarre but apparently coincidental car-bus incident at Selby and Victoria minutes after Sackett's murder, and her conversation with Ronald Reed a month or so later. Predictably, the matters of evidence—or, more to the point, the unreliability of memory in its absence—and the presence of Larry Clark were at the heart of counsel's questions.

Q: You said Ronald Reed was [at the Iglehart apartment]?

A: Yes. . . .

Q: Why didn't you arrest him?

A: He wasn't necessarily a suspect at the time. We suspected that he was, but we didn't have any very specific information yet. . . .

Q: Why didn't you write a report about that?

A: I did.

Q: Why don't we have it?

A: I don't know. There were a lot of reports that must have gotten lost in the process.

Q: And you indicated you thought Larry Clark was there. Is that right?

A: Yes.

Q: You don't know for sure?

A: I can't remember for sure, but if I recall, he was.

Q: But you are not positive?

A: No.

The former ICYL officials provided a more benign history of the organization than the prosecution had offered. They categorically denied, for example, that weapons were ever stockpiled in their building or that there was a shooting range in the basement. Former director Bobby Hickman, now seventy, remembered Reed, Clark, and other neighborhood youths of the time in a basically favorable light as well. "Ronnie was just an aggressive person," he told Paulsen during his cross. "He was a leader. He was a very intelligent young man, I thought."

Q: And Mr. Clark was more of a follower?

A: Well . . . I would like to say they were comrades or, you know, people who worked with one another. And in their close relationship, I don't know who was the leader and who was the follower. I just know that they were in tune to one another.

Bill Wilson, who later became Minnesota's human rights commissioner and a St. Paul city councilmember, was asked if there was anything about Clark "that would cause him to stand out amongst the crowd."

"Not to my knowledge," Wilson replied.

Q: Did you ever hear him advocate the killing of a police officer?

A: Never.

Mahmoud El-Kati, who until 1969 was known as Milt Williams, had taught at nearby Macalester College for more than thirty years. He often answered questions at considerable length, explaining aspects of African American history, the Black Panther Party (which, to his knowledge, he said, never had a chapter in St. Paul), and local protests circa 1970. Eventually, Handley asked him if he knew Larry Clark. El-Kati said he did.

Q: And was he also an activist?

A: Yes. Very bright, alert, ahead of the curve.

Q: And was he a hateful person?

A: No. Not in any sense that I know of.

Q: Did he advocate violence?

A: No.

Q: Did he advocate violence against the police?

A: No.

Q: Was he his own man?

A: Well, he thought for himself, if that's what you mean.

But El-Kati's tutorials, so far as they pertained to the Black Panthers, gave the prosecution the opportunity to introduce into evidence an issue of the Panther house organ from 1968. "We are offering this newspaper article for two purposes," Paulsen told the court during a heated argument at the bench about the document's admissibility. "One is to impeach [El-Kati's] testimony that the Black Panther Party would never advocate violence against police, that that was antithetical to their views, and, two, as substantive evidence of what the Black Panther Party really was, now that that door has been opened by the defense." Handley argued that the prosecution's references to the Panthers were "inflammatory and unfairly prejudicial" and that there was reason to suspect the newspaper excerpt in question had been doctored by the FBI during the bureau's notorious disinformation campaigns of the late sixties. After a long argument, Johnson overruled defense objections and allowed the state to examine El-Kati in front of the jury regarding the content of the Panther newspaper.

Quoting from an editorial signed by national Panther "minister of education" George Murray, Paulsen read aloud, concluding:

Black men, Black people, colored prisoners of America, revolt everywhere. Arm yourselves. The only culture worth keeping is a revolutionary culture change. Freedom everywhere. Dynamite. Black power. Use the gun. Kill the pig everywhere.

Paulsen then asked El-Kati, "Is it still your testimony that it was not a part of the Black Panther philosophy to use violence against police?"

"Yes," the witness answered, beginning an elaborate explanation that a student of Frantz Fanon or Noam Chomsky might appreciate. "I think that that's rhetoric and revolutionary rhetoric and, philosophically, everything they said could be justified in the same way as the Declaration of Independence. It was by violence they got this country freed. So I think you can't disengage it from the underlying reality. . . ."

Paulsen and El-Kati sparred over the meaning of the Panther rhetoric and later about the Panthers' ten-point party platform. To what extent the jury was following the conversation—or, for that matter, would factor the argument into their deliberations—was uncertain, but at one point the judge interrupted. "Mr. El-Kati," Johnson said, "I have to stop you. This is not a college lecture hall."

On a literally more down-to-earth level, the defense offered the testimony of a state crime laboratory technician named Donald Melander, who had analyzed the sack of debris the task force detectives had swept up in the ICYL building basement. "My results basically were inconclusive," Melander told Iversen. "I didn't find any metal fragments that would be consistent with bullets."

No more conclusive but considerably more intriguing was the testimony, during the afternoon of April 28, of Myrna Patrick, who, in May 1970, lived in a "multiplex" at 871 Hague Avenue. Around midnight on May 21–22, 1970, she said, she was startled by a noise: "A big bang. A loud bang." Looking out a front window, she saw a car "parked kind of at an angle" alongside the church at the corner of Hague and Victoria. She said the car was "medium brown in color" and pointed north on Victoria. Its passenger door was open. A moment later, when she returned to the window, the car was gone. A few days after the shooting, she told an investigator she had seen "someone running from the car," but she couldn't recall that now, thirty-six years later.

Again the problem of time and memory muddled a witness's testimony. On cross-examination, Patrick said the brown vehicle might have been an unmarked squad car and she didn't recall seeing anybody get in or out. The mystery car might also have belonged to "some poor unfortunate person who just happened to be driving by at the time, too—correct?" asked Susan Hudson.

"Could have been," Patrick agreed.

Glen Kothe later testified that he had not seen a car parked next to the church when he and Sackett arrived in front of 859 Hague, nor did he see a car in that spot when he ran back along the side of the house after hearing the gunshot that lit up the intersection.

*   *   *

As the defense plugged on, jurors could have been forgiven if they forgot about the defendant entirely. Larry Clark, the quiet man at the counsel table, was also virtually invisible during much of the testimony that followed El-Kati's glowing reference.

The crime scene reexamination by forensics expert Matthew Noedel neither discredited nor improved on the estimates and suppositions of the police investigators in 1970 and 2005. A man named Joseph Harrington, who worked for the dodgy businessman/civic leader/police informant Harold Mordh, described Mordh's electronic surveillance of the ICYL and its inconclusive results, adding nothing especially relevant to the narrative. (Mordh was convicted of income tax evasion, possession of an illegal weapon and illicit drugs, and financial irregularities involving his nursing homes in the early 1980s. He died following heart surgery in 1989.) If there were ever any tapes or transcripts from Mordh's surveillance activity, they apparently vanished decades ago.

Eighty-three-year-old retired patrolman James Mann described his experience working in the neighborhood in 1970 and drew one of the few laughs of the proceedings when he was asked to identify Clark in the courtroom. Clark, he said, was "the young black fellow sitting between the two white people at the counsel table." (The laughter lasted long enough for the judge to warn the gallery that he would clear the room if there were any more "outbursts.") Mann also reminded the assembly why he had been a lightning rod within the department, unloved, to say the least, by many of his mostly white colleagues. He talked about being shunned, in effect, when he arrived, off duty, at the Sackett murder scene, implying the reason was that he was black. He also told the court he was unaware that the Panthers had advocated killing police officers. "[N]obody ever talked about offing *me*," he said. "Nobody ever called me a pig, in fact." Asked if he had ever heard Clark, whom he knew, "advocate the killing of a police officer," Mann said no.

Even when Tom Dunaski took the stand and reiterated the major steps of the task force's investigation, Clark was mentioned infrequently. When Clark did make an appearance, it was almost always alongside Reed. Indeed, it was Clark's position in what for all intents and purposes was Reed's group that finally led to a curt exchange between Iversen and the grizzled detective.

Q: Did you ask [Eddie Garrett] about what Mr. Clark's role in [Reed's] organization was?

A: We did ask him.

Q: And did he tell you that Larry was close to Ronnie, but he didn't have any more power than any of the others in the organization?

A: That's correct.

Q: He then referred to Mr. Clark as always being a scapegoat for Ronnie Reed. Is that right?

A: That's his word, yes.

Q: You put "scapegoat" in quotes [in your report], correct?

A: That's correct.

Q: And are you aware of what the term "scapegoat" means?

A: It is whatever his definition of it is. . . .

Q: You asked [Garrett] about who had the leadership roles in the organization. Is that right?

A: That's correct.

Q: He did not give a title or a role for Mr. Clark as being a leader in the group, did he?

A: No, he didn't.

All told, the defense called twenty-one witnesses on Clark's behalf. Late in the day on May 2, with the jury out of the room, Iversen called the defendant himself to discuss his right to testify. She described for him the requirements of a witness and reminded him that the Constitution also gave him the right to remain silent.

Clark said, "I choose not to testify."

Moments later, the defense rested.

Despite the conviction of Ronald Reed eight weeks earlier, the prosecutors were not confident about the outcome of *State v. Clark*. Trial veterans that they were, neither Hudson nor Paulsen was inclined to take anything for granted—not even the precedent of a guilty verdict in the first half of the bifurcated case.

The closing arguments of the Clark trial had offered no surprises.

Iversen spent about half of her two-hour summation reprising the turbulent context of the Sackett murder and the second half discrediting the state's witnesses, many of whom, motivated by cash payments (totaling more than fourteen thousand dollars, she said) or reduced sentences, were not telling the truth. She also reiterated the possibility of an alternative conspirator: Kelly Day (who was "mentioned by every single witness in this case," she said with some exaggeration), Eddie Garrett ("an interesting man"), or perhaps Gary Hogan, the convicted bomber. "If being a friend of Mr. Reed is enough, then each and every one of those witnesses who testified against Mr. Clark should have been sitting in the chair that he was sitting in," she reasoned. For that matter, she asked, "[W]hy should you believe that it is necessary that anybody other than Mr. Reed and Ms. Trimble were involved in shooting this police officer? Why does there have to be a third person involved?" So the state can charge the defendants with conspiracy, she said, answering her own questions.

"Most of the testimony you heard was about the actions of Ronald Reed," Iversen said. "Many people claim Clark attended meetings, but no one can give any specifics of what Mr. Clark actually said at those meetings. . . . He was a friend of Mr. Reed's along with many others. [But] being a friend of someone does not make you guilty of homicide."

Paulsen, in a rebuttal argument, reminded the jury that the case was not about the times or the civil rights movement or police brutality. It was "about the murder of a police officer." He urged the jurors to ignore the "red herrings" and "straw men" (the brown car, the whereabouts of Arling Reese in May 1970, and so on) and concentrate on the facts. To wit: Reed had a plan to kill a police officer, and Clark helped him carry out that plan. Clark helped "by providing the base of operations" and "the place where the gun could be stored and hidden." Paulsen said, "Because he did that, he is an aider and abettor. And because it was pursuant to an agreement with Mr. Reed, and maybe others, he is a conspirator."

Judge Johnson gave the case to the weary jury at 7:40 PM on Wednesday, May 3. He ordered the panel sequestered in a downtown hotel overnight and, as it turned out, over the next two nights as well.

The jurors weren't the only ones who were exhausted. Hudson later called the two-part Sackett case the biggest, most difficult, and most tiring of her career. "I've had any number of challenging cases," she said. "I had, together with another lawyer, for instance, an eight-defendant homicide, which was a lot of work and took a long time. But I've never worked another case for the length of time I did on this one. And from the month or two before we started the first of the trials through the end of the second trial, it was pretty much a seven-day-a-week job." The fact that the trials involved a cop-killing only added to the pressure, she said. "Afterward, I remember being thrilled that I'd actually have time to wash my kitchen floor."

Both Hudson and Paulsen believed the defense made a strategic mistake by spending so much time discussing the era. That allowed the prosecutors to quote the Panthers' "Kill the pigs!" rhetoric, which could not have been in the defendant's best interest. Neither prosecutor was willing to suggest Clark's lawyers were seeking jury nullification, by which sympathetic jurors reach a not-guilty verdict despite accepting the evidence of the case, as some observers believe occurred at the end of O. J. Simpson's criminal trial. They said they did not believe the defense was trying to justify the violence of the times. "They just threw too much at the jury," Paulsen said afterward. "They should have focused on the lack of evidence against their guy." At the same time, the prosecutors were acutely aware of their own side's weaknesses—the scarcity of physical evidence and their several "problematic" witnesses. Then there were the uncertainties of the jury system itself. "I have lost cases that I was quite sure I was going to win, just as I have won cases I was quite sure I was going to lose," Hudson said. Both lawyers believed their odds of a guilty verdict had been a great deal stronger with Reed.

The amount of time it took the jury to reach a decision only added to their anxiety. Courthouse wisdom holds that the longer a jury stays out, the greater the likelihood of a not-guilty verdict. The Clark jury had deliberated for nearly thirty-three hours. But when the six women and six men trudged back into Courtroom 840 shortly after seven o'clock on Saturday evening, they told the judge they had found the defendant guilty on both counts.

There were loud sobs from Clark's family, hugs and handshakes on the Sackett side of the aisle. Jeanette Sackett Monteon embraced Dunaski, Mead, and Duff. Sackett Monteon, James Sackett Jr., and Julie Sackett offered statements to the court. Then Johnson sentenced Clark to life in prison, less the 478 days he had already spent in custody.

As he had with Reed two months earlier, the judge wished the prisoner good luck. But Clark did not reply.

4

"The passage of time is both an enemy and an ally," Jeff Paulsen said for neither the first nor the final time, speaking to reporters outside Courtroom 840 following the Clark verdict. "It's true that people die and memories fade, but it's also true that attitudes change and a case that could not have been successfully prosecuted in 1970 was successfully prosecuted now because people were willing, finally, to come forward and tell what they knew.

"The message from both verdicts, from both the convictions of Ronald Reed and Larry Clark, is that it's never too late to do justice."

Much later, Paulsen acknowledged that the "centerpiece" of the state's case in both trials actually had nothing to do with memory and had proved impervious to the passing of time. He was speaking about the carefully preserved recording of Connie Trimble's phone call, which had survived its own aging, a series of investigations and grand jury hearings, and a long-ago trial. "There was no question that was Trimble's voice on the tape," Paulsen said, "and once you have her making that call, and once it's established that she was Reed's girlfriend at the time, and once you have all those witnesses coming in and saying Ronnie and Larry hated cops and were trying to get a Black Panther charter and wanted to make a statement—then it all came together. But it was centered on that tape, that core piece of evidence, which was not dependent on anybody's memory or motivation." The recording was, to Paulsen's mind, the equivalent of a smoking gun.

"Trimble made the call, and Reed was with her when she made the call, and they went to Clark's house about three minutes before the shooting and the victim fell a hundred yards away. She can shade it all she wants at that point. She can say she doesn't think they ever left the house. But she made the call and that's what brought the officer to the scene and the officer was killed. Even if Reed didn't leave the house, even if he's not out there pulling the trigger, he's in on the conspiracy, and he's guilty of both aiding and abetting *and* conspiracy.

"Then there were the notes that were in Reed's pocket when he was arrested [in November 1970]," Paulsen went on, with the certitude of a man who has proven his case. "To me, those notes were a second smoking gun. Our whole theory of the case was laid out in those notes, in Ronnie's handwriting. *I'm going to hijack a plane. I'm going to kill people unless I get what I want. What do I want? I want Connie Trimble, Larry Clark, and Gary Hogan released from jail. I want free airtime for the Panthers' platform. I want $50,000 in gold.* You couldn't write a more incriminating script or one more in line with the government's theory. He didn't say anything about killing a cop, but if you take those notes together with Trimble's phone call and the other testimony, it all adds up."

Tom Dunaski, who had invested even more time in the case than the prosecutors, summed up the investigators' feelings in his inimitable fashion. "With Larry," he said, "I thought it could go either way. We weren't putting the gun in his hands. Plus, you never know what a jury's going to do. So it was pretty much I'd take the one and the other would be a bonus. With Ronnie, I'd been pretty confident. Larry was more touch-and-go. I was relieved we got both convictions."

"It was like winning the lottery to have the case not just solved but *resolved* in a courtroom," Neil Nelson said. "The chances of having another cold-case cop murder solved liked that, with no DNA or whatever—it will never happen again."

The older, retired cops such as Ed Steenberg and Joe Corcoran seemed confident the jury would judge history the way they believed they had lived it. "I had no doubt about the verdicts," Steenberg said. "It was the two of them and Connie. I think there were other people who were aware of the murder, but we'll probably never know if there was anyone else directly involved."

"It's a shame it took thirty-six years, but it was resolved today," Ron Ryan Sr. told the *Pioneer Press* outside the Reed courtroom.

Dan Bostrom said, "You never get over the loss, but [a guilty verdict] brings some closure."

The guilty verdicts did not settle the issue for everybody. After Reed's trial, Tyrone Terrill, the director of St. Paul's department of human rights, told the *Star Tribune,* "Somebody did it, but the question is: Are you sure you've got the right person?" The Reverend Devin Miller, described in the *Pioneer Press* as a "liaison between law enforcement and [St. Paul's] black community," called Reed's trial an "injustice" and asked, "Was the evidence really there, or was this trial really about something more?"

James Mann was typically contrarian following the verdicts, insisting, without elaboration, that the case was "never properly investigated." He added, "The man is dead, and no one knows who did it. That's the best I can say." So Reed and Clark were *not* the killers? he was asked. "I think any number of people could have been involved," Mann replied. "But there was no proof of one damn thing. No evidence."

Ron Edwards, the most resourceful of the local skeptics, referred in his blog to the infamous Dred Scott case of 1857, quoted Roger Taney, the U.S. Supreme Court's chief justice at the time ("There are just no rights that a Black American has that we . . . are obligated to respect and honor"), and declared during jury deliberation in the second trial, "Justice is indeed being denied to Larry Clark, just as it was denied to Ronald Reed." Edwards had been arguing since the men's arrests that the "establishment," desperate to solve the Sackett murder, had built its case on coercion, payoffs, and bad faith. "We are not here to defend Black men because they are Black," he wrote. "The guilty indeed belong in jail. We are here to defend Reed and Clark because we believe them to be innocent of the Sackett murder. Our concern is for unjustly jailed Blacks, of which we consider Reed and Clark to be in the Sackett case."

A week after the conclusion of Clark's trial, Reed spoke for himself in an interview with Shannon Prather of the *Pioneer Press.* "I didn't kill anybody," he said. "I didn't conspire to kill anybody." Beginning his life term at the state's Oak Park Heights maximum-security facility thirty minutes east of St. Paul, Reed denied he had ever been the angry young militant as portrayed during the trials. That was a persona created by the state, he said. "They wanted a conviction. They wanted a scapegoat. They wanted to close the case." He said he was the victim of law enforcement's obsession with cold cases. He denied that he and Trimble had been together the night of Sackett's murder but said he couldn't remember where he was at the time. He said he did not attempt to rob the Omaha bank, either. He was arrested for that crime, he said, because he was a suspect in the Sackett case.

When he was arrested and charged with the Sackett murder, Reed told the reporter, he was a "responsible, productive member of society." The label "cop-killer" was something he said he couldn't comprehend. "I can't identify with that," he said.

Reed was already preparing his appeal. With the help of another public defender, Melissa Sheridan, he would eventually submit no fewer than thirteen reasons—"claims of error," in legal terminology—why his district court conviction should be reversed. Reed argued, for instance, that the evidence presented at his trial was "insufficient as a matter of law to support his conviction." He argued that under 1970 law he would have been tried, as a nineteen-year-old at the time, in juvenile court, so the district court did not have jurisdiction in his case. He argued that Judge Johnson improperly deterred him from testifying on his own behalf by threatening to introduce the attempted Omaha bank robbery. He argued that Trimble Smith had lied in her testimony on behalf of the state. He argued that Johnson erred in not telling the jury that Trimble Smith's testimony required corroboration by other evidence.

On August 23, 2007, the Minnesota Supreme Court rejected Reed's claims. In a twenty-four-page opinion, the court found that none "constitute[d] reversible error."

Larry Clark also appealed his conviction. And his appeal, like Reed's, crawled through the overloaded judicial system at a snail's pace. In Clark's case, however, the outcome was a surprise. In a voluminous ruling handed down on August 28, 2008, the state's high court reversed Clark's conviction and remanded his case to district court for a new trial. Clark's appeal had included only five points of contention, generally similar to some of Reed's, and the court rejected four of them. The fifth argued that Johnson erred by not telling the jury that Trimble Smith was an accomplice in the Sackett murder and thus her testimony needed to be supported by other testimony. Reed had argued the same point—but responding to *his* appeal, the justices, while agreeing that the judge erred, said that in Reed's trial there had been sufficient testimony to corroborate Trimble Smith's account. In Clark's trial, while it was again "reasonable for a jury to consider [Trimble Smith] to be an accomplice," Justice Paul H. Anderson wrote, the evidence against Clark was generally weaker than it had been against Reed and not strong enough to offset the judge's omission.

Once again, Trimble Smith's role in the now thirty-eight-year-old drama was central to the story. She could not, under the Constitution's double-jeopardy clause, be tried again, but, the court said, she could "theoretically be charged with conspiracy to commit murder" and thus could be "reasonably considered an accomplice."

Reacting to the court's decision, the prosecutors said they didn't think they could have "theoretically" charged Trimble as an accomplice. They pointed out, moreover, that defense counsel in neither the Reed nor the Clark trial asked Johnson to instruct the jury on that point. "And, frankly," Jeff Paulsen said later, "the last thing [Clark's lawyers] wanted the jury to be told was that Connie Trimble was a co-conspirator in the murder. They didn't want Connie to be any part of it because Connie said she went to Larry Clark's house that night." Paulsen said he thought the accomplice ruling "might have signaled a larger issue the supreme court had—not so much with Clark's conviction, but with a mandatory life sentence for a guy who was more an aider and abettor than the principal."

Clark's trial counsel Connie Iversen said she was ready to go back to court. "I never put the case away," she told the *Star Tribune.* "It's still sitting here in boxes." Gurdip Singh Atwal, the assistant state public defender who helped with Clark's appeal, told a journalist that Clark was pleased with the ruling. He had been actively involved in the appeal and "upbeat" during the drawn-out process, Atwal said. "Whenever I talked to him, he was very positive, looking on the brighter side of things, which isn't easy to do in prison." Then again, Clark had more than the supreme court's decision to be happy about.

Seven justices sit on the Minnesota Supreme Court. Two of them, who were not members of the court when the case was argued in front of it almost a year earlier, did not take part in the Clark ruling. Of the five who did, four voted to reverse and remand. The fifth, Alan Page, argued that the entire case against Clark should be dismissed.

Justice Page, who three weeks earlier had turned sixty-three, was a celebrated member of the Minnesota Vikings when Patrolman Sackett was murdered. A native of Canton, Ohio, and a college All-American at the University of Notre Dame, he was in the salad days of a professional football career in 1970, one of the game's most feared defensive linemen and an eventual inductee in its Hall of Fame. The first African American to serve on Minnesota's high court, he had been an associate justice since 1993, following ten years of a post-football law career that included experience in both private practice and as a state assistant attorney general. Still physically formidable—at six-four and 240 pounds, he maintained a rigorous training regimen—he surprised people with his soft-spoken reticence, though there was little question where he stood on racial issues. His out-of-court interests included a large collection of slavery and racist memorabilia (slave chains, lawn jockeys, a fluorescent sign reading COLORED that once hung in an Alabama bus station) that he and his wife displayed in their Minneapolis home. The repugnant items reminded Page, according to a 2007 feature in the *Star Tribune,* that "not only have things not always been equal, they're still not, and that we need to make sure we don't go back to those ways."

In his nineteen-page opinion, Page wrote, "My review of the record leads me to the conclusion that the corroborating evidence relied on by the court is insufficient as a matter of law and therefore may not be used to support Clark's conviction. Because I further conclude that the remaining evidence, absent the accomplice testimony, is legally insufficient to support Clark's conviction, I would reverse Clark's conviction outright and not remand for a new trial. . . .

"The evidence the State relies on to support Clark's aiding and abetting conviction is the same circumstantial evidence the State relies on in support of Clark's conspiracy conviction. Again, there is no direct evidence of Clark's involvement in Officer Sackett's shooting. [T]he evidence of Clark's presence at United Black Front meetings, his agreement with Reed's statements about killing a police officer, statements of his own about black power and self-defense, and Clark's close relationship with Reed, standing alone, does nothing more than suggest that Clark is guilty because of his association with Reed and is insufficient to support an inference that Clark played a knowing role in the shooting of Officer Sackett.

"Moreover, [Arthur] Harper's testimony that Reed and Clark were seen leaving [Kelly] Day's apartment establishes nothing more than Clark's mere presence in Reed's company some 15 or 30 minutes before the shooting. That evidence does not, however, place Clark in Reed's company at the time of or after the shooting. Nor does it lead unerringly to the conclusion that Clark knew of the plan to shoot a police officer that night or that he played a knowing role in the plan."

Paulsen, Hudson, and Hudson's boss, Ramsey County Attorney Susan Gaertner, bristled at the supreme court's decision and considered Page's position flat-out wrong. The fact that they themselves (as well as their own investigators and many observers on both sides of the color line) believed the case against Clark had its weaknesses— was "touch-and-go," in Dunaski's words—did not mean they thought the verdict was reversible. In any event, it was now up to Gaertner's office to decide what to do next.

"We are carefully reviewing this decision to determine whether to go forward," she told the St. Paul Police Federation a few weeks after the ruling. "Be assured that we will do everything possible to see that the defendant is held accountable for his acts."

The passage of still more time, Gaertner acknowledged, would make a retrial of Larry Clark more difficult, fraught with unknowns. Would testimony from the first trial be admissible in the second? At least one important witness, Eddie Garrett, had died of a heart attack in March 2007. The whereabouts of many of the others was uncertain, as was their willingness to face, for a second or a third time, not only hostile counsel but angry, perhaps vindictive members of the community. None of the state's lawyers, much less her handlers in the police department, wanted to deal again with Trimble. On the positive side, the state didn't have to hurry. Clark was in prison and would stay there while the issue was decided.

So instead of a matter of weeks, as Gaertner told a reporter shortly after the supreme court ruling, the seemingly interminable

Sackett case dragged on for another six months—well into a new year. And then it came to a sudden and unanticipated conclusion.

On February 19, 2009, Ramsey County and Larry Clark reached a plea agreement that would make no one, with the likely exception of the defendant, happy. Clark entered, and Judge Johnson accepted, what is known as an Alford plea (named after a North Carolina criminal defendant at the center of a 1970 U.S. Supreme Court case), by which the defendant does not admit guilt but concedes that the state has enough evidence to convict him. Clark entered the plea to a single count: conspiracy to commit premeditated murder. The deal stipulated five years of prison time, then a year on supervised release. However, because Clark had already served more than four years since his arrest in January 2005, he would be provisionally free in eleven months.

An Alford plea serves a purpose—terminating a seemingly interminable case—but it is the kind of "back-room deal" that infuriates crime victims, police unions, and newspaper readers who write angry letters to the editor. Some states do not allow the plea, and the federal government uses it sparingly. After the Clark agreement was announced, David Titus, president of St. Paul's police federation, called it "outrageous." Letters to the *Pioneer Press* demanded the removal of both Gaertner and Johnson, who had been reelected a district court judge in November 2006. James Sackett Jr., after a long, thoughtful pause, told a journalist, "It is what it is."

It was the first Alford plea that Jeff Paulsen had been a part of in his twenty-year prosecutorial career. (Susan Hudson, in a like amount of time, had been involved in only a few.) But this was a highly unusual situation, he explained later. "It's very rare where you convict beyond a reasonable doubt, get a remand for some technical error, then work out an agreement with a person who wants an Alford plea," he said.

"I don't believe the county attorney would have gone for an Alford plea pre-trial, but post-trial, after we had already proven our case, it wasn't as big a hurdle. We could have rounded up our remaining witnesses and tried Clark again. We still had faith in our case. But reading between the lines of the supreme court opinion, it seemed like there was the possibility that even if we won again, they might reverse. It seemed, reading between the lines, that they might not have wanted to affirm a life sentence for somebody who even according to the government's theory wasn't the shooter. So this was a compromise."

If Clark had taken the deal the state had offered before the trials and agreed to testify against Reed, Paulsen said, he probably would have ended up serving about the same amount of time, which may or may not have made anyone feel better.

"He's guilty, and he knows he's guilty," Jim Sackett Jr. said. "He really can't go out and say, 'I didn't do it.' If we had gone through another trial, another five weeks, the outcome would probably have been the same. He was found guilty and did time. Hopefully, when he gets out, he'll violate probation and go back in."

A few weeks before the two sides reached their agreement, Sackett and his mother joined Paulsen, Hudson, and the investigators for lunch at DeGidio's, a red-sauce Italian eatery on West Seventh. The lawyers explained how an Alford plea worked and how it would affect Clark's sentence. "We're willing to make another try," Paulsen told them. "But this is what could happen: We could lose everything." Still, he made it clear that it would be up to the family to decide whether the state should accept the deal.

The Sacketts did not want Clark to go free. They believed he should serve more time than stipulated by the proposed deal. Only one more year in prison didn't seem right—it would not come close to all the years they had suffered with their loss. On the other hand, they, too, believed Clark was an aider and abettor, not the instigator or the shooter, so making a deal with him would not be the same as making a deal with Reed, which would have been impossible to accept. Almost as difficult would be sitting through another trial. Beginning with Trimble's trial in 1972, Jeanette Sackett had persevered through three of them. Three times she had listened to the arguments, alibis, and ghostly recorded voices, and three times she had looked at the blown-up photos of the crime scene and heard a medical examiner describe her husband's fatal wounds. People who had never been through the experience could not imagine how stressful and exhausting it was—how much it took out of you, how it ground you down. And what if they retried Clark and the jury found him not guilty of the charges?

The prosecutors neither recommended the plea agreement nor spoke against it. They asked Jeanette what she thought. She said her gut feeling was to accept it, but she wanted to talk to the rest of the family. Which she did. And they told her to do what she believed was best. "We all signed off on it," Jim Jr. said later.

"I just didn't want to go through that again," Jeanette said about the prospect of another trial. "I don't think I could have handled it." She said she worried about what the investigators would think, after all the time and hard work they had put into the case. But Dunaski, Mead, and Duff could sense the relief behind her decision. Whatever you feel is best for the family, they told her.

On that raw February day, after the two sides had agreed to the controversial plea, fifty-eight-year-old Larry Clark was driven back to prison. Thanks to their agreement, he now had less than a year to serve before he was—conditionally, at least—a free man.

That afternoon Jeanette, Jim Jr., and Simon Monteon sat down once more with the prosecution team before heading home and resuming their lives. Jeanette had no second thoughts about the decision. "That was the right move," she told the lawyers. She was sixty-five years old. Jim Sackett Sr. would have been sixty-six. She knew her life and her children's lives would have been very different if Jim had come home as usual after his shift on May 22, 1970, but there was no point dwelling on that now.

It was over.

5

Actually, it wasn't over for everybody. While Larry Clark bided his time until his January 2010 release, Ronald Reed, from his seven-by-eleven-foot, single-occupancy cell at Oak Park Heights—the state's modern, maximum-security correctional facility outside of Stillwater—continued to struggle for *his* freedom.

On August 12, 2009, Reed petitioned the district court for post-conviction relief. Represented by a well-known local criminal attorney named Howard Bass, Reed argued four points: his prosecution was precluded by the statute of limitations, his right to defend himself at trial had been denied, his court-appointed counsel both at trial and on direct appeal was ineffective, and "newly discovered evidence" revealed that Connie Trimble Smith had given false testimony, which entitled him to a new trial.

Three months later, Judge Johnson, concluding that Reed had "failed to allege sufficient facts," denied the petition without an evidentiary hearing.

On January 8, 2010, Reed, again represented by Bass, appealed for the second time to the Minnesota Supreme Court, arguing points regarding his right to represent himself, the statute of limitations, the adequacy of counsel, the liability for aiding and abetting, and Trimble Smith's trial testimony. After another long wait, the supreme court, on December 29, 2010, affirmed the lower court's ruling.

On March 28, 2011, Reed, now serving as his own lawyer, petitioned the United States Supreme Court for a writ of certiorari. He asked the court to review his case and to be allowed to "proceed in forma pauperis," that is, with the court covering the cost of the petition. It was, legally speaking, his last resort, and it was a long shot. Every year the court receives thousands of so-called cert petitions and denies all but about a hundred of them.

The following June, the court denied Reed's.

Tom Dunaski and Scott Duff formally retired after thirty-seven years on the job. The department's celebration for its 2009 retirees, at the Prom Ballroom in suburban Oakdale in May, drew dozens of family members, friends, and colleagues. Among those wishing Dunaski and Duff well that evening were Jeanette and Jim Sackett Jr., Simon Monteon, Jeff Paulsen, Susan Hudson, and other members of the Sackett task force. Along with Jane Mead, Paulsen, and Hudson, Dunaski and Duff had been honored in 2007 by the International Homicide Investigators Association during the group's annual gathering in Las Vegas for the Cold Case Investigation of the Year. In 2006 Dunaski had received the U.S. Attorney's annual Law Enforcement Recognition Award for his work on the Sackett case.

True to form, neither Dunaski nor Duff actually retired. As the decade expired, each was taking on special projects for the department and other agencies.

Duff joined fifteen other erstwhile homicide investigators hired with the help of an eighteen-month federal grant to revisit more than 150 cold cases dating back several decades. Among other cases, Duff drew the 1965 robbery-murder of an African American businessman named Royal Gooden, which had gone unsolved for lack of credible information. "The good folks didn't know who did it, and the bad folks weren't about to share what they knew," said one longtime Summit-University resident, neatly summing up the ageless problem. As it turned out, all three of the prime suspects were dead when Duff reviewed the case almost forty-five years later.

In the spring of 2010, Dunaski was asked by then Ramsey County sheriff Bob Fletcher to help with the investigation of yet another cold case—the triple murder, in March 2007, of a St. Paul man, his girlfriend, and the woman's teenaged daughter in an apparently drug-related bloodbath. In January 2010, a Ramsey County grand jury had indicted two men, Tyvarus Lindsey and Rashad Raleigh, who were already in prison following their convictions on different murder charges, and Dunaski—now known to colleagues as "the Closer"—was brought aboard to help build the case against them for trial. (Lindsey and Raleigh were convicted in federal court in June 2011 and sentenced to concurrent life sentences the following November. And, again, the small world of local law enforcement was apparent. Jeff Paulsen prosecuted the case, and before its conclusion Fletcher had been replaced as county sheriff by Matthew Bostrom, the son of Dan Bostrom, one of James Sackett's supervisors in 1970.)

Dunaski was working on that case when, on May 1, a police sergeant from Maplewood, on St. Paul's northern border, was shot and killed while taking part in a manhunt for a pair of carjackers near Lake Phalen. Joseph Bergeron's killer, who was killed himself a short time later during a brief but ferocious struggle with David Longbehn, a city patrolman, turned out to be a twenty-one-year-old local man identified as Jason Jones.

In a polo shirt and cargo pants, full of bluster and banter and talkative as always, Dunaski could have been mistaken for a senior drill sergeant in civvies, though the .40-caliber Glock on his hip and the sheriff's department star on his belt made his line of work apparent. Because this was St. Paul and because he was Tom Dunaski, he knew all three of the principals in the latest homicide: the fallen officer, the killer, and the cop who killed the killer. "I knew him when he was a little kid," he said of Jones. "His mom was a juvenile prostitute, an informant of mine. I remember she'd drag the kid along with her, wet from the rain, snot smeared all over his face. He didn't have a whole lot of chances growing up."

The Sackett case was old news, over and done with for the cops who, even in "retirement," had fresher crimes to preoccupy them. Still, for everybody who worked on it, the Sackett case was and would always be something special and, for many among its large cast of characters, unforgettable. For some, the case might never truly end. Ronald Reed, for example, as Dunaski reminisced, was waiting for a response to his latest appeal. "He was a smart kid, with a lot going for him," Dunaski said, drawing an implicit comparison with Jason Jones. "He was popular back at Central High. He had some talents— it just depended on how he wanted to use them. He was a leader.

He had visions of being something special in his community. And he was from a good family, very good people. I don't know what happened. People you talked to from back then would say, 'There was a change in him.' He went somewhere, to a rally or something, and it was like a light went on. He was different after that. He seemed to have this mandate when he came back."

Clark was "just a soldier," Dunaski said. "He carried the baggage. So he got five years in jail where he got three square meals a day. Now he's out. Maybe he's back in Nebraska.* I don't know. We haven't followed him. He was just a flat line, never got anything going on his own. Maybe I'm wrong about that, but I never saw any sign of it."

Dunaski had kind words for the late Eddie Garrett and for John Griffin, who had in fact been granted an early parole from federal prison after his testimony in the Reed trial and was living out of state.

"I came to really like the guy," Dunaski said of Griffin, "and not just because he went to bat for us. Here's this guy who was really an asshole back in the day. He was a real Black Panther, supposedly the only guy from around here who was actually initiated into the organization while the other guys were just wannabes. Then he got into heroin and was a real gangster. When we first went back to him [in federal prison], he was content with where he was. But then we finally broke through the shell and got to him. It's not like *we* did such a great job—he just decided that this was it. He wasn't promised anything. But we found we liked each other, these two opposites, oil and water, ending up having some respect for each other, having some things in common to talk about. Now he's out and working at a business, and I can't give him enough credit. He's kind of a success story after all those years."

Nothing had happened since the trials ended to create any doubts about the detectives' conclusions. Dunaski believed the original investigators had it right from the beginning. Though they never told him as much, Dunaski said he felt the frustration among the earlier detectives because they did not close the case in the weeks

---

*According to an acquaintance, Clark was living in the Twin Cities after his release. He had a job and a wife and attended services at his north Minneapolis mosque.

and months following Sackett's murder. "They were good, nose-to-the-ground detectives," he said. "They were old-school homicide—you know, fedora kind of guys. It had to be frustrating for them." In a courthouse hallway after the Reed verdict, Earl Miels had hugged Dunaski. "Nice job, kid," Miels told him.

Still, questions remained—some unanswered and some unanswerable, attached like barnacles to the ancient case. Whatever happened to the rifle? Dunaski and Duff were certain they would find the weapon in the house on Concordia. As it turned out, they could only be confident that it had been there at one time, hidden in the basement ductwork. Had there been other witnesses? Was there a neighbor coming home from work or a night on the town who might have seen a couple of young men with a rifle a few minutes after midnight? What became of the person who supposedly lived down the block or across the alley from Clark, who was rumored to have heard the shot and seen someone with a gun running either toward or away from Clark's house? If such a person existed, neither the detectives who wore the fedoras nor their hatless successors found him.

But because the case was closed, Dunaski no longer lost sleep over those questions. One of the last things he saw before turning off the light at night was a small, rectangular plaque that hung on a bedroom wall. The plaque, designed by Jane Mead and presented to every member of the task force, was inscribed *To the Team* and bore a reproduction of Sackett's shield, Badge 450, above the words *Never Forgotten* and *We Stand as One on the Thin Blue Line.*

Almost a dozen years younger than Dunaski, Mead was still on the job in 2010, a senior member of a seven-person St. Paul homicide squad that was investigating upward of a dozen murders a year. Her children had grown up and married, and since the Sackett investigation she had become a grandmother. Like her task force partners, Mead looked back at Sackett as the case of a lifetime, the most memorable experience of a long, productive career.

Mead believed the case had changed her. Even though she had been a St. Paul cop for almost twenty years when the team began looking into the Sackett files, she was surprised to learn there was so much she didn't know about the city. The middle-aged men and women the task force talked to on the Hill would say, "You don't know what it was like back then." One older man spoke passionately about the sewer-construction project that he and other African Americans picketed in 1969 because the contractor refused to hire blacks. The protest was a big deal at the time, front-page news and a cause célèbre among the growing numbers of politically active residents that included Milt Williams (later Mahmoud El-Kati) and Katie McWatt; several protesters, both black and white, were arrested for defying orders to disperse. Other black people told Mead and her partners about being harassed and roughed up by cops who were accustomed to having their way in the "ghetto." Many of the retired officers she talked to said the same thing—"You don't know what it was like back then"—though they recalled the experience from a different point of view, describing an inner-city landscape that had grown dangerous for law-abiding citizens and the police alike. Raised in a white community, surrounded by white law enforcement officers and firefighters, Mead had been fully aware of only the latter side of the gaping divide.

By the time she was working the streets as a St. Paul cop, times had not necessarily improved but they had definitely changed. She had dozens of African American, Hispanic, and Asian colleagues as the department began to better reflect the multicolored demographics of the city, and the drug culture tended to direct most of the violence toward rival gang members rather than the police. The idea of a revolutionary assassination of an officer seemed weirdly old-fashioned.

Like Dunaski, Mead had grown fond of several of the Sackett witnesses, even though many of them were distrustful and contemptuous of the police, at least at the beginning. "We really liked Eddie Garrett, and felt really bad when he died," she said. Mead also liked and felt sorry for Connie Trimble, and said so during the trials, though she knew that offended Jeanette Sackett, to whom she had grown close. "They were older now," she told a reporter, speaking of those witnesses. "They were not what they were in the day."

"You live and breathe with these people, and you hear about their struggles," Mead explained. "People do horrible things, but you learn they have good parts, too. I guess it's that empathy thing, where you can almost always get a better idea of why people are the way they are if you look at the world from their point of view."

*   *   *

Among many of the officers who were in the department on May 22, 1970, the Sackett murder held the kind of mnemonic power that the Kennedy and King assassinations and the 9/11 attacks held for most Americans. Everybody remembered where he or she was when the startling bulletin, like a thunderbolt, shattered the calm of an ordinary day or evening. As the Sackett case made clear, however, memory was not always reliable. Some of the cops who later said they were on duty that night were not. Others who suggested they would have been the ones responding to Trimble's O.B. call if this or that had not diverted them were similarly mistaken. It was not the least of the ironies surrounding the Sackett case that, as Dunaski pointed out, the one squad that shouldn't have caught that fateful call—a traffic car with neither the capacity nor the equipment to handle a medical emergency—was the one that did.

Ed Steenberg, who with his partner John LaBossiere was in the first car to arrive at 859 Hague after the ambush, not only thought about what happened that night but wondered what might have gone down differently. He and LaBossiere walked the Selby Avenue beat until the department decided it was safer to put all patrolmen in cars. They knew and were known by many of the young people who lived in the neighborhood. So what would have happened, Steenberg asked himself, if he and LaBossiere had reached the Hague address ahead of Sackett and Kothe? The idea of the sniper lowering his rifle and saying, "Oh, wait—I know those guys!" was a stretch, and Steenberg, a man with a hearty sense of humor who rose to the rank of deputy chief, answered his own question with a chuckle. It's unlikely familiar faces would have made a difference. And even if they had, he mused, "I would imagine that the next night, or the night after that, it would have happened—they would have killed someone else."

Bill Finney was quite sure the killer or killers would not have fired at James Griffin or Jimmy Mann. They were even better known in the neighborhood than Steenberg and LaBossiere, and, more to the point, they were two of the four black officers in the department at the time. Beyond that consideration, Finney believed the target's identity would not have mattered so long as the target was dressed in blue.

A few years ago, Glen Kothe, now in his middle sixties, had grown tired of going to the funerals of old friends. Three retired cops that he knew had died on the same day. They were not falling in the line of duty but succumbing to illness and age. As an antidote to the lengthening fatality list, Kothe began hosting what he called a "celebration of life"—an annual potluck dinner for local law enforcement retirees and their spouses. Once a year he set up a couple dozen folding tables in the big, barn-like building where his wife trained dogs, and for the better part of three hours he worked the crowd like the proprietor of a Munich *Biergarten*—shaking hands, slapping backs, and reminiscing with a hundred other survivors. Beer was indeed available to wash down the homemade chili and lasagna, but this was a celebration, not a wake, so the old cops stayed sober.

Kothe didn't drink anymore himself. For a long time after his partner's death he drank enough "for a dozen guys," and then he finally had enough. There were other changes, too. After decades of avoidance, he and Jeanette Sackett, while waiting to testify at Reed's trial, started talking again. But tormenting memories of that long-ago night still crept into his consciousness. Something he would see on TV or read in the paper would trigger a flashback. He tried not to think about it, but once a year, no matter what, not thinking about it was impossible.

"May 22 is never a good day for me," he told his friends.

James Sackett Jr. spent less time thinking about the case after the guilty verdicts were handed down. "Occasionally I do," he said three years later, "but not as much."

Sometimes people recognized him. They would notice the resemblance he bore to his father and say something. At the hospital where he worked, his identification badge revealed only his first name, yet every once in a while someone would look at him and then look at the badge and then ask, "Is your last name Sackett?" Sometimes the curious individual was an elderly cop who had served with his father. Once it was a nurse, now retired, who had been working in the Ramsey County emergency room the night his father was brought in.

"A couple times a year I'll run into somebody," he said quietly. Such an encounter was always difficult, but there was a positive side to it as well. "It's good that they remember. It's good that the story hasn't been entirely forgotten."

Afterword

R eviewing the thousands of pages of investigative files and courtroom transcripts that pave the long trail of the James Sackett murder case, I found it distressing but not difficult to reach the conclusion shared by successive Ramsey County juries in the late winter and early spring of 2006—that Ronald Reed and Larry Clark were guilty of conspiracy to commit, and of aiding and abetting, first-degree murder.

It was distressing for the obvious reasons: a dutiful public servant and family man had been gunned down because of the color of his shirt, and two very young men, teenagers actually, had condemned themselves to lives as fugitives and, eventually, prisoners of the state. The conclusion wasn't difficult because the prosecution's narrative was compelling and because there was no satisfactory alternative story. Even when the credibility of some of the state's witnesses was challenged, the larger story remained intact, partly because there was no other plausible way to think about the event it described.

But this is a white man speaking. You don't immerse yourself in a history such as this without being reminded that a white man, even an educated and empathetic liberal, is likely to have a different perspective on matters of law enforcement and the criminal justice system than many black men and women. Much has been said about that difference, by Richard Wright, James Baldwin, and Henry Louis Gates Jr., among many important African American writers and scholars, and by astute white journalists such as Jeffrey Toobin and Alex Kotlowitz. "When race is involved truth becomes myth, myth becomes truth, and your perspective—myth or truth, truth or myth—all depends on which side of the river you live on," Kotlowitz once said. After O. J. Simpson's criminal trial, Gates wrote, "As blacks exulted at Simpson's acquittal, horrified whites had a fleeting sense that this race thing was knottier than they'd ever supposed—that, when all the pieties were cleared away, blacks really were strangers in their midst."

Gates quoted fellow African American intellectual Cornel West saying, "Now we recognize that in a fundamental sense we really do live in different worlds."

In St. Paul, in the wake of the Reed and Clark trials, that difference was open and obvious. While police officers slapped each other on the back and Sackett's family spoke of "closure," many African Americans cried "no proof . . . no evidence" and "injustice." Almost five years after the verdicts, one older black man told me that the trials were a "fraud." Another said, "There was a lot of stuff in the case the [state] brought that I think was different from what really happened." The city's African American community is no more monolithic than its modern police department, and many blacks, including police chiefs Finney and Harrington, expressed strong support for the guilty verdicts. For that matter, some of the critics (as did a majority of the Minnesota Supreme Court) made a point of distinguishing between the Reed and the Clark outcomes, conceding the merits of the state's case against Reed while challenging its argument against Clark. Nonetheless, the overarching skepticism about the legal process itself was clear. The skepticism did not surprise me, but its insistency among thoughtful and responsible citizens long after the judgments had been rendered was troubling.

Yet just as disturbing was the fact that none of the skeptics, to my knowledge, was either able or willing to offer another, convincing explanation for Sackett's murder. In a court of law, the accused is not required to offer a counter-narrative to the government's case; in the larger community, presumptions of innocence and guilt are wilder creatures, less easily confined. *Someone* assassinated the officer, and it's inconceivable, given the connectedness within the Summit-University neighborhood, that the identity of the actual assassin (or assassins) would not be known. If Reed and Clark didn't do it, for God's sake who did?

Much of the post-verdict criticism pointed at the reward money, cash payouts, and reduced prison sentences offered to witnesses who would testify for the state. It's difficult for me to believe, however, that an individual would expose himself to the enmity of friends and neighbors and perjure himself for a few thousand dollars or a couple of months' rent. (No one claimed or was paid the Bureau of Criminal Apprehension's hundred-thousand-dollar reward.) A significant reduction of a long prison term would seem to be a more powerful incentive, but even that would carry sizable risks and no guarantees. In any event, the Reed and Clark juries—yes, white juries in a white court—were informed of the inducements, but they chose to believe at least the core of what the key witnesses were telling them.

Reading the trial transcripts as well as the many police interviews and extensive grand jury testimony, I believed the witnesses, too. The facts were discernible even in Connie Trimble's disordered responses, beginning with her admission that she made the May 22 phone call and that she, Reed, and Clark were present at the scene moments before Sackett was shot. Whether I believed that Reed and Clark were in her sight the entire five to seven minutes that she said they were present at Clark's house didn't matter as much as the fact that they were there, within a few feet of the spot where the shot was likely fired, within moments of the shooting. Reinforced by the several witnesses who described Reed's statements during the weeks and months before and after the murder—most of whom were not paid or offered sentence reductions—Trimble's words, stripped of the obvious improbabilities, carried the hard ring of truth.

Of course it is possible that Reed and Clark did not kill Patrolman Sackett. Or that one did and the other was not directly involved. Unless or until one or both confess to the crime, or an eyewitness swears that he or she saw one or the other fire the fatal bullet, it's possible to believe that someone else *could* have pulled the trigger. For now, though, given the information that's available to us, the testimony implicating both men, in my opinion, precludes a reasonable doubt.

Might other persons have been materially involved in the murder plot, the murder itself, or its cover-up? To me, that seems more than merely possible.

Trimble placed only Reed, Clark, herself, and Clark's girlfriend, Diane Hutchinson, at the Clark house a few moments after midnight on May 22, and Hutchinson, by Trimble's account and her own, was asleep with her children. Other witnesses saw Arthur Harper, Eddie Garrett, and Kelly Day in the immediate neighborhood before and/or shortly after the murder. Harper was a thief who had murdered a man during a robbery in 1969, and Garrett was the Vietnam War vet who had warned officers to "watch the rooftops." But, lingering speculation aside, neither man was part of the pool-hall rumble dominated by Reed and Clark following the murder, nor, according to people who knew them at the time, did either man possess, in one acquaintance's words, the "lion's heart" of an assassin. John Griffin, who described himself as the only legitimate Black Panther on the Hill during the period, was in prison in May 1970.

Which leaves, foremost among other possibilities, Kelly Day, Reed's pal since third grade. Day seemed to be everywhere at the time, involved in everything. A young man with ready access to guns and explosives, he was not only Reed's close friend but also tight with Griffin, who told authorities that Day showed him the Sackett murder weapon after Griffin returned home from prison in 1971. By his own admission, Day was a co-conspirator in the airplane hijacking that never came off; he was also the confidential informant who tipped the police to the supposed plot and then warned Reed—according to Reed—that the cops were about to pounce. And it was Day who much later boasted to Neil Nelson that he knew everything about the Sackett murder (but wasn't going to tell).

Considering his relationships and activities, I'm willing to take Day at his word. In fact, he laid out much of the tale in his signed statement to Cecil Westphall in February 1972, though he refused to repeat the account at Trimble's trial. Little wonder that Tom Dunaski was beside himself when Jane Mead spotted Day's obituary that December morning in 2002, as their reinvigorated investigation was just getting under way. As events turned out, while I don't believe that justice delayed resulted in justice denied in this instance, I can't help but think that justice would have been served much sooner if Day had told what he knew in court.

Reed himself acknowledged that Day had a role in the drama, even while denying his own involvement. When we talked at Oak Park Heights prison in late 2011, he said that Day, apparently "playing a kind of double-agent role," concocted the tale he told Westphall with the idea of recanting everything later on, believing that would scuttle the state's cases against both Reed and Trimble. "I did it for you," Reed said Day told him after Reed was released from prison in Nebraska. Reed not only believed Day but insisted he didn't hold a grudge. In fact, he told me, he visited Day when his friend was sick and later attended his funeral. "I forgave him for what he did, for implicating me—[for] setting me up to be killed" by vengeful cops as payback for Sackett. He said he believed that Day, facing prosecution for drug-related offenses and possibly other crimes, as well as physical intimidation by the police, had been squeezed to the point of betraying his friend.

Reed, now sixty-one, walked into the small, supervised office where our two meetings took place unescorted, unrestrained, and seemingly at ease with himself and his surroundings—a compactly built, clean-shaven, light-skinned man with hair shorn to his scalp and rimless glasses that glittered in the overhead light. Wearing a heavy-duty gray sweatshirt and baggy jeans, he looked more like the tradesman he was ten years ago than the convicted murderer he was today. He told me he spends most of his time, when not working in the institution's mental-health unit ("My title is 'mentor'"), reading and studying theology. He is not eligible for parole until 2023.

In the course of our conversation, I told him that if I had been a member of his district court jury, presented with the state's argument and witnesses, I, too, would have voted to convict. For probably any number of reasons, including the color of my skin, he didn't seem surprised. He made it clear, however, that I would have been mistaken—that he was an innocent man. Actually, what he said was this: "It was tragic and reprehensible what happened to Officer Sackett. I think about the man and his family every day. The pain and the suffering—I'm not so cold and callous that I don't understand that there are two sides. I also understand about the law enforcement community and their attitude. I understand all that. At the same time, when you know you didn't kill anyone and that to my knowledge I didn't assist killing anyone—I didn't provide anyone with a weapon, I didn't sit down and conspire with anyone—to know that whoever killed Officer Sackett has never been held accountable is to me an injustice." He said he was profoundly troubled knowing that he was hated by people who didn't really know him for something he didn't do.

Because of his relationship with Connie Trimble, he said, the police had decided to focus on him from the beginning; the prosecution built its case on the lies of paid and coerced informants, and he was faced with the historic reality of a hostile system. "So how am I going to go before a white jury with a white judge, and they're telling them I killed a white police officer because I hate white people?" he asked me, with rising emotion. "What am I supposed to say? How can you defend yourself against that? There's no rifle, there's no nothing. You either believe Connie or not. You say you believe her when she says I told her to make the call, but you don't believe her when she says I didn't [kill the officer]."

Reed had by this time exhausted his legal appeals, but he said his family and friends were still working on his case. He said he was confident that "someday" the truth would come out. "Dunaski, Paulsen—they know that [Garrett, Griffin, and the other prosecution witnesses] were lying. They don't know who did it. They believed I did, and that was enough for them to build a case. All they needed was a story."

A final thought: as tragic as the assassination of Patrolman Sackett was, it could have been the beginning of a larger, even bloodier saga.

Given the volume of guns on the street and the number of angry young people with their hands on them, it's reasonable to wonder why there weren't additional serious attempts on the lives of police officers in the Twin Cities circa 1970. Given, for that matter, the trigger-happy reputation of St. Paul's cops at the time and the provocations both real and rumored, why weren't there additional deadly attacks on African Americans? In the weeks immediately following Sackett's murder, while officers patrolling the Hill were armed to the teeth and riding four to a car, there was no spasm of homicidal revenge. Were both the "militants" and the cops so dumbstruck by the Sackett killing that neither side was willing to raise the ante and hazard the next step toward an all-out race war?

The situation might have changed on that dreadful Saturday afternoon three months later. If the second bomb that Gary Hogan planted in the downtown Dayton's locker had gone off, the toll among the police, firefighters, and others in the building could have been catastrophic. But the second bomb was discovered and defused, so that possibility remains only a sickening hypothesis. Luckily, cooler heads on the Hill and downtown combined with pure dumb luck to preserve a lasting—albeit relative and uneasy—calm.

The gory histories that emanated from New York, Chicago, Los Angeles, and other cities during the era (and since) remind us how fortunate one community has been that, for all its differences and conflicted colors, a greater tragedy was avoided.

Acknowledgments

I want to thank the dozens of individuals who spoke to me—in many cases on several occasions and at considerable length—about the subject matter of this book. Most of you are mentioned by name in the text. Please know that without your help this book would not have been possible. I'm especially grateful to Jeanette Sackett Monteon, James Sackett Jr., and Julie Sackett, as well as to Glen Kothe, Stuart Montbriand, William MacDonald, Robert Winger Jr., Daniel Bostrom, and Gerald Dexter—the family, friends, partners, and supervisors of Patrolman Sackett. Speaking candidly and repeatedly about the worst days of their lives surely wasn't easy.

Kate Cavett's oral histories of St. Paul's African American community, collected in her remarkable book *Voices of Rondo*, were invaluable. So were her oral histories of former St. Paul police officers, including several who were on the street on May 22, 1970. So were the many kind introductions to her friends and admirers in both the Summit-University neighborhood and the police department. Retired St. Paul officers and department historians Fred Kaphingst and Edward Steenberg dutifully answered my many questions about police work circa 1970 and since. Sergeant Jane Mead was my guide through the labyrinthine police records of this complicated case. Most of my many visits to the department's Grove Street headquarters were conducted during the watch and with the permission of then chief John Harrington (now a state senator) and homicide commander Timothy Lynch (now retired). Thank you all.

My thanks also to Jack Rhodes, former chief of staff at the Ramsey County Attorney's office, and erstwhile Ramsey County Attorney Susan Gaertner, for providing access to case files as well as explanations and insights; to Jill Garrison, Joseph Cassell, David Marchetti, and Debbie Erickson, for trial transcripts, additional Ramsey County district court documents, and courtroom detail; to Brett Aurit, for police department crime statistics; to Sarah Russell and Rico Lopez of the Minnesota Department of Corrections, for facilitating my conversations with Ronald Reed, and Sarah Berg for additional DOC data; to Mary Beth Redmond at St. Paul's Central High School, for dusting off old yearbooks; and to Lynn Sullivan at the Omaha, Nebraska, public library, for help re-creating the attempted robbery of the Ames Plaza Bank and subsequent trials.

I drew important information from the reportage provided by several newspapers and websites, including, in the Twin Cities, the *Pioneer Press*, *Star Tribune*, and *Minnesota Spokesman-Recorder*. Nick Coleman, Bill Gardner, Mara Gottfried, Paul Gustafson, David Hanners, Howie Padilla, Joy Powell, and Shannon Prather, among others, kept local readers such as myself abreast of the developments that followed the resurrection of the case in 2002. Ron Edwards offered his own point of view from the Twin Cities' African American community. KSTP-TV's Tom Hauser deserves kudos for locating and interviewing Connie Trimble in 1994.

Larry Millett's *AIA Guide to the Twin Cities*—especially the sections describing St. Paul's neighborhoods and architecture—was once again indispensable to this born-and-bred Minneapolitan. Nobody, in my opinion, has written more or better about the Twin Cities past and present. David Vassar Taylor's *African Americans in Minnesota* and Mary Lethert Wingerd's *Claiming the City: Politics, Faith, and the Power of Place in St. Paul* were among several additional books that gave me historical context and data.

My friend Jeffrey Thompson provided essential advice and counsel throughout the research and writing process. My son, Joseph Swanson, offered encouragement and valuable feedback from start to finish.

For the second time in my charmed writer's life, I have benefited from the intelligence, talents, and good humor of the team at Borealis Books, including press director Pamela McClanahan, managing editor Shannon Pennefeather, sales and marketing manager Mary Poggione, publicity and promotions director Alison Aten, marketing associate Leslie Rask, and design and production manager Daniel Leary. Ann Regan is not only a superlative editor in chief, she's a trusted partner in crime. Thank you all for another scintillating adventure in publishing.

My gratitude, finally, to Libby, Katie, Joe, and Kathryn. I can't imagine attempting, much less accomplishing, anything worthwhile without your love and support.